都兰纺织品珍宝

青海省文物考古研究所　编著

许新国　安吉莉卡·斯利弗卡　著

文物出版社

阿贝格基金会

英文翻译　艾美霞〔美〕

中文翻译　王东宁

摄　　影　宋　朝

文物出版社

责任编辑　王　戈

责任校对　陈　婧

责任印制　张道奇

阿贝格基金会

责任编辑　瑞谷拉·肖特　王东宁

Textile Treasures of Dulan

Institute of Cultural Relics and Archaeology of Qinghai Province
Contributions by Xu Xinguo and Angelika Sliwka

Cultural Relics Press
Abegg-Stiftung

English Translation by Martha Avery

Chinese Translation by Wang Dong-Ning

Photographs by Song Chao

Cultural Relics Press

Editor   Wang Ge

Copy Editing   Chen Jing

Printing   Zhang Dao-Qi

Abegg-Stiftung

Editors   Regula Schorta, Wang Dong-Ning

目 录

TABLE OF CONTENTS

序 一

这本《都兰纺织品珍宝》的出版前后经历了二十多年的漫长历程。20 世纪 90 年代初期，阿贝格基金会开始收藏整理中亚丝织品，进而涉足这一丰富多彩且令人激动的世界纺织史的研究领域，并于 1999 年在瑞士组织召开了第一届国际中亚纺织品的研讨会，时任青海省文物考古研究所所长的许新国先生出席了研讨会，并作了大会发言。

2003 年，经北京科技大学冶金材料史研究所韩汝玢教授引荐，阿贝格基金会研究所所长瑞谷拉·肖特博士和我首次访问了位于西宁市的青海省文物考古研究所，从此正式开启了阿贝格基金会与青海省文物考古研究所的合作关系。我希望并相信今后我们双方会继续合作下去。

青海都兰对我们来说是奇妙与神秘的代名词，它丰富多元的出土文物见证了 6 世纪曾经统治这一地区吐蕃政权的无比辉煌。从 20 世纪 80 年代开始，许新国先生带领青海省考古队在此挖掘了系列墓葬群，其中出土的各色珍贵的纺织品极具特色而令世人瞩目。虽然出土的纺织品由于受墓葬环境的影响多为残片，但是它们所代表的文化特质和历史价值都是无可比拟的。

都兰出土的这批纺织珍品不仅显示出丝织物本身的艺术和工艺特点，而且还提供了在这段特定历史时期不同区域、不同文化群落之间多元的交流信息。只有通过对这些纺织珍品耐心细致的科学研究，才能初步还原当时的历史片段，才能体验都兰地区在其文化交流巅峰时段所拥有的璀璨艺术和精湛技艺。

青海省文物考古研究所和阿贝格基金会在过去的岁月中建立了紧密的合作关系，从最早开始合作的原所长许新国先生，到继任所长任晓燕女士（任职 2011 ~ 2016 年），直至后任所长李智信先生（任职 2017 ~ 2019 年）三届领导班子对这个国际合作项目都是不遗余力地支持，在此我代表阿贝格基金会对青海省文物考古研究所表示衷心感谢。值得一提的是双方合作中的一个重要环节，就是从 2004 年开始德国纺织品修复专家安吉莉卡·斯利弗卡受阿贝格基金会聘请，在青海省文物考古研究所对都兰出土丝织品进行专业修复和整理工作。之后，安吉莉卡每年至少一次到西宁与考古所的同事们一起工作。对她来说，西宁几乎成了她的第二故乡。而瑞谷拉·肖特博士和我也曾多次访问西宁，每次都受到考古所领导和同行们的热情款待。

另一位需要特别致谢的关键性人物是北京科技大学韩汝玢教授。从合作项目起始，韩教授就努力促使这两个文化历史背景和组织结构迥异的合作伙伴一起携手克服一切难关，从而结出丰硕的研究果实。没有韩汝玢教授的丰富经验和远见卓识，阿贝格基金会与青海省文物考古研究所还有和其他中国考古研究机构之间的合作关系是不可能建立并持续下来的。随后与韩教授一起加入双方合作团队的王东宁女士也已经成为项目翻译编辑的重要合作伙伴。

这本图书能够最终出版发行，首先要感谢的是本书作者之一许新国先生。他从接触阿贝格基金会开始，就认定要与我们共同合作。同时，我们也非常感谢文物出版社的专业摄影师宋朝先生。他在很短的时间内克服了重重困难，完全掌握了拍摄纺织品的特殊技能，使图书中每件纺织珍品都能得到高质量展现。这本都兰纺织品中英文双语的研究图书是我们与文物出版社的第二次合作，我们非常幸运地得到了文物出版社及李缙云先生的大力支持。尤其是整部书稿的责任编辑王戈女士，她热情的投入，才使阿贝格基金会与青海省文物考古研究所的合作成果能够顺利出版发行。

多米尼克·凯勒

阿贝格基金会董事长

FOREWORD

This volume of Textile Treasures from Dulan is the result of a long journey. It started some twenty years ago when Xu Xinguo, the then-director of the Institute of Cultural Relics and Archaeology of Qinghai Province, spoke at the Abegg-Stiftung in Riggisberg, Switzerland, at the first conference on textiles from Central Asia. The Abegg-Stiftung had just begun to be involved in this rich and exciting new field of textile world history. In 2003 Regula Schorta, director of the Abegg-Stiftung, and myself, together with Professor Han Rubin of the University of Science and Technology Beijing, Institute of Historical Metallurgy and Materials, travelled for the first time to Xining to start a cooperation that continues until today and will continue into the future. Dulan was for us an almost mythical term with all its varied remains of the apogee of the Tubo empire in the last third of the first millennium. In the course of time, the Archaeological Institute with Xu Xinguo as its leader had excavated a number of the tumuli and the treasures they contained, with woven textiles a significant part. Textiles as organic material are very susceptible to the wear and tear of time and climate, and so the archaeological finds are mostly fragmented, but nevertheless of great importance and value. These textiles contain a great deal of information on the skills and creative excellence of the craftsmen and craftswomen who created them. They are proof of a rich cultural exchange that reached far to the West and East. Only step by step are we able to scientifically encode this information, but besides all this background we can simply admire the aesthetic and technical brilliance of these remains of a great era.

Over the years, contacts between the Archaeological Institute and the Abegg-Stiftung have become closer. Xu Xinguo was followed as the director first by Ren Xiaoyan (2011–2016), then by Li Zhixin (2017–2019). All three have always been highly supportive of our cooperation, for which we are very grateful. An important part of this cooperation was and still is the time that Angelika Sliwka spent in Xining as technical expert on behalf of the Abegg-Stiftung, first in 2004, from 2007 yearly, sometimes twice a year. For her, Xining has become almost a second home. Regula Schorta and I have visited Xining on several occasions and have always enjoyed very generous exchanges. From the beginning, a key figure in this exchange has been Professor Han Rubin, who with her foresight and openness, her knowledge and wisdom, her experience and generosity, has made the contact between two institutions with very different backgrounds and history possible and fruitful. Without her, this cooperation, also with other Chinese Archaeological Institutions, would not have been possible. Later on the journey Wang Dong-Ning joined our team and has been a very helpful, indeed an inspired, go-between, translator, and collaborator.

We sincerely thank Xu Xinguo, the author, who has from the beginning been a vigorous supporter of our joint activities. We are also much indebted to photographer Song Chao who has mastered the difficult task of making photographs of ancient textiles interesting.

This is the second volume that we have the good fortune to publish with Cultural Relics Press. We are most grateful to Director Li Jinyun, and especially to the editor in charge Wang Ge, who has been responsible for the entire production of this volume and has taken a singular personal interest in making our publishing cooperation most fruitful.

Dominik Keller

Abegg-Stiftung

President of the Board of Trustees

序 二

　　《都兰纺织品珍宝》是有关青海考古出土纺织品研究方面的第一部著作，是青海省文物考古研究所与瑞士阿贝格基金会（Abegg-Stiftung）合作的结晶。它的问世是青海考古工作中一件值得庆贺的大事。

　　都兰县位于青海省柴达木盆地的东南部，隶属于海西蒙古族藏族自治州。这里在古代是羌、吐谷浑、吐蕃等民族的聚居地，分布着众多的古遗址、古城址和古墓葬。都兰墓群分布广泛，绵延数百里，是一处不可多得的、重要的中华历史文化遗产。1982 年以来，青海省文物考古研究所展开了对热水血渭墓地、智尕日墓地、夏日哈乡大什角墓地、香加乡莫克里墓地的调查，并会同北京大学文博学院，对热水血渭墓地察汗乌苏河南岸的吐蕃墓葬进行了发掘，出土纺织品数百件。这些纺织品时代历经北朝、隋、唐，不乏新的发现和启示，具有重要的学术价值。

　　本书选取都兰热水乡血渭墓地出土的纺织品珍宝，包括锦、绫、绢、缂丝、纱等，其中织金锦、缂丝、嵌合组织显花绫、素绫等均属国内首次发现。这批丝织品大部分为中原汉地织造，小部分为中亚、西亚织造。具有浓厚异域风格的粟特锦，发现数量较多，其中一件织有中古波斯人使用的婆罗钵文字的织锦弥足珍贵。

　　自汉代始，我国的丝绸生产技术水平已有很大的发展和提高，丝绸远销中亚、西亚和欧洲，受到当地人民的喜爱和赞许，于是有了"丝国"之称，沟通中西、横贯亚洲的商路也被誉为丝绸之路。根据文献记载，途经青海地区的道路，在不同历史时期曾被称为"羌中道""河南道""吐谷浑道""青海道"等。中国内地经由西宁到拉萨的路线，现在一般称为唐蕃古道。都兰出土的纺织文物证明，从北朝晚期至中晚唐时期（6 世纪末～9 世纪上半叶），青海道是丝绸之路上的一条重要的干线。正是由于联系中西交通的丝绸之路青海道和唐蕃古道的兴盛，使先后占有此路的吐谷浑、吐蕃政权的地位日趋重要，并在不同时期，肩负了东西方政治、经济和文化交流的重任。

都兰地区出土的纺织物及其他文物还证明，在吐蕃控制下的 7 ～ 8 世纪，东西方贸易经过该路的规模是前代无法比拟的。可以说，都兰地区是当时中原和吐蕃以及西方贸易的中心之一，是沟通丝绸之路中亚廊道和南亚廊道的枢纽。其历史地位绝不亚于河西走廊各重镇。

　　都兰墓群令人震惊和举世瞩目的文物以及独特的历史地位，吸引了世界各地专家学者的目光。为便于各国学者和爱好者共同研究、鉴赏都兰出土丝织品，世界著名的古代纺织品收藏、保护和研究中心——瑞士阿贝格基金会和文物出版社、青海省文物考古研究所三方决定合作出版本书。阿贝格基金会董事长多米尼克·凯勒（Dominik Keller）对本书出版给予全力支持，瑞谷拉·肖特教授（Dr. Regula Schorta）给予多方指导，安吉莉卡·斯利弗卡（Angelika Sliwka）对我所丝绸修复、保护工作进行了长期指导和帮助，为本书的出版奠定了良好的基础，使这批丝绸能以全新的面貌展示在世人面前。许新国先生自 1982 年从事都兰热水墓群发掘工作三十余年来，全身心投入热水墓群文物及吐蕃文化研究，成果斐然，本书的出版完全基于他卓有成效的发掘、研究工作。北京科技大学韩汝玢教授为我所与阿贝格基金会的合作牵线搭桥，促成该书出版。

　　相信本书的出版，将极大地促进都兰吐蕃考古、中西文化交流以及民族、经济、宗教、艺术等一系列重大历史课题的研究。

李智信

青海省文物考古研究所所长

2017 年 5 月

FOREWORD

Dulan Textile Treasures is the first work on the study of textiles unearthed in Qinghai Province using archaeological methods. The book is the result of cooperation between the Institute of Cultural Relics and Archaeology of Qinghai Province and the Abegg Foundation of Switzerland (Abegg-Stiftung). Its publication is a great event, a worthy celebration of archaeological work in Qinghai Province.

Located in the southeast of the Qaidam Basin, Qinghai Province, Dulan County lies within the Haixi Mongol and Tubo Autonomous Prefecture. In ancient times, Dulan County was the home of nations such as the Qiang, Tuyuhun, Tubo, and others; it contains numerous ancient sites, cities, and tombs. Dulan tombs are widely distributed in areas spanning hundreds of miles, and constitute a rare and important element of China's historical and cultural heritage. Since 1982, the Institute of Cultural Relics and Archaeology of Qinghai Province has explored the Xuewei Cemetery and the Zhigari Cemetery in Reshui Town, the Dashijiao Cemetery in Xarag Town, and the Mokeli Cemetery in Xiangjia Town. With the cooperation of the College of Arts and Technology, Beijing University, the Institute explored the Tubo Tomb of the Xuewei Cemetery south of Qagan Us River. Hundreds of pieces of textiles were unearthed. Originating from the Northern, Sui, and Tang dynasties, these silk fabrics have led to many new discoveries and revelations, and are of great academic significance.

Most of the silk fabrics described in this book were unearthed from Xuewei tomb number 1 in Reshui Town, Dulan County. These silk fabrics include patterned weaves, damask weaves, tabbies, tapestries (kesi), and gauzes; among them a gold-woven band, wide silk kesi, damask-like weaves, and unpatterned twill were found in China for the first time. Most of these silk fabrics were woven by the Han nationality in the Central Plains of China, with some woven by people in Central Asia and Western Asia. Among the western products, Sogdian brocades, woven in a strong exotic style, comprised a relatively large quantity. One rare piece is particularly precious due to its woven inscription in middle-Persian Pahlavi script.

Since the Han dynasty, China's silk technology has been greatly developed and improved. Chinese silk has been exported to Central Asia, Western Asia, and Europe, and has been loved and praised by people from various countries. Consequently, China became known as the "Silk Country" and the trade routes between China and the West, crossing Asia, were known as the "Silk Roads". According to documents, the roads in Qinghai Province were called Qiang Road, Henan Road, Tuyuhun Road, and Qinghai Road during different historical periods. The route from the mainland of China to Lhasa via Xining is now commonly known as the "Tang-Bo Ancient Road." The silk relics unearthed in Dulan County demonstrate that from the late Northern dynasty to the middle and late Tang dynasty (the end of the sixth century to the first half of the ninth century), the Qinghai Road was an important trunk line on the Silk Road. Because the Silk Road, the Qinghai Road and the Tang-Bo Ancient Road, which linked traffic between China and the West, flourished, the position of the Tuyuhun and Tubo regimes became increasingly important. In different periods, they shouldered the responsibility of political, economic, and cultural exchanges between the East and West.

Silk and other cultural relics unearthed in Dulan County have shown that during the seventh and eighth centuries, under the control of the Tubo regime, the scale of East–West trade passing along the road was unmatched compared to previous generations. Dulan County was a centre of trade between Central China, Tubo, and the West at that time. The region was the hub of the Silk Road corridor between Central Asia and Southern Asia, and its historical status was as important as that of the major towns along the Hexi Corridor.

Dulan tombs have attracted the attention of experts and scholars from all over the world because of their astonishing cultural relics and unique historical status. In order to facilitate joint research and appreciation of the silk fabrics unearthed in Dulan County, the following organizations decided to cooperate in the publication of this book: the Abegg-Stiftung, a world-famous centre for the collection, protection, and research of historic textiles, the Cultural Relics Publishing House, and the Institute of Cultural Relics and Archaeology of Qinghai Province. Dominik Keller, Chairman of the Abegg-Stiftung, has fully supported the publication of this book, and Dr. Regula Schorta, Director of the Abegg-Stiftung, has offered guidance on multiple occasions. Angelika Sliwka, textile conservator-restorer of the Abegg-Stiftung, has provided long-term guidance and assisted our silk restoration and conservation work, which has laid a good foundation for the publication of this book and enabled the silks to be displayed in a completely new way. Since 1982, Mr. Xu Xinguo has been engaged in the excavation of Reshui tombs in Dulan County. He has devoted himself to researching the cultural relics of Reshui tombs and Tubo culture. The publication of this book is based on his fruitful excavations and research work. Professor Han Rubin of the University of Science and Technology, Beijing, assisted the author's collaboration with the Abegg-Stiftung and was crucial for the creation of this book. We believe that its publication will greatly promote the study of Tubo archaeology and cultural exchanges between China and the West, as well as research on a series of major historical issues such as nationality, economy, religion, and art.

Li Zhixin

Director of the Institute of Cultural Relics and Archaeology of Qinghai Province

May 2017

第一章　都兰出土纺织品初探

许新国

都兰县位于青海柴达木盆地的东南部，隶属于海西蒙古族藏族自治州，在古代是羌、吐谷浑、吐蕃等民族的聚居地，分布着众多的古遗址、古墓群。

1982～1999年，青海省文物考古研究所带领并参与了对都兰80余座古墓的发掘，出土了一大批精美的丝绸、金银器、铜器、漆器、木器、古藏文木简牍、装饰品等珍贵文物。这本图书中所采用的最具有代表性的纺织品大部分是都兰热水大墓及其周围陪葬墓1982～1985年考古挖掘和采集品，在书中以DRM1、DRM1PM2、DRXM1、DRXM、DRXM1PM2字母标注。图书中采用的其他纺织品还包括了20世纪90年代夏日哈墓葬出土品，标注为DXM；夏日哈大什角墓葬为DXDM；露斯沟墓葬为DRLM和DRLC；以及都兰热水南察汗乌苏河附近墓葬DRM、DRXM（图1）。通过几十年的发掘和研究，我们认为青海都兰的古墓群应归属为吐蕃文化，是吐蕃统治下吐谷浑邦国的遗存（图2）。

图1　都兰墓葬位置示意图 Location of Dulan Cemeteries

By Xu Xinguo

INTRODUCTION

Dulan County is located at the southeastern corner of the Qaidam Basin in Qinghai Province. Administratively, it is part of the Haixi Mongol and Tibetan Autonomous Prefecture. The area was settled in ancient times by the Qiang, Tuyuhun, and Tubo (Tibetan) peoples, and many ancient cemetery sites of these ethnic groups can be found throughout the county.[1]

From 1982 till 1999, the Institute of Cultural Relics and Archaeology of Qinghai Province has excavated more than 80 ancient tombs in Dulan County, and has unearthed exquisite cultural artifacts including silks, gold and silver wares, bronze and copper articles, lacquer, timber items, wooden slips inscribed with ancient Tibetan script, and decorative items. The textiles gathered in this volume have been chosen to represent the wide range of different materials in terms of patterns, weave structures, and other decorating techniques. Most have been unearthed from one of the several chambers and accompanying burial pits of the great tomb at Dulan Reshui (Xuewei) during the 1982–1985 archaeological campaigns (designated by the abbreviations DRM1 and DRM1PM2, also DRXM1 and DRXM1PM2). Others have been found in the tombs excavated in the 1990s at Xarag cemetery (abbreviated DXM) and Dashenjiao cemetery in Xarag township (abbreviated DXDM) and at Lusigou (abbreviated DRLM and DRLC) as well as at Dulan Reshui South of Qagan Us river (DRM, also DRXM) (fig.1).[2] More than a decade of research on the majority of finds has revealed that all these burials belong to Tubo (Tibetan) culture, and more specifically are remains of the Tuyuhun tutelary state under Tubo rule (fig.2).

---

1 This chapter summarizes the results of our research on these archaeological sites and on the artifacts found. It relies in particular on: 许新国 Xu Xinguo, “中国青海省都兰吐蕃墓群的发现、发掘与研究 Zhongguo Qinghai sheng Dulan Tubo muqun de faxian, fajue yu yanjiu (The Discovery, Excavation and Research of the Tubo cemeteries in Dulan, Qinghai Province, China)”, 许新国 Xu Xinguo, 西陲之地与东西方文明 Xichui zhi di yu dong xi fang wenming (The Western Frontier and the East-West Civilization), Beijing: Beijing yanshan chubanshe, 2006, pp. 132–41. 许新国 Xu Xinguo, “都出上蜀锦与吐谷浑之路 Dulan chutu shu jin yu Tuyuhun zhi lu (The Shu silks unearthed in Dulan and the Tuyuhun Road)”, ibid., pp. 199–212.—Xu Xinguo, “The Discovery, Excavation, and Study of Tubo (Tibetan) Tombs in Dulan County, Qinghai”, Central Asian Textiles and Their Contexts in the Early Middle Ages, ed. Regula Schorta, Riggisberg: Abegg-Stiftung, 2006 (Riggisberger Berichte 9), pp. 265–90.

2 Editor's note: A handy summary of these excavations is included in: Tong Tao, The Silk Roads of the Northern Tibetan Plateau during the Early Middle Ages (from the Han to Tang Dynasty) as reconstructed from archaeological and written sources, Oxford: Archaeopress, 2013 (British Archaeological Reports BAR International Series S2521). For the precise localization of the sites, see 中国·青海省におけるシルクロードの研究 Chūgoku·seikaishō ni okeru shirukurōdo no kenkyū (Studies of the Silk Road in Qinghai province, China), ed. the Research Center for Silk Roadology, Nara: Nara International Foundation, 2002 (シルクロード学研究 Shirukurōdo-gaku kenkyū, Silk Roadology 14), in particular the table on p. 176.

吐谷浑原系辽西慕容鲜卑中的一支。4世纪初，部分鲜卑人在首领吐谷浑的率领下，经过阴山，西迁至今甘肃东南部和青海东部，创立了新国家。统治者的后裔即以其先祖之名为姓，国家则以吐谷浑为号。

663年，吐蕃攻灭吐谷浑，吐谷浑"故地皆入吐蕃"，吐谷浑国在青海地区存在了350余年。据文献记载，灭国之后的吐谷浑人虽然被吐蕃人统治，仍有自身的建制、自己的可汗、自己活动的特定区域，并以部落为单位，保持着自己民族的组织结构。

图 2　都兰墓葬发掘现场（1982 ～ 1985 年）　Excavation site, Dulan 1982 ～ 1985

The Tuyuhun originally stem from a branch of the Murong–Xianbei of the western Liao. At the beginning of the fourth century, a group of the Xianbei people, under the leadership of a man named Tuyuhun, crossed the Yinshan mountains and migrated westward into southeastern Gansu and eastern Qinghai, where they fought a military campaign against the various Qiang groups and established a new state. The descendants of the rulers of this state took the name of their original tribal chieftain as the name of the state: Tuyuhun.

In 663, the Tubo attacked and destroyed the Tuyuhun and put Tuyuhun lands under Tubo jurisdiction. The king of the Tuyuhun, Nuohebo, and his wife, Princess Honghua, were forced to flee to Liangzhou and request asylum there. The ancient lands of the Tuyuhun then came under the control of the Tubo, and this tutelary state continued in Qinghai for more than three hundred and fifty years. Historical texts show that although the Tuyuhun were ruled by the Tubo, they continued to have their own socio-political system and their own rulers (*khagan*), as well as their own specifically defined sphere of activity and tribal units, thus maintaining their own ethnic organizational structures.

留在故地的吐谷浑人作为吐蕃的邦国存在，役属于吐蕃。吐蕃委派"大论"一级的官员对其进行统治。他们要向吐蕃朝贡，交纳赋税，还要为吐蕃提供物资，当兵打仗。对于这部分吐谷浑人，文献上虽有记载，但他们的遗迹却至今未见。其准确的活动地域一直是学术界争论的焦点。而都兰的发现使我们有理由认为，吐蕃统治下的吐谷浑邦国的活动区域主要是在柴达木盆地，而其国的统治中心应在都兰至香日德一带。

首先从空间上看，都兰墓葬的分布范围与文献中记载的吐谷浑活动区域相吻合。根据我们的调查和发掘，都兰墓葬主要分布在夏日哈河、察汗乌苏河、柴达木河流域，目前已经发现近千座墓葬。而这一区域正是吐谷浑人活动的中心地带。

其次从时间上看，这批墓葬出土文物所跨越的历史年代与吐谷浑国活动的时代相符。例如，都兰出土北朝晚期至初唐时期流行的丝绸数量较多，而这一时期柴达木盆地尚在吐谷浑国的有效控制下，丝绸的持有者只能是吐谷浑人。

再从出土文物本身所反映的文化来看，史书记载吐谷浑人使用汉字，汉化程度极深。这一点在都兰出土的文物中得到了印证。例如夏日哈出土的一件鸳鸯栖花锦，背面墨书有"薛安"二字（图版 No.25）。热水出土的一枚印章上刻有篆文"谨封"（图 3）二字，另一件热水出土的残漆器底部也刻有汉字。从都兰墓葬中保留的殉犬之习俗来看，热水血渭一号墓就殉有完整狗八只。与文献记载的东胡鲜卑人"生前畜犬，死后殉犬"之习俗一致，符合"肥养一犬……使护死者神灵归赤山"的鲜卑旧俗。此外，都兰墓葬中所出的带扣、带饰等，也在一定程度上反映出鲜卑风格（图 4）。

图3 都兰墓葬出土"谨封"印章 Seal excavated in Dulan bearing the characters "jin feng"

图4 都兰墓葬出土带饰 Gold and turquise ornament excavated in Dulan

The Tuyuhun people who remained on their original lands now existed as a Tubo tutelary state, and presented tribute to the Tubo kings. They also paid taxes, supplied the Tubo with materials, and fought for them as soldiers. Although the Tuyuhun do appear in historical records, there were once no material remains of them, and their actual sphere of activity long remained a topic of contentious academic debate. The Dulan discoveries give us reason to believe that the main sphere of the activities of the Tuyuhun state under Tubo rule was located in the Qaidam Basin of Qinghai and that the political center of their state was in Dulan County. What follows is supporting evidence for our conclusion.

First, we believe that in spatial terms the distribution of the tombs in Dulan County conforms with the description of the locales of Tuyuhun activities in historical documents. Surveys and excavations show that the main areas in which the tombs are distributed are the Xarag Us, Qagan Us, and Qaidam river valleys (fig. 1), in which almost one thousand tombs have been discovered to date. This area was the center of Tuyuhun activity.

Second, in temporal terms, the relics found in these tombs span a number of historical periods that match the period in which historical texts record that the Tuyuhun were active. For example, we have unearthed a fairly large number of silks that were fashionable in the period from the late Northern Dynasties through the early Tang; throughout this period the Tuyuhun were in effective control of the Qaidam Basin, and it is most likely that the owners of these silks were the Tuyuhun.

Third, the level of Han acculturation revealed by the unearthed artifacts conforms with what we know of the Tuyuhun from historical records. The Tuyuhun used the Chinese written script. On a warp-faced compound twill bearing a motif of mandarin ducks resting among flowers two Chinese characters forming the name Xue An are written in ink on the verso of the piece (cat. no. 25). A seal excavated in Reshui bears the characters *jin feng* ("respectfully sealed") in seal script, and a damaged lacquer item unearthed at Reshui is also incised with Chinese characters (fig. 3).

Fourth, the finds at the Dulan tombs conform with what we know of the Donghu–Xianbei practice of sacrificing dogs after the death of their owner, so that they would protect the soul of the dead on its return ascent to the Crimson Mountains. Eight complete skeletons of sacrificed dogs were found at the M1 site in Reshui Xuewei. Additionally, a number of belt clasps and decorative items clearly reflect Xianbei styles (fig. 4).

与此同时，我们也注意到都兰这批墓葬与西藏山南和藏北的吐蕃墓存在文化因素相同的一些特征，比如圆形封土、梯形封土、流行屈肢葬、二次葬和火葬，以及殉葬完整马匹等。都兰墓葬中出土有古藏文的木简、木牍（图5），表明这一时期古藏文的使用较为普遍，加之墓葬所属年代最晚已达中唐时期，正是吐蕃统治这一地区的年代，因此我们主张都兰这部分灭国后吐谷浑人的墓葬还是应归属到吐蕃文化系统。

吐蕃的埋葬制度和习俗，文献中记载较少，考古发掘的资料也不多。都兰的发掘使我们对该领域有新的认识。

都兰墓葬群有以下几个特点。第一，讲究对葬地的选择，一般均"依山面河"，一座大墓的周围往往有数十座小型墓葬。中小型墓葬也是数座连成一排，或是集中在同一条沟内。这些应是"聚族而葬"制度的反映。第二，墓葬都有封堆，分梯形和圆形两种。有的为夯土构成，有的堆以砾石后再覆盖夯土。封土堆均有遗迹，在夯层之间铺有沙柳枝条，夯土下方构筑平面为等腰梯形的石墙。夯土边缘常常砌有土坯或泥球，并在其外侧涂以红色石粉。特别值得一提的是热水血渭一号墓的墓上建筑。该墓为双覆斗式封土，上层封土由黄土、沙土、砾石、巨石等组成。排有七层穿木，并构筑梯形混凝夯土墙和梯形石墙。发现器物陪葬墓和动物陪葬墓两座，均未见人骨。第三，墓室均位于封堆梯形石墙的正中下方，均为竖穴形制。墓室上方盖有柏木，其大小与墓室大小成正比。柏木上再覆砾石一层。墓室常见长方形、方形和梯形，并分单室、双室和多室。另外，也发现有带回廊的。一种

图5　都兰10号墓出土古藏文木简
Wooden slips with ancient
Tibetan inscriptions, from Dulan
tomb M10

However, we also notice that the tombs built in the Dulan area after the destruction of the independent Tuyuhun state show elements of cultural conformity with Tubo tombs in the Shannan and Zangbei areas of Tibet. Round and trapezoidal burial mounds can be found in all these places, and crouched burial, secondary burial, and cremation were practiced in all three areas. Also, the sacrificial burial of animals is known in all these areas, especially the practice of sacrificially burying entire horses is similar to the Dulan finds. The discovery of ancient Tibetan inscriptions on wooden slips, correspondence, plaques, and wooden articles (fig. 5) shows that the ancient Tibetan language was commonly used in the area at this time. At the latest, the tombs can be dated to the late Tang, which was the period of Tubo rule.[3] Their unique cultural features and the cultural variations exhibited by the unearthed artifacts reflect the multiethnic nature of the Tuyuhun within the Tubo cultural structure. They should be regarded as a regional type within Tubo culture to distinguish them from Tubo tombs in the Shannan and Zangbei areas of Tibet.

There is little recorded in historical documents about the Tubo burial system and customs, and few archaeological excavations have been conducted. The Dulan excavations have, however, provided us with a stream of new discoveries and advances in this area of research. Dulan burials generally backed on to mountains and faced rivers or streams, although some burial sites were located on the tops and slopes of mountains, or at the point where the ridges of mountains met the ground below, so that the tomb then formed part of the adjoining mountain ridge. Usually several tombs, sometimes more than ten, were concentrated in a particular area. A large tomb was often surrounded by several tens of small tombs. These phenomena suggest that a system of clan burial sites existed at that time. Sometimes a number of medium-sized and small tombs were arranged in a row or concentrated in the same ravine, and these probably reflect a system of family burials. The tombs are always covered with an earth mound, trapezoidal or rounded in form. Some were made of tamped earth, others were covered with small stones that were covered in turn by tamped earth. The earth mounds invariably contain traces of desert tamarisk fronds, and on the flat earth below the tamped mound there would be a waisted, tapered stone wall. The edges of the tamped earth often bear traces of mud balls and are often faced with red ocher on the outside. The superstructure of tomb M1 at Reshui Xuewei has attracted particular attention. The tomb mound itself consists of a double-arc structure. The upper mound is formed from loess, shale, pebbles, and large rocks through which seven layers of timber pass; there is also a stepped composite wall of tamped materials and a stone wall. The superstructure also contains two secondary burials of either artifacts or animals, both

---

3 Several graves have been dated with the help of dendrochronology, see, for example: Li Mingqi, Shao Xuemei, Yin Zhiyong, Xu Xinguo, "Tree-Ring Dating of the Reshui-1 Tomb in Dulan County, Qinghai Province, North-West China", *PLoS ONE* 10/8 (2015), e0133438 (https://doi.org/10.1371/journal.pone.0133438). Wang Shuzhi, Zhao Xiuhai, "Re-evaluating the Silk Road's Qinghai Route using dendrochronology", *Dendrochronologia* 31 (2013), pp. 34–40.

分前后两室的墓葬，前室为石砌，后室为木椁。墓底一般以石块和木板铺地。第四，有葬具的一般分两种，一种为近似方形的木质棺箱，一种是仅有底板和侧板、无盖板的棺箱。而无葬具的则是将尸体直接放置于地板或地石上。这类无葬具的墓葬数量较多。第五，葬式多见屈肢葬，分俯身和侧身两种。二次扰乱葬也有一定数量。仰身直肢葬罕见，火葬数量亦较少，且葬式分单人葬、男女合葬及三人合葬等。第六，随葬品的数量及种类因墓葬大小而有所不同，这是当时贫富差别和等级制度的明证。第七，都兰墓葬中有殉牲的现象，一是以分割的动物肢体殉葬；二是将兽骨置于墓葬的耳室中；三是以单独墓葬出现，作为大墓的陪葬；四是以组合遗迹形式出现。比如热水血渭 1 号墓南面平地上的陪葬遗迹，由 27 个圆坑和 5 条陪葬沟组成。整个布列范围长 30 米，宽 50 余米，殉牛头、牛蹄者 13 座，殉完整狗者 8 座，陪葬沟里殉完整马 87 匹，殉牲规模之大非常罕见。

without human bones. The tomb chambers were all centered below the stone wall and all resembled a pit in form. Set apart from the earth pit, walls made of small rocks and pebbles are frequently seen. The tomb chambers were covered with cypress logs, and the size of these corresponded with the size of the tomb. A layer of pebbles was placed over the covering logs. Tomb chambers were rectangular, square, or trapezoidal in shape, and tombs could be single-, double-, or multi-chambered. A circular ambulatory was another feature of some tombs. One type of tomb consisted of a front and rear chamber, with the front chamber being a stone crypt and the rear chamber being a timber outer-coffin chamber. The floor of most tombs was paved with stone or timber boards.

Two types of burial furniture were discovered. One type approximated a rectangular timber coffin casket; the other was a coffin casket consisting only of a bottom board and side panels. Most graves lacked any tomb furniture, and the corpse was placed directly on the ground or on stones covering the ground. Most burials were of contracted (or crouching) corpses, and these were placed facing down (prone) or on their side. There were also a significant number of secondary disturbed burials. Supine burials with the corpse facing upward were rare, and cremations were even fewer. There were burials of single bodies, of couples consisting of a male and female, and burials of three persons. There were also large variations in the quantity of burial goods, indicating a social system in which there were gradations of wealth and status.

The practice of sacrificing animals occupies an important place in manuscripts describing Tubo funeral practices, and this is supported by the discoveries at Dulan. The following different forms of animal sacrifice have been found at Dulan: the sacrificial burial of dismembered animals; animal bones placed inside chambers of tombs; the burial of sacrificial animals in independent graves that form secondary graves for a large tomb; and composite forms incorporating the three previous types. For example, tomb M1 at Reshui Xuewei featured secondary burials in its superstructure as well as an area with 27 round sacrificial burial pits and five sacrificial burial trenches. The entire complex of pits and trenches covers an area measuring 30 meters in length and 50 meters in width, and contains a total of 13 graves with sacrificed heads and hooves of oxen, eight sets of the remains of complete dogs, and 87 complete horses.

一　丝绸之路青海道

位于青海柴达木盆地的都兰地区，是古代丝绸之路上的一个重要中转站。根据文献记载，由西宁至兰州、西宁经大通到张掖、西宁经青海湖和柴达木盆地进入新疆和敦煌、西宁经海南州到川西北、沿岷江而下入蜀之路都是古代丝绸之路的分支。一般学术界认为，丝绸之路青海道只是河西走廊的辅助路线。仅在河西路因战争原因不通畅时才绕道青海道。另外，还有一种意见认为，青海道兴盛只限于吐谷浑国控制的 5～6 世纪，在 7～8 世纪吐蕃占领这一地区后，便衰落不振。然而都兰墓葬中出土的丰富的文物种类和特质，都反映了当时这一丝绸之路中转站的繁盛景象，而且证明从北朝晚期至中唐的漫长时间内，青海道一直被作为一条交通要道使用。除丝织品外，都兰出土的其他各种类型的文物都显示出不同层面东西文化的碰撞和交融。例如墓葬出土的一种带双腹耳的灰陶罐，同青海东部及河西汉晋墓中的同类器物接近，沿袭特点明显，显然受汉地影响。其他出土文物中属于中原汉地的文物还有一批"开元通宝"铜钱、小宝花铜镜及大量的杯、盘、碗等漆器等汉地制造器物。而属西方文化的出土文物则包括粟特金银器（图 6）、突厥银饰件、玛瑙珠、红色蚀花烛、铜盘残片和铜香水瓶等。因此，我们认为这批丰富的珍宝，绝大多数都是吐蕃与中原、中亚、西亚进行贸易的结果，说明在吐蕃控制下的 7～8 世纪，丝绸之路青海道不仅繁盛而且贸易规模也是前代无法比拟的。

图 6　都兰 1 号墓出土衣饰
Gilt silver panel with a standing phoenix, from Dulan tomb M1

Qinghai Road and its Role

The Dulan area in Qaidam Basin, Qinghai Province, is an important intermediate station on the ancient Silk Road. According to historical records, there were communication routes known as Silk Roads running from Xining in Qinghai to Lanzhou, from Xining to Datong and Zhangye, from Xining via Koko Nor (Qinghai Lake) and the Qaidam Basin to Xinjiang and Dunhuang, and from Xining to northwestern Sichuan and down the Minjiang River into Shu. These roads have been variously named the Qinghai Road, Henan Way, and Tuyuhun Way. This has long been recognized by scholars. However, most scholars have also considered that the Qinghai Road was only an auxiliary route of the Hexi Corridor, and was used only when the Hexi Road was cut because of warfare. Another view is that the Qinghai Road flourished only in the fifth and sixth centuries during the period of Tuyuhun rule, and that in the seventh and eighth centuries, after the Tubo took control of this area, the road fell into decline and ceased to be used as a trade route.

Given the evidence of the artifacts unearthed from Dulan, we must now revise that point of view. We believe that Qinghai Road was not only used throughout the long span from the late sixth to the end of the eighth century but was a key position in the East–West transportation and communications routes. Besides the extensive quantities of textiles, many artifacts unearthed from Dulan indicate cultural interactions and exchanges. For example, in some of the tombs large quantities of Kaiyuan *tongbao* copper coins have been found, as well as bronze mirrors with small *baohua* floral motifs. These were clearly goods imported from the Central Plains. A large number of lacquer objects, such as cups, bowls, and plates, were also manufactured in Han areas. In addition, many artifacts from the ancient West were also discovered at Dulan, including Sogdian gold and silverware (fig. 6), Turkic silver ornaments, beads of agate, glass, and carnelian, the remains of a copper platter, and a copper perfume phial. The large number of artifacts from east and west found in Dulan are adequate evidence of the importance and the role of the Qinghai Road.

The unearthed articles thus demonstrate that in the seventh and eighth centuries, under Tubo control, the Qinghai Road was not only open to traffic but also to trade on a very significant scale. The Qinghai Road played a key role whose importance was not in the least inferior to that of the Hexi Corridor.

二　都兰丝织品

都兰吐蕃墓葬出土大量遗物，其中丝织品数量之多、品种之全、图案之美、技艺之高、时间跨度之大（北朝晚期至唐代晚期）是前所未有的。据统计，这批丝织品共有残片 350 余件，不重复图案的品种达 130 余种，112 种为中原汉地织造，约占品种总数的 86%；18 种为中亚、西亚所织造，约占品种总数的 14%。西方织锦中有独具浓厚异域风格的粟特锦，数量较多，其中一件锦上织有罕见的中古波斯人使用的婆罗钵文字。毫无疑问，这批都兰丝织品的发现具有极其重要的学术价值。

（一）　种类

都兰出土的丝织品几乎包括了目前已知的唐代所有的丝织品种，而且其中的抛梭织法的锦、织金锦带、嵌合组织显花的绫、素绫、宽幅缂丝、绊锦等品种在国内均属最早实例，夹缬和蜡染织物也占一定比例，这对研究唐代丝绸生产技术有着重要的意义。

丝织物品种主要根据丝织物的组织结构、织造工艺及外观效果来区分。唐代织染署中的织纴之作分为布、绢、绝、纱、绫、罗、锦、绮、绸、褐等十作，这就是当时对纺织品种的一种分类法。十作中，除布为麻织品、褐为毛织品外，其余均属丝织品。这一分类与今天基本接近。在此，我们按锦、绫、罗、缂丝，以及平纹类织物（绢、纱、绝、绸），绸与绊的次序作一概要介绍。

Silk articles from Dulan

The silk textiles excavated from the Dulan Tubo graves are unprecedented in a number of ways, including their quantity, variety, beauty of patterns, levels of technique, and the span of time they cover, from the late Northern Dynasties to late Tang, that is, from the late sixth to mid-ninth century. More than 350 fragments of silk-woven articles display more than 130 types of unrepeated, unique, patterns. Among these, 112, or 86% of the total, are Han silks produced in the Central Plains region; 18, or 14%, are of west Central Asian or western Asian manufacture. Of the west Asian fabrics there is a fairly large number of distinctive Sogdian silks (*sute jin*), that is, compound weaves, which have the rich flavor of exotic lands. One textile fragment (cat. no. 78) is of particular interest. With an inscription woven into it in Pahlavi, an eighth-century Persian script, it is one of very few such examples ever found.

Varieties and types of weave [4]

The silk textiles excavated from Dulan include all types of silk textiles of the Tang dynasty known to have been produced at this time. Indeed, several excavated fragments are the earliest extant examples of certain techniques. These include compound weaves with weft floats on the reverse, a gold woven ribbon, self-patterned tabby using the warp/weft pattern step method, plain silk twill, kesi of a considerable width, *beng* fabrics, and so on. Textiles excavated from Dulan also include a certain number of clamp-resist and wax-resist dyed textiles. These textiles are highly significant for our research into the technologies of Tang-dynasty silk production.

The classification of silk-woven items generally relies on the underlying structure of the weave, weaving techniques, and the appearance of the results. During the Tang dynasty, a classification was made by the Weaving and Dyeing Bureau that created some ten different categories as follows:[5] cloth (*bu*), tabby silk (*juan*), coarse silk (*shi*), simple gauze (*sha*), silk twill or twill damask (*ling*), complex gauze (*luo*), compound weave (*jin*), patterned tabby (*qi*), shaded silks (*jian*), and coarse cloth (*he*). This was a way of differentiating distinct weaving products at the time. Of the ten, one is woven of bast fibers (*bu*), and one is woven from wool (*he*). All the others are made from silk. The classification is basically similar to the way we classify different weaves today. Below is a general introduction to several of these weaves: *jin, ling, luo, kesi*, plain weave types (including tabby silk *juan, sha, shi,* and *chou*), *jian*, and *beng*.

---

4 The following sections draw on: 许新国 Xu Xinguo, 赵丰 Zhao Feng, " 都兰出土丝织品初探 Dulan chutu sizhipin chutan (A tentative study of silk fabrics unearthed at Du Lan)", 中国历史博物馆馆刊 *Zhongguo lishi bowuguan guankan (Bulletin of the Chinese National Museum)* 15–16 (1991), pp. 63–81 [English translation: "A Preliminary Study of the Silk Textiles Excavated at Dulan", *China Archaeology and Art Digest,* 1/4 (1996), pp. 13–34].

5 Li Linfu [of the Tang dynasty] et al., 唐六典 *Tang liudian (The six statutes of the Tang dynasty)*, Beijing: Zhonghua Shuju, 1992, *juan* 20:576.

1. 锦

织彩为纹曰锦。都兰出土丝织品中以锦最为丰富，从组织结构上来说，可以分为平纹
经锦、斜纹经锦、斜纹纬锦和织金锦等。经锦依靠多彩的经丝表里换层而显花。它在中国
出现的年代极早，在春秋、战国时期已相当成熟，但当时都是平纹经锦。平纹经锦在都兰
出土物中实例不多，最有特色的是红地云珠吉昌太阳神锦（DRM1PM2：S109，图7，图
版No.7），以红、黄两种色彩的经丝构成1：1的经二重组织。大量的是斜纹经锦，这是
一种隋代前后才出现的新型组织。此类锦往往以四五种色彩的经丝通过分区排列，并以1：
2的经二重组织显花，使织锦图案上出现色条效果。其代表作有橙地对波连珠狮凤龙雀纹
锦（DRM1PM2：S150－2，图版No.4）、橙地小窠连珠镜花锦（DRM1PM2：S127，
图8，图版No.60）、黄地连珠对马纹锦（DRM1PM2：S17，图版No.11）等。

图7　平纹经锦（图版No.7）　Warp-faced compound tabby（cat. no. 7）

图8　斜纹经锦（图版No.60）　Warp-faced compound twill（cat. no. 60）

Jin 锦

To weave colours into patterns is given the name *jin*. The excavated fragments from Dulan include a wealth of *jin* weavings. These can be divided into categories according to their woven structure, such as warp-faced compound tabby *jin*, warp-faced compound twill *jin*, weft-faced compound twill *jin*, *jin* woven with metallic threads, and so on.

Warp-faced compound *jin* relies on different colours of warp threads that alternately appear on the front or the back of the weave in order to create the pattern. This type of weave appeared in China at an extremely early date and was already a mature technology at the time of the Spring and Autumn and Warring States periods. At that time all such weaving was warp-faced compound tabby. There are not many examples of warp-faced compound tabby among the excavated articles from Dulan, but one of the more unique is the *jin* with red ground, cloud-pearl roundels, and auspicious sun-god (fig.7, cat. no. 7), which uses red- and yellow-coloured warp threads to form a compound warp-faced weave with two series of warps. Most excavated examples are warp-faced compound twill *jin*, a new weave that did not appear until around the time of the Sui dynasty in China. This kind of *jin* frequently used four to five colours of warp threads lined up in discrete areas, and often used a compound structure with three or more series of warps to create the pattern. Key examples of *jin* weaves that allowed coloured pattern designs are seen in the excavated items of an orange ground *jin* with opposing aligned-pearl wave design with lions, phoenix, dragon, and peacock patterns (cat. no. 4), an orange-ground *jin* with small aligned-pearl roundels enclosing a mirror-pattern (fig.8, cat. no. 60), and a yellow-ground *jin* with aligned-pearl roundels enclosing confronted horses (cat. no. 11).

除经锦之外，都兰还出土了大量的纬锦。纬锦采用纬丝表里换层进行显花，组织结构是斜纹纬二重的 90 度转向。经二重中的夹纬，列纬二重中就是夹经，但在纬经中除少量采用单夹经如黄地大窠连珠狩虎锦（DRM1PM2：S102，图版 No.20）等外，绝大多数纬锦均采用双夹经，如红地中窠连珠对牛纹锦（DXM1：S5，图版 No.62），而且夹纬都加有强捻，图版 No.20 为 S 捻，图版 No.62 为 Z 捻。纬锦中较为特殊的是红地中窠含绶鸟锦，这是一类锦，以花瓣、小花或连珠等作图案，参见图版 No.75（图 9）。通常以紫红色为地，藏青、橘黄、墨绿等色显花。在色彩变换频繁处，所有纬丝全部织入，是 1：3 的斜纹纬二重组织。而在色彩变换不多的地部，就单织某两种或三种纬丝，为 1：1 或 1：2 的斜纹纬二重组织。多余的纬丝在织物背面抛梭而过，不织入织物而浮在织物背面。这种锦无论从图案看还是从织法看，都是西域地区的产物，但从名称上来看，却与唐宋文献中常见的"绒（茸）背锦"或"透背锦"相吻合。值得指出的还有一件蓝地龟甲花织金锦带，宽仅 3 厘米（图版 No.31）。在 1：1 基础平纹地上再以隔经的大循环平纹金箔显花，在地部则把金箔剪去，这一织法明显地采用了手工编织技术。在我国史料的记载中，丝织物使用金箔的记载早在三国时已经出现了，但织金锦的最早实物目前应为此件。

图 9　斜纹经锦（图版 No.75）　Weft-faced compound twill (cat. no. 75)

In addition to warp-faced compound *jin* weaves, large numbers of weft-faced compound *jin* were excavated from Dulan. Weft-faced compound *jin* uses the weft threads to display patterns by exchanging weft threads laying on the surface and those laying on the back of the fabric. The weave structure is turned 90 degrees compared to warp-faced compound twill weave. Among warp-faced compound weaves, both the inner weft passing through the pattern shed and the binding weft passing through a tabby or twill shed are single weft threads, but among weft-faced *jin*, other than a small number of silks that utilize single main warp ends, such as a silk with large aligned-pearl roundels enclosing a tiger-hunting scene (cat. no. 20), the greater number of weft-faced compound *jin* use a double main warp, such as a red-ground jin with aligned-pearl roundels enclosing confronted oxen (cat. no. 62), and so on. Moreover, the main warp ends are all given a strong twist, with the first example mentioned (cat. no. 20) having an S-direction twist, the second (cat. no. 62) a Z-direction twist.

One very special group of silks, all weft-faced compound *jin*, depicts a roundel enclosing a bird holding a ribbon in its beak against a red ground (for example, fig. 9, cat. no. 75). This is a type of *jin* that often uses petals, small flowers, or aligned pearls as motifs, and often has a deep-red ground and blue-green, tangerine-yellow, and dark-green patterning. Where colours interchange in a complex manner, all weft threads are entered into the weaving; when only a few are used, some of the others are left floating on the backside of the fabric, tossed behind with the shuttle. Thus, the compound weft-faced twill structure with four lats (weft systems) changes locally to a two or three lats weft-faced compound twill weave, with floating wefts. Both in terms of pattern and weave, this kind of weave is invariably a product of the Western Regions. The name given to this kind of weave in China can be seen in records dating from the Tang and Song dynasties: it corresponds to what is known as 'backed *jin*,' or 'penetrating through the back *jin*' (*rongbei jin* or *toubei jin*).

One piece that is worthy of special mention is a ribbon, *dai*, with tortoiseshell pattern, woven gold on a dark olive green ground (cat. no. 31). This is only 3 cm wide. On a tabby ground it has flat strips of gold foil woven in to create the pattern. The gold has been cut in areas where it is not needed for patterning, a method of weaving that clearly relates to entering the weft by hand. There are historical records of weaving gold foil strips into items as early as the Three Kingdoms in China (220–265 CE). This excavated textile is the earliest actual example seen in China to date.

2. 绫

绫在都兰的发现也是大量的，按其组织可分为三类，即平纹地暗花绫、斜纹地暗花绫和素绫。

平纹地暗花绫又包括以下两种。一是平纹地上斜纹显花。这种组织即以前考古界通常称的"绮"的组织，是对汉代之后绫织技术的直接继承。这种组织的绫发现极多，占全部出土绫的80%左右，如团窠双珠对龙绫，柿蒂绫（图10，图版No.28、29、41），山形斜纹黄地绫（DRLM1：S11-4，图版No.43）等。二是一种新发现的绫组织。它以平纹为地，显花部分则由方平或变化方平组织提花与平纹地配合形成变化斜纹，称之为嵌合组织。比如龟甲绫（DRM1PM2：S62，图版No.30）的显花组织，则是由平纹与经2、纬4的变化配合而成的。这种结构组织在国内目前还是首次见于报道。

斜纹地暗花绫的组织有两种。一是四枚异向绫，又称同单位异向绫，即以1：3的左斜纹和3：1的右斜纹互为化地组织，如黄色对波葡萄花叶绫（DRM9：S6-2，图版No.39）即为一例。二是同向绫，又称异单位同向绫，常常以2/1右向斜纹为地，1/5右向斜纹显花。

素绫的组织是2/2斜纹结构，这在新石器时代的草、竹编织物上十分常见，但应用在丝织物上却很晚。DRM6中发现了不少此类残片，是2/2斜纹组织，同时也是素面（无纹）斜纹丝织物的首次发现。

图10 平纹地上斜纹显花（绮，图版No.28）
Twill-on-tabby damask-like weave (*qi*; cat. no. 28)

Ling 绫

A large number of textiles employing a *ling*, or twill damask-like weave, were discovered at Dulan. The different structures of this weave can be divided into three categories: twill-on-tabby damask, twill-on-twill damask, and plain twill, of which the first and the second include several subtypes. One uses a tabby ground with 3:1 twill to display the pattern. Archaeological circles have commonly called this kind of weave *qi*. It is a direct continuation of the damask-weave technology of the Han dynasty. This type of damask weave is extremely common, accounting for some 80% of all excavated damask-like weaves. The type includes roundels enclosing all kinds of paired dragons with double pearls, all kinds of persimmon patterns (fig.10; cat. nos 28, 29, 41), zigzag patterns (cat. no. 43), and so on. The next is a kind of new discovery of damask-like weave that uses tabby as the ground, with the pattern made up of extended tabby squares or rectangles of two or four warp and weft threads overlapping with the tabby ground to form a 'distorted' twill. We call this an integrated or embedded weave (*qian he*). The Dulan example is a tortoiseshell pattern damask (cat. no. 30) that employs the 2-warp/4-weft step pattern system. This is the first time this weave has been reported in China.

There are two kinds of twill-weave damask: one is a four-end twill damask with opposite grain direction, also called 'same unit, alternate direction.' It uses a structure of weft-faced 1/3 Z twill and warp-faced 3/1 S twill, such as the example with opposing-wave pattern (cat. no. 39). The second combines two different twills with the same grain direction, and this is also called 'alternate unit, same direction' damask. A quite common combination uses 2/1 Z twill as ground, 1/5 Z twill for pattern.

Plain *ling* weave has a 2/2 twill structure. This kind of weave was used in reed and bamboo weavings of the Neolithic period; the use of the technique in silk weaving is very late. Many fragments of this weave type were discovered in DRM6. This is the first discovery of a 2/2 unpatterned twill weave that is woven of silk.

3. 缂丝

缂丝又称克丝、刻丝，其名出现于宋代，但从织造技艺来看，在唐代已经具备。缂丝是一种通经断纬的织物，以平纹为基本组织，依靠绕纬换彩而显花。都兰出土的蓝地十样小花缂丝（DRM1PM2：S70，图11，图版No.33）是目前所知极少的唐代缂丝中有特别价值的一件，纬向宽度为5.5厘米，尚非通幅，说明有别于唐代其他的缂丝带。但它的风格又与宋代缂丝有较大区别，并不严格按照换彩需要进行缂断，有时在同一色区内亦呈镂空之状，表明此件缂丝在缂织技术发展史上具有重要的地位。

4. 平纹类织物

平纹类织物是最普通的织物，可以根据经纬丝的原料、纤度、密度等变化产生许多品种。绢是一般平纹织物的通称。都兰出土平纹织物中最为常见的是绢，根据经纬密度的不同分为两个小类。一类密度较大，织造致密，经密65～70根／厘米，纬密约40～50根／厘米。这类绢或可称为缣。另一类密度较小，经密在40根／厘米，纬密在30根／厘米上下。此类丝线较粗的织物或可称之为绌，虽然密度小，但纤度粗，最后的效果仍是厚密。

图11　缂丝（图版No.33）　Kesi（cat. no. 33）

Kesi 缂丝

The name *kesi* first appeared in the Song dynasty, but the technique itself was already in existence in the Tang dynasty. *Kesi* (silk tapestry) is a kind of weaving with continuous warp while the weft is discontinuous. The basic structure of the weave is tabby, and the weft threads, which have different colours, are introduced only where needed to make the pattern or figure. The example excavated from Dulan (fig.11, cat. no. 33) is of particular value as it is an extremely rare example of a Tang-dynasty *kesi*. It has a blue field with small quatrefoil flowers. The weft-directional width of the piece is 5.5 cm, showing that it is different from other Tang-dynasty *kesi* bands. However, its style is yet again quite different from Song-dynasty *kesi*. The wefts, for example, do not turn only according to colour changes, but sometimes within a certain region of colour a slit is left. These characteristics place it at a particular point in the development of the *kesi* technique.

Tabby-weave textiles

Tabby weaves are the most common textiles. The different types can be classified simply by the type of material used for warp and weft, by density of threads, and so on. *Juan* is the general name for basic tabby weaves. The most commonly seen tabby items excavated at Dulan are *juan,* which can be divided into two types depending on the density of warp and weft threads. One kind has a relatively dense and tight weave, with the density of warp at about 65–70 ends per cm, and the density of weft at about 40–50 threads per cm. This kind of *juan* can also be called *jian* 缣 , which is defined as 'fine silk'. Another type has a relatively low density of threads, with a warp count of about 40 threads per cm and weft count of about 30 threads per cm. This relatively thick or rough kind of fabric is also called *shi*. Although the thread density is low, the thickness of the threads is greater so that the result is rather sturdy.

5. 綟与绊

以上几个大类的丝织品种主要根据织物组织结构的不同来区分，但统与绊情况较为复杂。从工艺上来看，它们属于"织采为文"的范畴，故常被人们称作"统锦""晕统锦""绊锦"等。但从组织结构来看，它们分别采用锦、绫，甚至是绢的组织。其变幻的装饰效果主要来自经丝色彩排列的变化或经丝本身色彩的逐段变化。

綟原是一种染缬效果。《续日本纪》云："染作晕綟色，而其色各种相间，皆横终幅。假令白次之以红、次之以赤、次之以红、次之以白、次之以缥、次之以青、次之以缥、次之以白之类，渐此浓淡，如日月晕气杂色相间之状，故谓之晕綟以后名锦。"[1]这段话已把晕綟的来历说得十分清楚。唐代织纤十作中专有綟作，当是专门织綟的作坊。都兰出土的綟采用斜纹经二重和山形斜纹两类组织。晕綟小花锦（DXM1:S6－1，图12，图版No.36）属于前者，经丝地部色彩排列为橙、黄、绿、蓝、绿、黄、橙等反复。其上再显小花，表现出锦上添花的效果，这或就是唐代史料中所说的晕綟锦。而山形斜纹常由两种色丝间隔排列，形成明显的两种色道，可称为綟道。都兰出土褐黄綟道素绫（DRM1PM2:S56，图版No.42），采用3/1山形斜纹。綟道与晕綟的主要区分在于綟道没有晕色过渡。

此外，都兰还发现了平纹组织的扎经染色织物。其工艺是先将经丝分组扎经染色，然后合而织之，我们可以称其为绊锦（DRM9:S6－1，图版No.38）。绊是日本学者对此类扎经染色织物的通称，但论其词源，还是来自中国。

---

1 《笺注倭名类聚抄》卷三"布帛部"。

图12　綟锦（斜纹经锦，图版No.36）
Jian (warp-faced compound twill, cat. no. 36)

Jian 繝 and *beng* 絣

The major categories of weave as described above are mainly differentiated on the basis of weave structure. *Jian* and *beng* present a more complex situation. They are colour-patterned weaves, and therefore often called *jian jin* or *yunjian jin,* or *beng jin*, and so on. In terms of technique, however, they use the same structures as *jin, ling*, and even *juan*. Their blurry ornamental result is derived from the way the silk colours are lined up, or from the alternating colours of the silk warp yarn itself.

Jian was originally the result of a kind of dying method. In a commentary to the *Shoku Nihongi (Chronicles of Japan)* a textile is described with "an arrangement of colours including red, vermilion, red, white, green, white, and so on, including deep and pastel or soft colours, such as the interplay between sunlight and moonlight, so that this is called 暈繝 *ungen* [in Chinese *yunjian*], and was later called 锦 *nishiki* [in Chinese *jin*]". [6] This quotation describes the origins of *yunjian* very clearly. The Tang classification of ten types of weave includes *jian,* and there was a workshop during Tang times that specifically made *jian*. Two types of striped weaves have been excavated from Dulan. The first type is represented by the little-flower *jin* (fig.12, cat. no. 36), which is a warp-faced compound twill. Its warp threads are arrayed in repeating colours of tangerine-orange, yellow-green, blue, green, yellow, tangerine-orange, and so on, with small flower patterns on top so that it appears as if the flowers had been strewn on a field. This may well be the *yunjian jin* referred to in Tang historical records. The second type commonly uses two kinds of coloured silk in its array, to form clearly delineated stripes of colour. A piece excavated from Dulan (cat. no. 42) belongs to this category and uses a 3/1 warp chevron twill. The difference between such striped fabrics and *yunjian* striped weaves is that the latter achieves an effect of shading by colour gradation.

Another piece was discovered at Dulan that is a tabby weave with assorted colour-dyed warp. The technique was to dye the warp threads first in groups, and then to put them together and weave them. The example is a narrow band (cat. no. 38), which could be called *beng jin*. The term *beng* comes originally from China, although Japanese scholars also typically use it as their term for this warp-dyed textile (*kasuri*).

---

6 "Shoku Nihongi. Chronicles of Japan, continued, from A.D. 697 to 791" (Books IV–VI), translated and annotated by J. B. Snellen, *The Transactions of the Asiatic Society of Japan,* second series, vol. 14, 1937, p. 259.

（二） 相关问题探讨

从都兰出土的丝织品中，仅就与品种密切相关的几个问题作一初探。

1. 经锦和纬锦的区别

在鉴定北朝至唐代丝织品的过程中，往往会遇到经锦与纬锦，主要是斜纹经锦与斜纹纬锦的区别问题。这一问题在过去的研究中颇多争议，夏鼐先生指出这是一个重要问题，应早日解决[2]。现在，通过都兰丝织物的鉴定，对这个问题形成了比较明确的认识。如前所述，斜纹经锦和斜纹纬锦的显花原理、显花方法均是相同的，仅在显花丝线上有经纬之别。因此，鉴定经锦的关键就是鉴别经线和纬线，最可靠的标准是确定幅边，与幅边平行者为经线，与幅边垂直者为纬线。

都兰出土织锦中有很大一部分都带有幅边，由此可以看出，经锦幅边与纬锦幅边的区别。经锦由于是经线显花，经线密而多，纬线疏而少，在幅边外则通过减少经线层数与纬线交织成单层三枚斜纹组织，经锦的幅边细密、平整。纬锦则由纬线显花，纬密经稀，在幅边外纬线无法依靠其他手段得到减稀，纬锦的幅边往往用较粗的麻线作经与高密度的纬线交织，以承受大量纬线的挤拉，外观也就较为粗糙。在许多纬锦上，还经常出现一条宽1～3厘米的1:1纬二重组织的界边，这条边将整匹的纬锦图案分成若干段。从实物使用情况来看，此边主要是为了便于剪裁，故而可称为裁剪界边。这种情况不但在都兰出土丝织品中可见，在吐鲁番出土丝织品上也屡见不鲜，甚至在敦煌画塑中也有所反映。

② 夏鼐《新疆新发现的丝织品——锦、绮和刺绣》，《考古学报》1963 年第 1 期，45 ～ 76 页。

An exploration of key questions

The silk textiles excavated at Dulan raise a number of questions that have yet to be resolved. Here are several key questions we would like to address.

Distinguishing between warp-faced jin and weft-faced jin

In evaluating Northern Dynasties to Tang period silk textiles, one often encounters the problem of differentiating between warp-faced and weft-faced weaves, particularly warp-faced compound twill and weft-faced compound twill. This question has been addressed in the past. Xia Nai, for example, noted long ago that this important question should be resolved at the earliest possible time.[7] Now, as a result of evaluating Dulan silk textiles, we can arrive at a clearer resolution of the issues.

As noted earlier, the overall principles and methods of figuring or making a pattern on warp-faced and weft-faced compound twill fabrics are the same, the only difference being that the silk threads used for the patterning are either warp or weft. Because of this, the key to evaluating warp-faced *jin* lies in differentiating between warp and weft threads. The most reliable standard for this is confirming the selvages, for threads in alignment or parallel to the selvages are warp, and those that are perpendicular to the selvages are weft.

A large percentage of the woven *jin* fragments excavated from Dulan have selvages, so we are able to make use of this distinction. Since warp threads create the pattern on warp-faced compound weaves, the warp threads are both denser and greater in number, whereas the weft threads are sparser and fewer in number. Weft-faced compound weaves use weft threads to create the pattern: in this instance, the weft is the denser and the warp is more sparse. There is considerable pull on the weft threads due to the patterning: in order to hold the edge, a hemp thread was often put in to bolster the warp at the selvage, so that the selvage looks somewhat thicker and rougher. On many weft-faced compound twills, there is a 1 to 3 cm border or demarcating strip in weft direction with two lats only; this border divides the entire pattern of these weft-faced weaves into many sections. Looking at the actual circumstances of using the fabric, this border exists mainly to facilitate cutting the fabric, therefore it is called a 'cutting border.' Such borders are seen not only in silks excavated from Dulan, but are common in silks from Turfan, and they are even portrayed in paintings at Dunhuang. Some people believe that the thicker hemp threads on weft-faced compound twills making up the selvage should be considered a loom-head (transverse selvage), and they determine the 'cutting edge' to be a 'selvage.'[8] In fact, the characteristics of a selvage are clear: the weft threads should reverse directions at a selvage, whereas at a 'cutting edge' this is not the case.

---

7 夏鼐 Xia Nai, 新疆新发现的古代丝织品 —— 绮、锦和刺绣 "Xinjiang xin faxian de gudai sizhipin—qi, jin, he cixiu (Ancient textiles discovered recently in Xinjiang—qi, jin, and embroidery)", 考古学报 *Kaogu Xuebao (Acta Archaeologica Sinica)* 1, 1963, pp. 45–76.

8 See, for example, Wu Min, "The Exchange of Weaving Technologies between China and Central and Western Asia from the Third to the Eighth Century Based on New Textile Finds in Xinjiang", *Central Asian Textiles and Their Contexts in the Early Middle Ages*, ed. Regula Schorta, Riggisberg: Abegg-Stiftung, 2006 (Riggisberger Berichte 9), pp. 211–42.

有的学者认为，纬锦上粗麻线的幅边应为轴头，而把剪裁界边定作幅边。其实幅边的特征相当明确，纬丝在幅边处应有转绕，而裁剪界边却不具有这个特点，轴头在一般情况下亦无此例，故而经锦与纬锦是不难鉴别的。通过幅边的确定，可以把一大批经锦和纬锦区别开来。对这些经锦、纬锦进行织造技术及外观效果上的分析比较，又可为没有幅边情况下的经锦、纬锦鉴别提供依据。

Ⅰ. 纬锦的表层显花丝线密度远远小于经锦。据我们实测，纬锦表层显花丝线密度一般在 20 ～ 30 枚／厘米上下，不超过 40 枚／厘米；而经锦的表层显花丝线密度均大于 40 枚／厘米，一般在 50 ～ 60 枚／厘米上下。

Ⅱ. 经锦显花丝线很少超过三组，即多为 1∶1 和 1∶2 显花。而纬锦常在四组到五组之间，即为 1∶3 或 1∶4 显花。其原因是经锦多用一组色丝，要使经密增加 50 ～ 60 根／厘米，会超出一般的穿综能力，影响开口清晰。而纬锦若增加色丝组数最多只影响生产速度而已，并无技术难题。

Ⅲ. 经锦的显花丝线在显花处呈梭状，覆盖不严，导致色彩不纯。而纬锦的显花丝线粗而平整，表面具有台面效果，覆盖严实，色彩统一。

Ⅳ. 绝大部分纬锦都采用双夹经甚至是三夹经，少数采用单夹经，但所有这些经线均加有强捻，而经锦均用单丝作夹纬。因此，凡采用双根作夹丝，并加以强捻的锦，一般均可定为纬锦。这种双夹经的技术对于保证纬锦的台面和平整起到了重要的作用。

Through determination of the selvages we can differentiate between most warp-faced *jin* and weft-faced compound twills, and we can then do a comparative analysis of weaving technology and the resulting appearance of the textile. However, even when there is no selvage, we can find evidence for differentiating between warp- and weft-faced compound weaves in the following four ways.

One. The density of threads on the upperside of a weft-faced compound weave is far less than that of a warp-faced compound weave. By our estimation, the density of patterning threads in a weft-faced *jin* is generally around 20 to 30 passes per cm, not over 40 per cm, whereas the density for warp-faced *jin* is always greater than 40 series of warps per cm, usually around 50 to 60 per cm. One thread per pass and per warp series respectively is visible on the textile's upper side.

Two. Rarely do the threads used for patterning in warp-faced compound weaves exceed three in a series, most have two and three series, whereas with weft-faced compound twill the number is generally between four and five weft threads in a pass to make the pattern. The reason is that to add one more warp series or colour the density of threads must be increased by 50 to 60 ends per cm, which generally exceeds the shaft capacity, making it difficult to get a clear shed opening for the shuttle. With weft-faced *jin*, however, increasing the number of colours or lats influences at most the speed of operation—there is no technical difficulty.

Three. In the case of warp-faced compound weaves, the coverage of patterning silk threads is often uneven, making colouring impure or not perfect, whereas with weft-faced compound weaves the silk threads of the patterning are thicker and even and the surface has a flat effect, the coverage is tighter or closer, and the colouring is more unified.

Four. Most weft-faced compound weaves utilize double main warp ends or even triple main warp ends; only a small number use single main warp ends, but all of these warp threads are strongly twisted. Warp-faced compound weaves all use single silk threads as inner weft, passing through the pattern shed. Because of this, all textiles using double inner threads that are strongly twisted can generally be considered weft-faced compound weaves. This double main warp technology plays an important role in guaranteeing the flatness and smooth surface effect of weft-faced *jin*.

2. 织物的幅宽

我们都知道唐代丝织物的规格在当时律令中有严格的规定，"皆阔尺八寸，长四丈为匹"[3]。以前曾有人验之于敦煌契约文书，基本是吻合的[4]；今验之于都兰出土的丝织物，亦较吻合。都兰出土织物许多有双幅边，能测出完整的幅宽。其中最多的是绢，幅宽均为53 ~ 58.5 厘米，以唐尺一尺合今 30 厘米计，幅宽为 1.77 ~ 1.95 唐尺，与一尺八寸的标准相差无几。

经锦和绫织物中亦有双幅边者，但从实测情况看，除了黄地连珠对羊锦（DRM1PM2：S59，图版 No.17）幅宽为 52 厘米外，其他均在 50 厘米以下，离唐代标准幅宽约差两寸，最大的差四寸，这可能是因为锦绫的织造工艺较为复杂，偷工减料所得的利益颇大之故。

唐代还有一种丝织物的计量单位是"张"，主要流行于中亚地区。吐鲁番文书证实，这一计量单位在当地使用甚早。具体尺寸是长 8 ~ 9.5 尺，宽 4 ~ 4.5 尺[5]。北朝时期的尺度标准略小于唐代，可知张的幅宽约为匹的幅宽的 2 倍稍多些，而在长度上则大大小于匹，约为 1/5。

其实，张与匹的规格区别最初曾是西方织锦与东方织锦、纬锦与经锦的重要区别标志。但随着东西纺织技术交流的深入，纬锦中也有采用经锦幅宽的，中原纬锦也有采用张作尺度的。纬锦并不都以张为计量单位，但可以说，以张为计量单位的都是纬锦。

3 《唐令拾遗》"赋役令"。
4 王进玉《敦煌遗书中的丝织物》，《丝绸史研究》1987 年第 1 ~ 2 期。
5 例如，吐鲁番文书中提到的 75TKM99.6(b)，614 年，参见唐长孺编《吐鲁番出土文书》卷一，94 ~ 95 页，文物出版社，1992 年；75TKM88.1(b)，506 年，《吐鲁番出土文书》卷一，99 页。

The width of woven articles

Tang-dynasty statutes carry strict regulations regarding the standard measurements to be observed for silk textile pieces:"all [textiles have] widths of one *chi* eight *cun*, [and] lengths of four *zhang*, which is one *pi* (bolt)."[9] This standard has been measured against contractual documents found in Dunhuang, and it basically corresponds.[10] Applying the standard now to silk textiles excavated from Dulan, we find that it also basically corresponds.

Many of the textiles excavated from Dulan have both selvages so we can measure the complete width of the fabric. Among those with two selvages, the largest number are *juan*, or normal silk tabby. The width falls between 53 and 58.5 cm. Since the Tang-dynasty *chi* measured around 30 of today's centimeters, the width as defined in *chi* was 1.77 to 1.95 Tang-dynasty *chi*. This is not far off from the standard noted in the Tang statutes of "one *chi* eight *cun*."

Some warp-faced *jin* and *ling* textiles excavated from Dulan also had two selvages, but in measuring these pieces we find that they all measure less than 50 cm in width, or at least 2 *cun* under the Tang-dynasty standard. An exception is DRM1PM2: S59 (cat. no. 17), which is 52 cm. The greatest disparity from the standard Tang width was some 4 *cun*, which may have been due to the relative complexity of the weaving technology of *jin* and *ling*, or it may have been due to the benefits derived from skimping on materials.

Another term of measurement in the Tang dynasty was *zhang*. The measurement unit *zhang* was used mainly in Central Asian regions, and also designated a piece of fabric of a given size. Documents from Turfan give evidence that this measurement unit was used in Turfan from an early date, and that the actual length of a *zhang* was around 8–9.5 *chi*, with a width of around 4–4.5 *chi*.[11] Since the Northern Dynasties' standard measurement of a *chi* was smaller than it was in the Tang period, it can be assumed that the width of a *zhang* was roughly twice the width of a *pi*. The length of a *zhang* was much smaller than a *pi*, however, roughly one-fifth that of a *pi*.

In point of fact, the original difference between the standard measurements of *zhang* and *pi* was simply the difference between *jin* textiles woven in the West and those woven in the East. The two measurements can be an important indicator of the difference between weft-faced compound weaves and warp-faced *jin*. As intercourse between eastern and western regions increased with the passage of time, some weft-faced compound weaves began to use warp-faced *jin* widths. Weft-faced compound weaves produced in the Central Plains also began to use the *zhang* measurement. Naturally, not all weft-faced compound weaves use the *zhang* as a unit of measurement, but we can say that any textile that does use *zhang* as the unit of measurement is a weft-faced *jin*.

9   新唐书 *Xin Tang shu* (*New history of the Tang dynasty*), Beijing: Zhonghua shuju1975, *juan* 48:1271.

10   王进玉 Zheng Jinyu, 敦煌遗书中的丝织物 "Dunhuang yishu zhongde sizhipin (Textiles in Dunhuang documents)", 丝绸史研究 *Sichou shi yanjiu (Research on the History of Silk)* 1–2, 1987.

11   For example, for document 75TKM99:6[b], a loan contract dated 514, see 唐长孺 Tang Zhangru (ed.), 吐鲁番出土文书 *Tulufan chutu wenshu (Excavated documents from Turfan)*, Beijing: Wenwu chubanshe 1992–1996, vol. 1, pp. 94–95, and document 75TKM88:1(b), another loan contract, dated 506, see *Tulufan chutu wenshu*, vol. 1, p. 89. See also Zhao Feng and Wang Le, "Glossary of Textile Terminology (Based on the Documents from Dunhuang and Turfan)", *Textiles as Money on the Silk Road, Journal of the Royal Asiatic Society* Series 3, 23, 2 (2013), pp. 349–387, in particular pp. 386–387.

3. 东西方织锦的区别

都兰位于丝绸之路青海道上。受东西方文化的影响，在唐代，丝绸生产已遍及丝绸之路沿线，故而在都兰同一墓群中出土来自东西方的织锦也是很自然的。

我们所说的东方，主要是指阳关以内的唐朝疆土，西方主要是指西域，以中亚地区为主，甚至包括西亚。这两个地区的历史条件不同，风土人情有别，从纺织文化的角度来看应分属于两个不同的文化圈。它们生产的织锦也肯定有所区别。这一问题早已引起人们的重视，但要分辨清楚却非易事。我们主要从都兰出土织锦鉴定所得的体会来探讨东西方织锦的区别。

Ⅰ. 东方织锦的传统是平纹的经显花，后来才有斜纹和纬显花，而中亚地区的传统织法则是纬显花。这一点已为众多的学者所证实。因此，一般可以将经锦列入东方织锦之列。我们的任务主要就是把纬锦中的东方织锦和西方织锦区别开来。

Ⅱ. 从大效果来说，纬锦都具有厚实、平挺、覆盖严实的特点。但相比之下，西方织锦这一点更好，表层出现的色丝几乎呈长方形，整个形成一个台面，露出的明经斜向整齐，说明织造技术相当高。

Ⅲ. 纬锦多采用双夹经，或采用单夹经，但夹经均加强捻，捻向有 S 捻和 Z 捻两种。据研究，中国的传统是采用 S 捻，而中亚地区的特点是采用 Z 捻，这是一个相当普遍的现象。因此，在都兰纬锦的鉴定中，可以将之作为区别东西方织锦的一个重要标志。

Differentiating between eastern and western jin

Dulan is situated on the Qinghai portion of the Silk Road, and so has been influenced by both eastern and western cultures. During the Tang dynasty, silk production extended all along the Silk Road, so it is natural for textiles from both East and West to be found in any single grave in Dulan.

When we say East, we usually mean territory of the Tang dynasty that lies within the Yangguan post. By West, we mean mainly the Western Regions, principally the Central Asian area but also Western Asia. The history, customs, and human circumstances of these two regions have been distinct, so they should be regarded as belonging to two separate cultural spheres in terms of weaving technology. The *jin* textiles that each region produced have their own distinct characteristics. Although this subject has long received scholarly attention, it is not in fact easy to differentiate between the two. Based on the understanding that we have been able to gain from evaluating Dulan textiles, we list below the main points of difference between eastern and western patterned compound weaves.

One. The tradition in eastern *jin* is compound tabby with warp-faced patterning; only later did weft-faced patterning and twill appear. In the Central Asian region the traditional weaving method was to use the weft for patterning. This point has already been acknowledged by most scholars in the field and, because of it, warp-faced *jin* pieces can basically all be entered into the ranks of eastern *jin* textiles. Our main responsibility, therefore, is to differentiate between eastern and western weft-faced *jin* textiles.

Two. In terms of the results for woven textiles, all weft-faced compound weaves are characterized as being thick and tough, flat, and with a tight or close coverage. In contrast, western textiles are better in the sense that the surface is extremely regular: the delineation of twill is very even in western weaves, showing that the weaving technology is extremely high.

Three. Weft-faced compound weaves mostly use double main warp ends, or use single main warp ends but with the main warp threads given a strong twist, with either S direction or Z direction. Our research suggests that the tradition in China is to use the S-twist direction, while Central Asian textiles are characterized by a Z-twist direction. This is a relatively widespread phenomenon. It can be an important standard in differentiating between eastern and western weaves when evaluating Dulan weft-faced compound weaves.

Ⅳ. 东西方织锦的色彩差异很大。中亚织锦的配色对比强烈、鲜明，染色牢度极佳，保存也较一般织锦好。东方织锦的配色显得较为明快、清秀、协调，染色牢度明显不如西方织锦。具体的色调差别也很大，如中亚地区用紫红、藏青（有时近黑）、暗绿、血牙黄、白等，在都兰出土物中尤以紫红地为多；而东方用红多呈橙红（或称退红）、普蓝、草绿、褐黄，尤以黄地为多，效果明显不同。

Ⅴ. 东西方织锦的图案题材也有很大区别。在纬锦中，东方织锦主要是织宝花团窠或写生折枝花纹样，很少有连珠纹等直接模仿西方织锦的产品。中亚织锦采用较多的还是团窠中安置含绶鸟、对牛、对马、灵鹫等主题纹样，而且其纹样造型几何化，轮廓鲜明，不像东方织锦那样明显具有写实风格。此外，中亚织锦的图案较为复杂，连珠中也寻求色彩的变换，团窠之间的间隔极少，几乎靠在一起，这与东方团窠的花地分明、自由从容、明快淡雅形成鲜明的对比。

东西方织锦的区别大致可分，但产地研究更难。东方织锦中心不外四川和中原两大地区，西方织锦的产地却尚无结论。据敦煌文献记载，部分波斯人和中亚粟特人曾进入中国西部，都兰出土的西方织锦极有可能是这些人制造的。它的制作地点应该是在米兰、敦煌、都兰之间。在这一时期，这部分人属于吐蕃统治。中亚的粟特锦和波斯锦受到吐蕃人的喜爱。目前，丝绸之路上的西方织锦以都兰出土者为大宗。

Four. The difference in colour use between eastern and western compound weaves is striking. Central Asian textiles use strongly contrasting bright colours, and the colour fastness of the dyes is excellent. The colours have often been extremely well preserved. Eastern colours appear more delicate, pretty, and harmonized, and the colour-fastness of dyes is far lower than that of western textiles. The dyestuffs used to make colours also vary between eastern and western textiles. Central Asian textiles predominantly use dark red as the ground, whereas eastern pieces use predominantly a yellow ground. The red in eastern pieces is more orange-red, also called faded red, whereas it is dark to purple-red in western pieces. Western green sometimes approaches black, whereas eastern green is more a grass-green, and the yellow, instead of being ivory-yellow as in western pieces, is more a brownish yellow. The use of these different colours in eastern and western *jin* produces very different aesthetic results.

Five. The subject matter of patterns shows clear differences. Among weft-faced compound weaves, eastern pieces mainly use flower roundels or realistic branches; very rarely do eastern products directly copy such western motifs as aligned-pearl patterns. Central Asian compound weaves display more roundels that enclose birds with ribbons in their beaks, opposing oxen, opposing horses, eagles, and other such subjects, and their aspect is particularly rigid and geometric. Outlines are clear-cut, unlike eastern patterns that have a more realistic and painterly style. In addition, Central Asian patterns are relatively more complex. They attempt colour changes among aligned pearls, and the interval between the roundels is so small that they nearly touch one another. Eastern roundels are looser and more fluid, they are lively, simple, and elegant, forming a clear contrast with western designs.

One can make the above general distinctions between eastern and western *jin* textiles, but it is harder to specify their actual place of production. The centers of eastern production were the two large areas of Sichuan and the Central Plains, but there is as yet no resolution on the issue of the locations of western production.

According to written records from Dunhuang, Persians and Central Asian Sogdians *established several cities in the western* part of China. We feel that there is a strong possibility that the western *jin* textiles excavated from Dulan were made by these people. The place of manufacture should be among the three centers of Miran, Dunhuang, and Dulan. During the period we are discussing, people in these areas were under Tubo rule. Central Asian Sogdian *jin* and Persian *jin* fabrics had become highly coveted by Tubo inhabitants. To date, the largest number of western-produced compound weaves from along the Silk Road have been excavated from Dulan.

第二章　都兰纺织品珍宝

许新国　安吉莉卡·斯利弗卡

都兰县隶属于海西蒙古族藏族自治州，在古代是羌、吐谷浑、吐蕃等民族聚居地，分布着众多的古遗址、古墓群。

在第一章中，从纺织技术的角度叙述了都兰热水血渭大墓（DMR1）及其周围陪葬墓（DMR1PM2）考古发掘和采集出土的纺织品，主要是毛织品，还有丝织品和棉织品。书中还选用了夏日哈墓葬（DXM）、夏日哈大什角墓葬（DXDM）、露斯沟墓葬（DRLM & DRLC）出土的其他纺织品。为了能够清晰认识都兰出土纺织品的特点，本章选取了具有代表性的 82 件纺织品，包含了一百多种纹样织法，并对其分别作详细介绍。其中一半以上的纺织品出于热水血渭大墓（DRM1、DRM1PM2、DRXM1、DRXM1PM2），9 件来自露丝沟墓葬，10 件出自热水南察干乌苏墓（DRM9、DRXM9、DRXM26）。书中记录了最初的考古发掘编号、保管收藏号及织物尺寸，并根据国际标准 CIETA 对织物的组织结构进行了分析。每件织物都有简要说明文字，以标识箭头明确其经线的方向。图版中有时两件织物会缝在一起，或原为成组残片，为方便叙述，我们用简单示意图表明其关系。

By Xu Xinguo, with weave analyses by Angelika Sliwka

Textile Treasures of Dulan

Dulan County is located in the Haixi Mongol and Tibetan Autonomous Prefecture. The area was settled in ancient times by the Qiang, Tuyuhun, and Tubo (Tibetan) peoples, and many ancient cemetery sites of these ethnic groups can be found throughout the county. In the Introduction, we gave a brief outline of the archaeological excavations in Dulan County, introduced the main types of textiles found in the area, and discussed some key questions arising from these finds. The following pages present a selection of characteristic and important examples of these textile treasures in more detail. The 82 catalogue numbers describe more than one hundred different patterned textiles. More than half of them have been excavated from the large tomb M1 at Reshui Xuewei (DRM1 and DRM1PM2, also DRXM1 and DRXM1PM2), ten from Dulan Reshui graves south of Qagan Us river (DRM9, also DRXM9, and DRXM26), nine from Dulan Lusigou grave group (DRLM and DRLC), and seven from cemeteries in Xarag township (DXM and DXDM).

The catalogue entries all comprise find number, inventory number, measurements after conservation, detailed technical analysis of weave structure established according to the guidelines of the Centre International d'Etude des Textiles Anciens CIETA, as well as a short commentary. Every textile is shown in full view, with additional detail images where appropriate. Height, width, and the arrow indicating the warp direction always refer to the full image. Sometimes two textiles are stitched together, or several fragments can be reassembled. In these cases, diagrams help to identify the individually numbered textiles and fragments.

绿地对波连珠狮凤龙纹锦　(DRM1PM2:S85；QK002034)　6 世纪末

长 11 厘米、宽 6.7 厘米，经向 ↔。

2/1Z 斜纹经重组织。经线：弱 S 捻丝，有黄、橄榄绿或蓝二色。经密 120 ~ 132 根／厘米（1:1，每组为 60 ~ 66 根／厘米）。纬线：很细近本色，无明显加捻丝，双根并股，明纬、夹纬交替，纬密 28 ~ 30 根／厘米。幅边已失。

绿地显黄花。用连珠纹构成对波骨架，以小花为连组。残存有两个对波圈，一圈对狮，一圈对凤，纹样较为清晰。对狮蹲踞，是全侧面形象；对凤的形象十分优美。

LATE SIXTH-CENTURY JIN, GREEN GROUND, OPPOSING ALIGNED-PEARL WAVES WITH LION AND PHOENIX MOTIFS (DRM1PM2:S85; QK 002034)

Height 11 cm, width 6.7 cm (warp direction ↔).

Warp-faced compound 2/1 Z twill with two series of warps.

Warp: silk, slightly S-twisted, yellow, olive-green to blue; 120–132 ends per cm (60–66 ends per warp series and cm).

Weft: silk, no noticeable twist, very fine, undyed(?), paired; 28–30 picks per cm, passed alternately through a twill shed and a pattern shed.

No selvage preserved.

Green ground with yellow patterning. Framework is made of aligned-pearl-pattern opposing waves, with small flowers as connecting knobs. The remaining fragment has two opposing wave enclosures, one with confronted lions inside, one with phoenixes. The pattern is relatively clear; the confronted lions are crouching and in profile, the aspect of the confronted phoenixes is very appealing.

蓝地对波缠枝对鸟纹锦 （DRM1PM2:S36；QK003591） 6世纪末

长11厘米、宽7.5厘米，经向↔。缀附残片，长2.8厘米、宽4.8厘米，经向↔。

2/1Z斜纹经重组织。经线：S捻丝，含深蓝、红、黄和其间的绿等四色。经密在1:2处约为180根/厘米，在1:3处约为240根/厘米，每组约为60根/厘米。纬线：近本色很细的无捻丝，明纬、夹纬交替，纬密为35根/厘米。幅边已失。

平纹经重组织。经线：无明显加捻，有黄、绿二色，经密约130根/厘米（1:1，每组约65根/厘米）。纬线：无明显加捻的近本色丝，明纬、夹纬交替，纬密约34根/厘米。一侧幅边尚存。

蓝地显绿、黄、棕色花。用缠枝和对波构成骨架，以小花为连组。残存两个对波圈，内均为展翅的对鸟或对鸭纹，呈全侧面形象。

LATE SIXTH-CENTURY JIN, BLUE GROUND, OPPOSING WAVE PATTERN MADE OF CURVING BRANCHES ENCLOSING CONFRONTED BIRDS (DRM1PM2:S36; QK 003591)

Height 11 cm, width 7.5 cm (warp direction ↔). Attached fragment (height 2.8 cm, width 4.8 cm; warp direction ↔).

Warp-faced compound 2/1 Z twill with four series of warps.

Warp: silk, S-twisted, dark blue, red, yellow, green (intermittently); c. 180 ends per cm in areas with three series of warps, c. 240 ends per cm in areas with four series of warps (c. 60 ends per warp series and cm).

Weft: silk, no noticeable twist, very fine, undyed(?); c. 35 picks per cm, passed alternately through a twill shed and a pattern shed.

No selvage preserved.

Attached fragment: Warp-faced compound tabby with two series of warps.

Warp: silk, no noticeable twist, yellow, green; c. 130 ends per cm (65 ends per warp series and cm).

Weft: silk, no noticeable twist, undyed(?); c. 34 picks per cm, passed alternately through a tabby shed and a pattern shed.

Selvage preserved on one side.

Blue ground with patterning in green, yellow (beige), and brown (red). Twining branches and opposing waves form the framework, with small flowers as connecting knobs. The fragment has two opposing waves enclosing profile depictions of geese or some other kind of birds, spreading their wings.

1 组织细节 Weave detail

一组三片（A、B、C）黄地对波牵驼狮象纹锦

（DRM1PM2:S149 - 1）　6世纪末

A. QK002038　长7.5厘米、宽41.5厘米，经向↕。

2/1Z斜纹经重组织。经线：无捻丝，由黄、白和深蓝，红与绿交替显色组成，经密约162根／厘米（1:2，每组约54根／厘米）。纬线：近本色无捻丝，明纬、夹纬交替，纬密约为24根／厘米。织物的左侧端存留幅边，一侧长端缝缀有十根细平纹织条边饰，颜色顺序为深蓝、浅黄、赭石、绿、黄、赭石、黄、绿、蓝绿、橄榄绿。

A.

THREE (A, B, C) LATE SIXTH-CENTURY JIN SILKS, WITH YELLOW GROUND OPPOSING WAVE-PATTERN WITH CAMELS BEING LED, LIONS, AND ELEPHANTS (DRM1PM2:S149-1)

A. (QK 002038) Height 7.5 cm, width 41.5 cm (warp direction ↕).

Warp-faced compound 2/1 Z twill with three series of warps.

Warp: silk, no noticeable twist, yellow, white, dark blue, green, and red (the latter three arranged in stripes); c. 162 ends per cm (c. 54 ends per warp series and cm).

Weft: silk, no noticeable twist, undyed(?); c. 24 picks per cm, passed alternately through a twill shed and a pattern shed.

One selvage preserved at the left side of the fragment.

A band composed of ten narrow strips of plain tabby (dark blue, light yellow, ochre, green, yellow, ochre, yellow, green, blue-green, olive-green) is attached to one long side of the fragment.

B. QK002843　残片总长 18.7 厘米、通宽 26 厘米，其中的驼狮象残片长 18.5 厘米、宽 16 厘米，经向 ↔。

驼狮象残片为平纹经重组织。经线：无捻丝，黄、白和深蓝与绿色交替显色组成，经密约 162 根 / 厘米（1：2，每组约 54 根 / 厘米）。纬线：米色无捻丝，明纬、夹纬交替，纬密约 28 根 / 厘米。幅边已失。

缀附残片也为平纹经重组织[1]。经线：无捻丝，黄、白色与深蓝、绿色交替显色，经密约为 180 根 / 厘米（1：2，每组约 60 根 / 厘米）。纬线：米色无捻丝，明纬、夹纬交替，纬密约 24 根 / 厘米。幅边已失。

缀附残片的一边缝有两色三根平纹织条的边饰，颜色次序为深蓝、棕、深蓝。

1 这块残片的图案分析参见图版 No.6。

B.

B. (QK 002843) Height 18.7 cm, width altogether 26 cm, width of camel, lion, elephant fragment height 18.5 cm, width 16 cm (warp direction ↔).

Warp-faced compound tabby with three series of warps.

Warp: silk, no noticeable twist, yellow, white, dark blue and green (the latter two arranged in stripes); c. 162 ends per cm (c. 54 ends per warp series and cm).

Weft: silk, no noticeable twist, beige; c. 28 picks per cm, passed alternately through a tabby shed and a pattern shed.

No selvage preserved.

3

Attached fragment:[1] Warp-faced compound tabby with three series of warps.

Warp: silk, no noticeable twist, yellow, white, dark blue and green (the latter two arranged in stripes); c. 180 ends per cm (c. 60 ends per warp series and cm).

Weft: silk, no noticeable twist, beige; c. 24 picks per cm, passed alternately through a tabby shed and a pattern shed.

A band composed of three narrow strips of plain tabby (dark blue, brown, dark blue) is attached to the left side of the fragment.

---

1   For the pattern of this fragment, see cat. no. 6.

C. QK002925　长 5 厘米、宽 27.5 厘米，经向 ↕。

正面为 2/1Z 斜纹经重组织。经线：无捻丝，由浅棕、乳白和蓝与绿色交替显色组成；经密约为 180 根 / 厘米（1:2，每组约为 60 根 / 厘米）。纬线：近本色的无捻丝，明纬、夹纬交替，纬密约 26 根 / 厘米。幅边已失。

背面为 1/2Z 斜纹纬重组织[2]。经线：米色 S 捻丝，夹经、明经 2:1 交替。夹经约 44 根 / 厘米，明经约 22 根 / 厘米。纬线：无捻丝，有米、绿、白、黄四色，四纬一组，纬密约为 30 根 / 厘米。

这组织物有两种组织结构，A 和 C 为斜纹经重，B 为平纹经重。所有的织物基本色彩是红与黄，分别由蓝和绿在各区域显花，红色为地，蓝、绿显花，黄色勾勒，均有幅边。整个图案可根据四件残片复原，应是由七个完整的和一个被分割成两半置于两边的对波圈构成。构成对波骨架的为单纯的带状线条，在两条对波线之间用六瓣小花连接。自一边始各对波圈中图案分别是一坐二立人物、对象、对狮、对牵驼、对虎。最边上的对虎纹样已经模糊，为纬视纹样。其次为牵驼纹，胡服装束的牵驼者牵了一双峰驼，作健步行走状，为经视纹样。对狮的变形较大，作蹲踞状，张口、扬尾，鬃毛竖立，亦为经视纹样。大象形象十分明显，以蓝色显示花纹，象鼻垂至地面，背上搭着坐垫，象牙亦清晰可见。居中的对波圈中是一纬视的人物纹样，在殿堂式建筑中，一交手人物盘坐于台上，两旁为手持三叉戟的立姿人物。然后又是对象、对狮、对牵驼和对虎等。该锦由多件残片组成，有的做成套状。

2 背面织物上显有大朵花纹的局部。

C. (QK 002925) Height 5 cm, width 27.5 cm (warp direction ↕).

Front side: Warp-faced compound 2/1 Z twill with three series of warps.

Warp: silk, no noticeable twist, light brown, cream, blue and green (the latter two arranged in stripes); c. 180 ends per cm (c. 60 ends per warp series and cm).

Weft: silk, no noticeable twist, undyed(?); c. 26 picks per cm, passed alternately through a twill shed and a pattern shed.

No selvage preserved.

Back side:[2] Weft-faced compound 1/2 Z twill with four lats.

Warp: 2 main warp ends to 1 binding warp end; silk, S-twisted, beige; c. 44 main warp ends per cm, c. 22 binding warp ends per cm.

Weft: silk, no noticeable twist, beige, green, white, yellow; c. 30 passes per cm.

---

2   The fabric has a large-size pattern of medallions(?) and interstice motifs composed of vegetal elements.

C. 正面（上），背面（下）Front side（top）and back side （bottom）

The weave for two of the fabrics (A, C) is warp-faced compound twill, for the third (B) warp-faced compound tabby. The overall colour impression is red and yellow, but actually the ground is red with blue and green patterning, yellow-coloured outlining, and all have selvages. The entire pattern can be reconstructed from four fragments. The full pattern was formed from seven complete enclosures made of opposing waves, plus one that was cut into two halves. The opposing waves are depicted in a single line; six-petalled flowers link the 'waves' in the places where they touch. Within the enclosures are one sitting and two standing people, confronted elephants, confronted lions, confronted led camels, and confronted tigers. The confronted tigers closest to the edge are rather unclear; they are depicted at right angles to the warp direction. Next are the camel patterns, with a *hu*-clothed person leading a Bactrian camel. This is depicted in line with the warp direction. The confronted lions are shown in a fairly distorted manner, in crouching posture with mouths open and tails uplifted, their manes upright. This also is to be viewed in warp direction. The depiction of the elephant is very clear, with blue displaying the pattern, the elephant's trunk is seen hanging down to the ground and on its back is a seat cushion. The ivory of the elephant tusks is clearly seen. In the central enclosure is a human figure woven depicted at right angles to the warp. He sits cross-legged on a platform in a palace-type building; on either side of him are people with tridents in their hands. Enclosures follow with confronted elephants, confronted lions, confronted led camels, and confronted tigers. There are several fragments of this *jin*, some of which form sets.

1 组织细节和幅边（A.） Weave detail and selvage (A.)

2 组织细节（B.），经向 ↕ Weave detail (B.), warp direction ↕

3 缀附残片的组织细节（B.） Weave detail of attached fragment (B.), warp direction ↔

3

4 组织细节（C.） Weave detail (C.)

5 背面的组织细节（C.） Weave detail, back side (C.)

橙地对波连珠狮凤龙雀纹锦　（DRM1PM2:S150 - 2；QK001864A）　6世纪末

整件织锦包括图版 No.15 在内，总长 36 厘米、总宽 23 厘米。由三块不同的锦拼接而成，分别长 12.6 厘米、宽 17 厘米，长 11.8 厘米、宽 3.5 厘米，长 12.6 厘米、宽 3.5 厘米，经向 ↕。

2/1Z 斜纹经重组织。经线：米色和红褐色丝线，无明显捻丝，经密约 96 根／厘米（1:1，每组约 48 根／厘米）。纬线：近本色无捻丝，双根并股，明纬、夹纬交替，纬密 22 根／厘米。幅边已失。

这片锦与图版 No.15 的锦缝制成一条幡带。幡带齿状边饰由六色细平纹织条拼组而成，从内向外颜色的顺序为白、红、黄、米、绿、蓝六色。

该片织锦是橙地对波连珠狮凤龙雀纹的经重组织，为红地米色花纹。织物的顶部有三个较为完整的对波圈，上为对龙，中为对孔雀，下为对狮。龙的造型相当灵动，中有一柱和一珠，颇有后世"二龙戏珠"的意境。对孔雀的造型初看与凤凰相近，但仔细观察又有所不同，其尾只有一条，中有圈纹，正观与流行的孔雀纹造型一致。对狮纹与前述绿地对波连珠狮凤龙纹锦（图版 No.1）略有不同，狮子颈上系有飘带，敦厚可爱。除这片锦织外，还有一件类似的锦织物（M1:S5），锦面上残存一个完整的对波圈，其中有对凤纹样，图案与前述绿地对波连珠狮凤龙纹锦（图版 No.1）的风格一致，但在造型上略有区别，凤冠如鸡，尾如绶带。第二片锦（M1:S5）的狮子对波圈可与图版织锦（DRM1PM2:S150 - 2）相接，动物纹的次序是龙、雀、狮、凤，均是纬视纹样。

从现有的资料来看，目前尚无同类型的织物发现，但其年代还是能够对照一些资料来进行判断。敦煌莫高窟第 420、427 窟都有菱格骨架的狮凤锦图案，狮子的造型有别于那种初期的正面大开口的形象，而与都兰的狮凤龙纹锦的狮子十分接近[3]，凤亦如此。尽管莫高窟彩塑服饰中的狮凤没有成双成对，但其造型却是一致的。第 420、427 窟的年代均属隋代，都兰对波连珠狮凤龙纹饰也应为隋代之物。值得注意的是孔雀的造型。吐鲁番曾出过两件连珠对孔雀纹饰，一件是出于 72TAM169，属于 558 年的墓葬[4]；另一件出于 66TAM48 墓葬，同墓出有 596 ~ 617 年的文书[5]。后者的孔雀造型与狮凤龙雀纹锦中的孔雀极类似，亦可证其年代在北朝末至隋代之际。

3 Dunhuang: Caves of the Singing Sands, Buddhist Art from the Silk Road, text by Roderick Whitfield, photographs by Seigo Otsuka, London 1995, vol. 1, pls. 64, 367.

4 原品藏于新疆维吾尔自治区博物馆，72TAM169:34。新疆维吾尔自治区博物馆《新疆出土文物》，图版 78，文物出版社，1975年，武敏《织锦》，图版 72，台北幼狮文化事业有限公司，1992年。

5 原品藏于新疆维吾尔自治区博物馆，66TAM48:6。新疆维吾尔自治区博物馆《丝绸之路——汉唐织物》，图版 28，文物出版社，1972年。

LATE SIXTH-CENTURY JIN, WITH ORANGE GROUND AND OPPOSING ALIGNED PEARL WAVE PATTERN WITH LIONS, PHOENIX, DRAGON, PEACOCK PATTERNS (DRM1PM2:S150-2; QK 001864 A)

Overall dimensions, including cat. no. 15: height 36 cm, width 23 cm. Assembled from three pieces: height 12.6 cm, width 17 cm; height 11.8 cm, width 3.5 cm; height 12.6 cm, width 3.5 cm (warp direction ↕).

Warp-faced compound 2/1 Z twill with two series of warps.

Warp: silk, no noticeable twist, reddish brown, beige; c. 96 ends per cm (c. 48 ends per warp series and cm).

Weft: silk, no noticeable twist, undyed(?), paired; c. 22 picks per cm, passed alternately through a twill shed and a pattern shed.

No selvage preserved.

This textile was sewn together to form a streamer with cat. no. 15. A band composed of six narrow strips of plain tabby (white, red, yellow, beige, green, blue) is attached along the pointed edge.

This specimen is a warp-faced jin with opposing aligned pearl waves enclosing lion, phoenix, dragon, and peacock patterns. It has red ground and beige patterning. The fragment shown here (DRM1PM2:S150-2) has three fairly complete opposing-wave enclosures in its top section, within which are confronted dragons on top, a pair of peacocks in the middle, and confronted lions below. The style of the dragons is lively, and between them a pillar and a pearl seem very similar in meaning to the latter-day 'two dragons chasing a pearl.' At first glance, the depiction of the peacock seems similar to that of the phoenix, but on detailed examination there are differences. The peacock's tail has just one 'line' on which are circle designs; seen properly it is the popular image of a peacock pattern. There are slight differences between this lion pattern and the previously described green-ground lion (cat. no.1), since a streamer is tied to the neck of this one, and it appears rather sturdy and appealing.

In addition to the textile shown here there is another fragment (find no. M1:S5), on which is a complete opposing-wave enclosure holding a pair of confronted phoenixes. The patterning of the phoenixes is the same as the *jin* described in cat. no. 1, but there are slight differences in the depiction: the crest of the phoenix here is like a cock's comb, its tail is like a ribbon. This second fragment (M1:S5) can be linked up to (DRM1PM2:S150-2) at the point of the roundel with lion. Because of this, we see that the sequence of patterning is dragon, peacock, lion, phoenix, lined up parallel to the weft direction.

At present there is no similar textile among currently available material that can aid in cross-referencing and evaluating this piece. *Jin* textiles were depicted on the murals at caves 420 and 427 among the Mogao Grottoes in Dunhuang. One shows lion and phoenix enclosed in a lozenge-framework; the depiction of the lion is very similar,[3] fairly distinct from early depictions when the

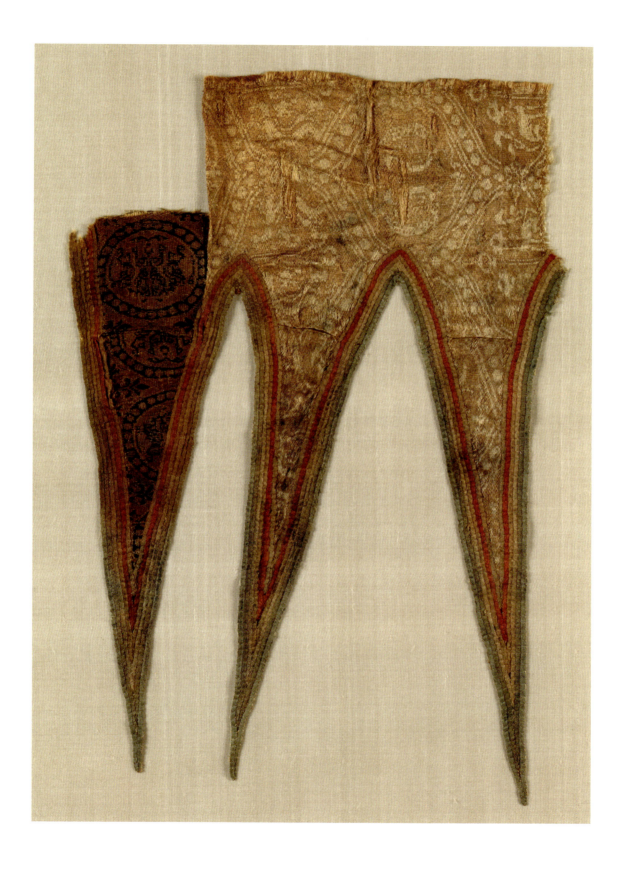

lion faces out frontally, with a large open mouth. The murals are very close to the lions of the Dulan *jin*, and the phoenix is also quite similar. Although the lions and phoenixes on painted clothing in the Mogao grottoes were not in couples, opposing each other, still their manner is the same. The 420 and 427 grottoes are dated to the Sui dynasty, so the Dulan textile should also be Sui dynasty.

Worth noting in this piece is the depiction of the peacock. Two examples of pearl-pattern roundels enclosing confronted peacocks were excavated at Turfan. One was from grave 72TAM169, dated to 558,[4] the other from 66TAM48, with written documents dating to 596–617 found in the same grave.[5] The peacock depiction of the latter was very similar to this lion phoenix dragon peacock *jin*, which helps confirm the dating of this textile to between the end of the North Dynasties and the Sui dynasty.

3   *Dunhuang. Caves of the Singing Sands. Buddhist Art from the Silk Road*, text by Roderick Whitfield, photographs by Seigo Otsuka, London 1995, vol. 1, pls. 64, 367.

4   Urumqi, Xinjiang Museum, 72TAM169:34, 新疆维吾尔自治区博物馆 Xinjiang Uighur Autonomous Region Museum (ed.), 新疆出土文物 *Xinjiang chutu wenwu (Cultural relics excavated in Xinjiang)*, Beijing 1975, pl. 78; 武敏 Wu Min, 织绣 , *Zhixiu (Weaving and embroidery)*, Taipeh 1992, pl. 72.

5   Urumqi, Xinjiang Museum, 66TAM48:6, 新疆维吾尔自治区博物馆 Xinjiang Uighur Autonomous Region Museum (ed.), 丝绸之路 —— 汉唐织物 , *Sichou zhilu. Han Tang zhiwu (Silk Road: Han to Tang fabrics)*, Beijing 1972, pl. 28.

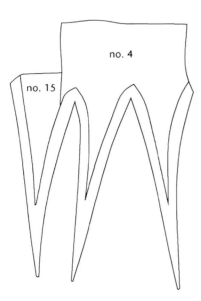

1 结构图 Numbering diagram

2 组织细节，经向↔ Weave detail，warp direction ↔

红地对波楼堞狮面锦 （DRM1PM2:S157-2；QK002393） 6世纪末

　　整件织锦包括图版No.6在内，总长41.5厘米、总宽23.3厘米。此锦长41厘米、宽12.3厘米，经向 ↔。

　　2/1S经重组织。经线：弱S捻丝，褐红色、米色、深褐色与绿、深蓝交替显色。经密约159根／厘米（1:2，每组约53根／厘米）。纬线：近本色很细的无捻丝，纬密约30根／厘米，明纬、夹纬交替。双幅边都存在，幅宽41厘米。

　　这片织锦和图版No.6缝制在一起。织锦的左边有一条七色平纹窄织条做边饰，颜色次序为黑、深棕、红褐、米、黄、深绿、浅绿。

　　这片织锦出自都兰热水1号大墓封堆2号陪葬墓中。全幅图案由五个对波圈再加两边的两区组成。居中的对波圈较小，其中有一对经向对称的狮子，步伐雄健，造型简洁。此外的对波圈两两沿纬向对称，本身的图案又沿经向对称。靠中间的圈由方格节状图案分隔，圈内有三个人物。两边为持械直立者，方脸，眉目不清，着绿袍，身持三叉戟状兵器，但中间一叉呈十字形。中间人物由于裁剪而不完整，但仍可看出坐于台上。三人均在一建筑物之中，屋顶飞檐和屋内立柱清晰可见。建筑物的地面呈水平状，但似有三角状基础支撑。建筑之外的对波圈由一狮面构成。该狮面庞大，充满经向循环。狮面正视，张开血盆大口，头部周围附有多层卷云状的鬃毛，下有一对狮爪，显然是伏踞时的姿态，十分狰狞。这个对波圈至此为止，两边还有一些余地，便用直线隔出两个经向对称的立兽，兽形模糊不清。

　　这件织锦图案所用的对波形骨架并不十分明显。中间的对波纹由直接的线条构成，然后是方格的节状线，最后是狮面的卷云状鬃毛。这种对波形骨架，与斯坦因在敦煌莫高窟发现的北朝几何填花龙虎朱雀纹锦[6]和新疆吐鲁番出土的北凉时期鸟兽纹锦相似[7]。这两件织锦的骨架主要由经向的卷云带和纬向的几何形直带（类似节状线）构成，无对波形，但已十分接近。此类织锦图案应属于列堞锦之类，成书于隋代的《拾遗记》中载有列堞锦之名，诚然有对周代的想象性描述，但实际上反映了北朝时期的情况："锦文似云霞覆城雉楼堞也。"都兰所出的狮面人物锦的骨架较之前二者虽有不同，但遗风犹存，故仍称其为楼堞式。

6 原品藏于大英博物馆，MAS 926(Ch.00118)；赵丰主编《敦煌丝绸艺术全集》，东华大学出版社，2007年，82、120页。
7 原品藏于新疆维吾尔自治区博物馆，72TAM177:48(1)；新疆维吾尔自治区博物馆《新疆出土文物》，图版56，文物出版社，1975年。

5

LATE SIXTH-CENTURY JIN, WITH RED GROUND AND OPPOSING WAVE PATTERNS ENCLOSING BATTLEMENTS AND LION FACES (DRM1PM2:157-2; QK 002393)

Overall dimensions, including cat. no.6: height 41.5 cm, width 23.3 cm; dimensions of fragment: height 41 cm, width 12.3 cm (warp direction ↔).

Warp-faced compound 2/1 S twill with three series of warps.

Warp: silk, slightly S-twisted, brownish red, beige, dark brown and green, and dark blue (the latter three arranged in stripes); c. 159 ends per cm (c. 53 ends per warp series and cm).

Weft: silk, no noticeable twist, very fine, undyed(?); c. 30 picks per cm, passed alternately through a twill shed and a pattern shed.

Both selvages preserved; loom width 41 cm.

This textile is stitched to cat. no. 6. A band composed of seven narrow strips of plain tabby (black, dark brown, reddish brown, beige, yellow, dark green, light green) is attached to its left edge.

This textile was excavated from the no. 2 subsidiary grave at the M1 Great Tomb Mound. The area between selvages is composed of five opposing wave enclosures with two strips on either side. The middle opposing wave pattern is rather small; inside it are a pair of confronted lions depicted at right angles to the warp direction, simply depicted pacing with masculine vigor. The other opposing wave enclosures are to be viewed in weft-direction, although the pattern is again warp-faced. The enclosures next to the middle are separated by a row of squares. Inside the enclosure are three people, on either side two stand holding weapons, with square faces, their faces indistinct, wearing green robes, hands holding trident-type weapons. One of the prongs has a cross shape on it: it is not clear if this had some original significance or was necessitated by limitations of the weaving technology. In the middle, the central person cannot be seen completely because the fabric was cut, but it appears that he is seated on a platform. All three people are in an architectural setting; the roof has flying eaves and supporting pillars that can be seen clearly. The building has a horizontal baseline, supported by a triangular-shaped foundation. Outside the structure is an opposing wave enclosure that forms the outside definition of a lion's face. The face is quite large and is to be viewed in weft direction; it is seen frontally, with open mouth, and its mane billows like clouds around its head. There are a pair of lion's claws under the face, as if it were crouching in ambush. The opposing wave pattern framework goes thus far, followed by some space on either side. Therein, divided by straight lines, are a pair of standing creatures that are again to be viewed in weft direction, their aspect very unclear.

The opposing wave framework of this weave is unclear and composed of different elements. The middle opposing wave is formed of straight lines, with a row of squares, and finally the lion faces with billowing mane. This kind of opposing wave framework resembles the North Dynasties geometric *jin* with dragon tiger peacock discovered by Stein at the Mogao Grottoes at Dunhuang.[6] It is also comparable to a *jin* excavated from Turfan in Xinjiang that dates from the Northern

Liang period and has a bird and beast pattern.[7] The framework of these two woven *jin* pieces is constructed of warp-directional rolling-cloud strips and weft-directional geometric bands. They have no opposing waves, but are nevertheless very similar. This kind of patterning should belong to the type of *liedie jin* (*jin* with arch pattern), a name that is to be found in the Sui dynasty work *Shiyi ji*. Although this is an imaginary description of the Zhou period, it in fact reflects circumstances existing during the North Dynasties: "The *liedie jin* patterns are like rosy clouds wafting through the town and the watchtowers."[8] The framework of the textile excavated from Dulan, with lion-faces and people, shows certain differences from these two but it retains the same style. Therefore, we call this a *loudie* (battlements) style, especially since the pattern really does show a building that could be called a tower.

5

6 London, British Museum, MAS.926 (Ch. 00118). Zhao Feng (ed.), *Textiles from Dunhuang in UK Collections*, Shanghai 2007, no. 82, p. 120.

7 Urumqi, Xinjiang Museum, 72TAM177:48(1). 新疆维吾尔自治区博物馆 Xinjiang Uighur Autonomous Region Museum (ed.), 新疆出土文物 *Xinjiang chutu wenwu (Cultural relics excavated in Xinjiang)*, Beijing 1975, pl. 56.

8 拾遗记 *Shiyi ji (Records of picked-up leftovers)*, Zhonghua shuju chuban, Beijing 1981, book 2, p. 50.

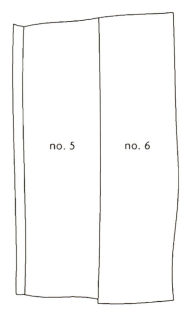

1 结构图 Numbering diagram

2 组织细节 Detail

黄地卷云太阳神织锦 （DRM1PM2:S157 - 1；QK002393） 6世纪末

此锦和图版 No.5 缝缀在一起，总长 41.5 厘米、总宽 23.3 厘米。此锦长 41.5 厘米、宽 11 厘米，经向 ↔。

平纹经重组织。经线：无明显加捻，由米色、褐红、绿色（与深蓝交替换色）分区显花。经密约 180 根／厘米（1:2，每组约 60 根／厘米）。纬线：为本色无明显加捻，纬密约 30 根／厘米，明纬、夹纬交替。双幅边完整，幅宽为 41.5 厘米。

该织锦采用一种由圆环相互搭接而成的四方连续展开的骨架式构图，我们将其称为簇四型。整个图案以卷云纹作环，以小团花作组（簇）连接。残片共有三件，其中 DRMIPM2:S157 - 1 保存得相对完整，而 DRMIPM2:S149 - 2 略为破损，被裁为两片。DRMIPM2:S149 - 2 保存着完整的幅边，幅宽 41.5 厘米，是明显的 1:2 平纹经锦。地色基本色彩为橙黄，用浅黄色部分显花并勾勒。主要花纹在不同区域中由蓝、绿等多色分区变换显示。全幅内有三个卷云圈。两边的两个圈纹样相同，并且对称，可分为四组。最上方是一对象，象作浅色，用蓝色勾边。其次为骑马射鹿，一男人骑在一奔驰的马上，回首弯弓搭箭，射向身后之鹿，鹿作惊慌回首嘶鸣状。第三组为对狮，黄地蓝线，形体较大。一前爪高举，余三爪着地。对称的狮子之间有一莲花座塔状物。最下一组为对骆驼，系双峰驼，驼背上有骑士，背后有忍冬叶状饰物。

中间一圈是母题花纹，为一人物坐在四马驾车之上的形象。纹样为纬视，纬轴对称。四马分成两组，两两向着相反方向奔驰，显然是采用了不同的透视法。四马所拉之车的车轮依稀可见，车体形态也由于透视角度不同而呈前窄后宽状，车上带有遮拦挡护之物。车内置有莲花状台座，座上坐有一人，有圆形头光，面目不甚清晰。此人双手下垂相合于腹际，犹如佛教之禅定印。头光之上有华盖，华盖上似有龙形饰物，两边挂有钟铃。在该人物两侧各有两小人，骑在鸟状物上，似为有翼天使或迦陵频伽，手中持锤状物挥舞，作击铃或驱赶马车状。在与该圈相邻的簇四圈外，装饰着对马衔花和忍冬草叶纹饰。在簇四圈与幅之间的圈外，饰有形象模糊的对兽。

1 组织细节 Detail

LATE SIXTH-CENTURY JIN, YELLOW GROUND, ROUNDELS OF ROLLING CLOUDS, CHARIOTEER (DRM1PM2:S157-1; QK 002393)

Overall dimensions, including cat. no.5: height 41.5 cm, width 23.3 cm; dimensions of fragment: height 41.5 cm, width 11 cm (warp direction ↔).

Warp-faced compound tabby with three series of warps.

Warp: silk, no noticeable twist, beige, reddish, green (striped dark blue); c. 180 ends per cm (c. 60 ends per warp series and cm).

Weft: silk, no noticeable twist, very fine, undyed(?); c. 30 picks per cm, passed alternately through a tabby shed and a pattern shed.

Both selvages preserved; loom width 41.5 cm.

This *jin* weaving uses a framework of tangent-roundel designs that extend in four directions. We give it the name 'clustered-fours-type jin.' The entire pattern is composed of roundels in rolling-cloud pattern, with small flower groups as connecting knobs. Three separate fragments of this textile are preserved, among which S157-1 is the best preserved, while S149-2 is slightly more damaged and has been cut into two pieces. S149-2 preserves both selvages, is 41.5 cm in width, and is a clear warp-faced tabby. The basic colour of the ground is tangerine-yellow; light-yellow is used for some of the patterning and also to outline. The principal pattern is made by alternating blue, green, and so on in various regions of the fabric. The loom width comprises three cloud-roundels, the two on the sides have similar patterns and are opposing. Inside are four groups, at the top of which is a pair of elephants that are outlined in blue, next are hunters on horseback hunting a deer, a man rides a prancing steed and is shown in turned-back posture ready to loose an arrow toward the deer behind him from his bow. The deer seems to be turning its head in alarm. The third group comprises confronted lions, with yellow ground and blue threads. Their shapes are relatively large. One lion's paw is upraised, the other three are on the ground; a lotus platform stands between the confronted lions. The bottom group are confronted Bactrian camels with a rider on the back of each and behind them decorative scrolls.

The middle circle constitutes the main pattern. It encloses a man sitting in a chariot drawn by four horses. The pattern is depicted at right angles to the warp, mirrored along a weft-parallel axis. The four horses are in two groups, each two going in opposite directions. Clearly this use of different perspectives is to show movement. One can distinguish the axles of the chariot that the horses are pulling. The shape of the chariot is also seen from different perspectives so that it appears narrow in front and broad in the back. A blocking rail can be seen on the front edge of the chariot. Inside the chariot is a platform; on it is a man with a round halo around a face that is simple and somewhat indistinct. The two hands of this man hang down, placed over his middle, like the hands of a Buddha performing the meditation (Dhyana) mudra. His feet tend sideways but his legs are not crossed. Above his halo is a ring of flowers, and on that is dragon-shaped ornamentation; bells hang down on both sides. On either side of this man are two smaller people, riding on bird-shaped animals as though they were winged angels or kalavinka birds. They hold hammer-shaped objects as they dance, either to strike the bells or to encourage the horse-chariot forward. Honeysuckle ornamentation twines outside these tangent roundels and there are confronted animals of indeterminate form.

6

红地云珠吉昌太阳神锦 　(DRM1PM2:S109；QK001863)　6世纪末

整件织锦包括了图版No.13在内，总长63厘米、宽84厘米，经向↔。

平纹经重组织。经线：红、黄无捻丝，经密160根／厘米（1:1，每组80根／厘米）。纬线：本色无捻丝，纬密约40根／厘米，明纬、夹纬交替。存留一侧幅边。三块残片和图版No.13丝锦连成一块U形织片，顶端有一条七色窄平纹条带做边饰，颜色次序为深蓝、深褐、红、黄、米、绿、蓝七色。

同一件幡上的三块残片，即S109-1、S109-2、S109-3，色彩保存完好。据其色彩、构图风格判断，应当属同一织物上的不同裁片。组织为1:1平纹经锦，为红地黄花两种色彩。在S109-3上还能见到幅边。整个图案由卷云连珠圈构成簇四骨架，并在经向的骨架连接处用兽面铺首作组，而在纬向的连接处则以八出小花作组。据前述黄地卷云太阳神锦的纹样排列推测，该锦全幅应由三个圆圈连接而成，其中作为母题纹样的太阳神圈应居中，狩战圈在太阳神圈一侧，而另一侧的圆圈已残损，估计两边的圈内纹样应该一致，亦应是狩战题材。

LATE SIXTH-CENTURY JIN, WITH RED GROUND, CLOUD-PEARL ROUNDELS, AND

AUSPICIOUS SUN-GOD (DRM1PM2:S109; QK 001863)

Overall dimensions, including cat. no.13: height 63 cm, width 84 cm (warp direction ↔).

Warp-faced compound tabby with two series of warps.

Warp: silk, no noticeable twist, red, yellow; 160 ends per cm (80 ends per warp series and cm).

Weft: silk, no noticeable twist, undyed(?); c. 40 picks per cm, passed alternately through a tabby shed and a pattern shed.

Selvage preserved at one side only.

Three fragments of this textile and cat. no.13 are joined to form a U-shape. A band composed of seven narrow strips of plain tabby (dark blue, dark brown, red, yellow, beige, green, blue) is attached to its upper edge.

Three fragments were sewn to the same streamer, namely S109-1, -2, and -3. The colour is well preserved and, judging by the colouring, composition, and style, these should be fragments from the same piece of weaving. The weave is warp-faced compound tabby. It uses only two colours, red for the ground and yellow for the patterning. On S109-3, the selvage is still visible. The entire pattern is composed of tangent roundels of rolling clouds, and the framework in the warp direction's tangent points has animal faces as connecting knobs. On the weft-direction, connecting points use eight-pointed little flowers for knobs. By looking at the previous piece, the rolling-cloud pattern with sun-godcat. no. 6, this *jin* should be composed of three roundels across the width of the fabric, between selvages. The primary subject of the sun-god should be in the center roundel, with hunting combat on one side, and probably the same on the other: the other side is missing, but the contents of both side roundels were probably the same.

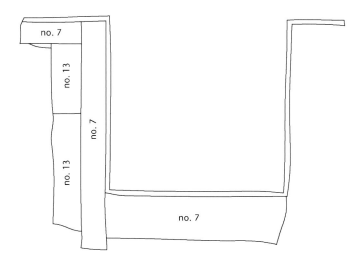

1 结构图 Numbering diagram

太阳神圈中的纹样基本清晰完整。这是一组六马拉车的群像，六匹有翼的神马分成两组，列于车体两边，相背而驰。车身前窄后宽，上有遮挡之用的栏杆。车轮清晰，可见放射状车辐。车上置有莲花形宝座，太阳神手施禅定印，头戴菩萨宝冠，身穿尖领窄袖紧身上衣，交脚坐于莲花宝座之上。太阳神的旁边是两个侧面向的持王杖、戴圆帽的人物，似为太阳神的卫士。太阳神身后有靠背，头部带有一圈连珠状光圈，应系头光。头光旁和靠背上方有两个半身人像，为侧面向，均戴幞头，为官吏形象。太阳神的头部正上方有一华盖，盖顶附有龙形饰物。在马车两旁有龙首幡迎风招展，十分生动。

在狩战圈中，纹样已被分割成两半，中间还有部分残缺。根据复原效果来看，圈中应有四组主要的纹样。按由上至下的顺序，第一组是一对骑驼射虎的纹样。骑驼者头戴圆形小帽，身穿窄袖短衫，下着长靴，骑在双峰骆驼之上，回首拉弓射虎。第二组是一对骑马射鹿的纹样。马首带有花形头饰，与骑驼者装束相同的骑士在马上回首拉弓射鹿，鹿身上可见圆点形斑纹。该组纹样的马身残缺。第三组纹样上半部已残，仅能见对人对兽，人在兽前，身穿长袍，下摆至膝。兽的四腿粗壮，为狮类动物。据此推测，这组纹样应系人物搏狮。第四组是一对手持盾牌和短剑的武士形象，相向而立，作搏战状。武士身后各有一只鹦鹉回首而视，鹦鹉边饰有灵芝状纹样。

在太阳神圈上部圈的空间处，装饰有云气纹和九个圆点，还有"吉"字和相对奔跑的动物。在太阳神圈下部圈外亦有一个"吉"字和一对带角的野山羊。在狩战圈上部圈外（应与太阳神圈下部圈外相连），有对鹿、云气纹、七个圆点和对狮纹。

2 组织细节 Detail

The sun-god motif in the center roundel is basically complete and can be read quite clearly. It portrays a group of six horses pulling a chariot. The six sacred winged horses are divided into two groups, each arrayed alongside one side of the chariot. They charge forward pulling the chariot. The front of the chariot is depicted as narrow and the back as wide, and on it is a restraining railing. The wheels are clearly seen, even the radiating spokes. A lotus-flower throne rests on the chariot. The sun-god is performing the meditation (Dhyana) mudra, and from the crown on his head one can see that he is depicted as a Bodhisattva. He wears a robe with narrow sleeves and pointed neck as he sits on the lotus-flowered throne. Beside him are two people shown in profile, each wearing round hats and each holding a sceptre. These appear to be the guardians of the sun-god. There is a backrest behind the sun-god with a halo issuing around his head made of aligned pearls—one could view it as rays of light emanating from his head. Beside the rays and on top of the backrest are two half-people, faces shown in profile. Each wears a Chinese-style *futou* headgear; they are officials. Above the sun-god's head is an ornamented canopy, surmounted by dragon-shaped ornaments. Beside the chariot are dragon-headed streamers that wave in the wind in a lively way.

7

3 组织细节 Weave detail

The pattern in the roundel with hunting combat scene has been cut into two halves, with a missing part in the middle. If reconstructed, there should have been four main pattern components. As listed from top to bottom: the first group is a pattern of a pair of camel riders shooting at tigers. The riders wear small round hats and short jackets with narrow sleeves, they have tall boots, and ride on the two-humped Bactrian camels. Their heads are turned as they pull the bow to shoot the tigers. The second group is a pattern of a pair of riders shooting at deer from astride a horse. There is patterned decoration on the head of the horse. Wearing the same things as worn by the camel riders, the horse riders also turn their heads around, pulling their bows in a backward stance as they aim at the deer. There are dot patterns on the body of the deer; the part with the horse's body is missing. The third group is missing its top half, but one can see a pair of people and wild animals. The people are in front of the animals, they wear long robes that go to their knees. The legs of the animal are thick and sturdy, like some kind of lion. The assumption is that this group portrays people hunting or doing combat with lions. The fourth group is a pair of warriors with short swords who stand facing each other, in a mutual combat stance. Behind the bodies of the warriors is a raptor turning its head around to look, and next to these birds are *lingzhi*-shaped clouds.

In the interstice above the sun-god roundel is cloud-pattern decoration and nine circular points, also the Han-Chinese character 吉 *ji*, which means lucky or auspicious. There are also animals that run and oppose each other. Under and outside the sun-god roundel is also a *ji* character, and a pair of ibex with horns. Outside the roundel of the hunting/combat scene (the one connected to the lower part of the sun-god roundel) appear a pair of deer, cloud patterns, seven circular points, and the pattern of confronted lions.

4 组织细节 Detail

黄地套环云珠人物锦 （DRM1PM2:S63；QK002849、QK002053）　6 世纪末

总长 5 厘米、总宽 34.8 厘米。其中一片 QK002849 宽 19.2 厘米，另一片 QK002053 宽 16.8 厘米，经向 ↔。

2/1Z 斜纹经重组织。经线：无捻丝，由黄、白、深蓝与绿交替显色。经密约 169 根／厘米（1:2，每组约 63 根／厘米）。纬线：本色双股无捻丝，纬密约为 30 根／厘米，明纬、夹纬交替。幅边已失。

黄色为地，蓝、绿色显花。该锦为残片，套环圈由卷云和连珠构成，卷云在外，连珠在内。每环大小已很难判定，现存一环仅有一弦，弦高 4.5 厘米，弦长 18 厘米。由此推算，此圆环直径约 22.5 厘米。

套环骨架把套环内的空间切割成两种形状的小空间，一是由两环的外侧和一环的内侧构成的类似三角形的圆锥形空间，二是由两环内侧构成的菱形空间。圆锥形空间的主要纹样是一人物，交脚坐于一台座上，头戴宝冠，身穿露领的紧身衣，双手屈臂上举，两侧还有两朵灵芝状云彩。人物留有络腮胡，是胡人形象。而菱形空间已残，其上方有一华盖顶，顶上有花状饰物。华盖下有三个人物，中间一人取正面形象，头戴宝冠，显得身份尊贵；旁边两人取侧身形象，均面朝中间的人物。人物下身残损。套环骨架曾出现在吐鲁番隋代织物上 [8]，此织物的年代可定为隋代前后。

8 原品藏于新疆维吾尔自治区博物馆，66TAM48:14、68TAM99:2。新疆维吾尔自治区博物馆《丝绸之路——汉唐织物》，图版 45、46，文物出版社，1972 年。

1　组织细节　Weave detail

LATE SIXTH CENTURY JIN, WITH YELLOW GROUND, CLOUD-AND-PEARL FRAMEWORK, AND PERSON (DRM1PM2:S63; QK 002849 AND QK 002053)

Height 5 cm, overall width 34.8 cm; two fragments fitting together: width of QK 002849: 19.2 cm, width of QK 002053: 16.8 cm (warp direction ↔).

Warp-faced compound 2/1 Z twill with three series of warps.

Warp: silk, no noticeable twist, yellow, white, dark blue and green (the latter two arranged in stripes); c. 169 ends per cm (c. 63 ends per warp series and cm).

Weft: silk, no noticeable twist, undyed(?), paired; c. 30 picks per cm, passed alternately through a twill shed and a pattern shed.

No selvage preserved.

Yellow ground with blue and green patterning. This textile is a fragment. It includes part of an enclosing framework made of rolling-cloud and aligned-pearl border. The original size of the pattern is hard to determine given the fragmentary nature of this textile; what remains of the one enclosure is merely a section. The section is 4.5 cm tall and 18 cm long; from this we estimate that the diameter of the original roundel would have been roughly 22.5 cm.

The intersecting framework of cloud-and-pearl border creates spaces in which various patterns are depicted. In the triangular-shaped space of the intersecting roundels a man is shown sitting on a platform with legs crossed. He wears a crown on his head, and wears an article of clothing that

shows the collar. His arms are bent at the elbow and lifted up beside his head on either side; next to each hand is a *lingzhi*-shaped cloud. The person is bearded and looks like a *hu* (barbarian) person. Another lozenge or diamond-shaped space is mostly missing, but there is a canopy over what was there on which are flower motifs. As can be seen on another fragment, not illustrated, there are three people under the flower canopy, the one in the middle faces frontally forward, wearing a crown so that he looks elevated in rank. The two beside him are shown in profile, their lower bodies lost. A silk with such looping framework has been found at Turfan and dates to the Sui dynasty,[9] and the period of this piece can also be approximately established as Sui.

9 Urumqi, Xinjiang Museum, 66TAM48:14, 68TAM99:2. 新疆维吾尔自治区博物馆 Xinjiang Uighur Autonomous Region Museum (ed.), 丝绸之路——汉唐织物,
   Sichou zhi lu. Han Tang zhiwu (Silk Road: Han to Tang fabrics), Beijing 1972, pl. 45, 46 (pl. 46, 47 in the 1973 edition).

2 组织细节 Weave details

黄地方格连珠小花锦　(DRM1PM2:S53；DRM1PM2：S95、QK002905；QK002801)　7世纪初

　　总长 15.7 厘米、总宽 10.7 厘米。其中 QK002905 的长 8 厘米，QK002801 的长 7.7 厘米，经向 ↔。

　　2/1S 斜纹经重组织。经线：无捻丝，由黄、白、深蓝与绿色交替显色，经密约 162 根／厘米（1:2，每组约 54 根／厘米）。纬线：本色无捻丝，纬密约为 26 根／厘米，明纬、夹纬交替。QK002905 的上端存留一侧幅边。

　　黄色为地，白色勾边显珠，蓝、绿两色交替显示主要花纹。图案以连珠形式的直线通过小团花点连接成图案骨架，方格之内的四角上均饰有忍冬花纹。方格中心是由十四片花瓣组成的小团花，团花外沿还有一圈白色的连珠。方格连珠小花锦在日本正仓院有收藏，色彩稍有不同[9]。根据记载，日本学者称其为"蜀江锦"，确切年代不明。这一难题可以在敦煌壁画上得到解决。莫高窟第 427 窟隋代洞窟中发现多种大同小异的方格连珠团花锦[10]，与此锦风格十分相似，据此可以将此锦的年代定在隋代前后。

9　原品藏于东京国立博物馆。*Jodai-gire. 7th and 8th century textiles in Japan from the Shōsō-in and Hōryū-ji*, by Kaneo Matsumoto, Kyoto 1984.

10　图版可参见 *Dunhuang. Caves of the Singing Sands. Buddhist Art from the Silk Road*, text by Roderick Whitfield, photographs by Seigo Otsuka, London 1995, vol.1, pl.366.

EARLY SEVENTH-CENTURY JIN, WITH YELLOW GROUND, SQUARES AND ALIGNED-PEARL SMALL FLOWERS (DRM1PM2:S53; DRM1PM2 :S95AND QK 002905; QK 002801)

Overall height 15.7 cm, width 10.7 cm; two fragments fitting together: height of QK 002905: 8 cm, height of QK 002801: 7.7 cm (warp direction ↔).

Warp-faced compound 2/1 S twill with three series of warps.

Warp: silk, no noticeable twist, yellow, white, dark blue and green (the latter two arranged in stripes); c. 162 ends per cm (c. 54 ends per warp series and cm).

Weft: silk, no noticeable twist, undyed(?); c. 22 picks per cm, passed alternately through a twill shed and a pattern shed.

Selvage preserved at the upper edge of fragment QK 002905.

To show the pattern the textile uses alternatively blue and green with white outlines on a yellow ground. A straight-line square framework is punctuated by small flower groups at the intersections of the lines. Inside the squares are honeysuckle patterns in the corners and small fourteen-petal flowers in the centers. Outside the flowers is a circle of white-coloured aligned pearls.

The Hōryū-ji temple in Japan has preserved a *jin* textile with squares and aligned-pearl small flowers that is similar though of slightly different colouring.[10] Based on historical records, Japanese scholars name this Shokkōkin (Shu or Western-Sichuan River *jin*). The dating of this piece from Hōryū-ji is unclear, but the difficulty of dating can be resolved by looking at a wall painting in Dunhuang. A large number of similar motifs have been depicted in the Sui-dynasty Mogao cave 427.[11] The motifs are by and large similar to this Dulan piece, with minor differences. We therefore determine the dating of this piece to be around the time of the Sui dynasty.

---

10 Tokyo National Museum. Kaneo Matsumoto, *Jodai-gire. 7th and 8th century textiles in Japan from the Shōsō-in and Hōryū-ji*, Kyoto 1984.

11 See, for example, *Dunhuang. Caves of the Singing Sands. Buddhist Art from the Silk Road*, text by Roderick Whitfield, photographs by Seigo Otsuka, London 1995, vol. 1, pl. 366.

绿地小窠连珠云花锦　(DRM1PM2:S61；QK002796)　7世纪初

长 10.2 厘米、宽 10.4 厘米，经向 ↔。

2/1Z 斜纹经重组织。经线：黄、绿无捻丝。经密约 112 根／厘米（1:1，每组约 56 根／厘米）。纬线：本色无捻丝，纬密约 30 根／厘米，明纬、夹纬交替。幅边已失。

此块织锦为绿地显黄色花。在 28 颗散状珠连成的团窠环中，饰几何小花，抽象、简洁，类似于后世的云状花。连珠圈外以十样小花作为辅花。这种十样花也是以六瓣小花为中心，然后四向伸出四朵花蕾。相似的图案在吐鲁番初唐时期墓葬中有出土 [11]，在敦煌莫高窟初唐时期壁画中也有发现，故其年代当定在初唐前后为宜。

11 藏品属于新疆维吾尔自治区博物馆，73TAM221:9，新疆维吾尔自治区博物馆《新疆出土文物》，图版 147，文物出版社，1975 年。另一件相同花纹的织锦可参见 68TAM104，新疆维吾尔自治区博物馆、日本奈良丝绸之路学研究中心《吐鲁番出土绵与出土织物》，图版 70a、71b，2000 年。

EARLY SEVENTH-CENTURY JIN, WITH GREEN GROUND AND YELLOW PATTERNING, LITTLE ROUNDELS OF ALIGNED-PEARL AND CLOUD PATTERNS (DRM1PM2:S61; QK 002796)

Height 10.2 cm, width 10.4 cm (warp direction ↔).

Warp-faced compound 2/1 Z twill with two series of warps.

Warp: silk, no noticeable twist, green, yellow; c. 112 ends per cm (c. 56 ends per warp series and cm).

Weft: silk, no noticeable twist, undyed(?), very fine; c. 30 picks per cm, passed alternately through a twill shed and a pattern shed.

No selvage preserved.

The textile has a yellow design on green ground. Highly geometric depictions of little flowers, quite abstract and simplified, can be seen in roundels formed of twenty-eight aligned pearls. These are similar to the cloud-type flowers that later came to be a common motif. Outside the aligned-pearl roundels, quatrefoil flowers serve as supplemental motifs. These have six-petalled small flowers at their center and then extend four-flower buds in the four directions. A similarly patterned piece has been excavated from an early-Tang grave at Turfan.[12] The pattern also exists on Tang-period wall paintings at the Dunhuang Mogao Grottoes. It is appropriate therefore to determine the dating of this piece as early Tang.

12 Urumqi, Xinjiang Museum, 73TAM211:9. 新疆维吾尔自治区博物馆 Xinjiang Uighur Autonomous Region Museum (ed.), 新疆出土文物 *Xinjiang chutu wenwu (Cultural relics excavated in Xinjiang)*, Beijing 1975, pl. 147. Another similarly patterned textile has been found in grave 68TAM104: 中国新疆维吾尔自治区博物馆 China Xinjiang Uighur Autonomous Region Museum, 日本奈良丝绸之路学研究中心, Japan Research Center for Silk Roadology (eds.), 吐鲁番地域与出土绢织物, *Tulufan diyu yu chutu juan zhiwu. Tulufan Basin and Paleo Silk Textiles*, Nara 2000, pls. 70a-b, 71b.

黄地连珠对马纹锦 （DRM1PM2:S17；QK002033 上、QK002842 下）　7 世纪初

　　QK002033 长 9 厘米、宽 9 厘米，QK002842 长 10 厘米、宽 9.3 厘米，经向 ↔。

　　2/1S 斜纹经重组织。经线：弱 S 捻丝，黄、白、深蓝与绿交替显色。经密约 162 根／厘米（1:2，每组约 54 根／厘米）。纬线：本色细无捻丝，纬密约 25 根／厘米，明纬、夹纬交替。每片织锦上存留一侧幅边，幅宽不知。

　　织锦以黄色作地，浅黄色勾勒，各区域中以蓝绿分区换色显示主要花纹，再由八瓣小花为组，连接连珠圈而成一种四方连续的排列形式。在连珠圈外，由十样小花组成辅助花纹。圈内的主题花纹为对马纹图案，马身有翼，马颈上系一对后飘的绶带，马头饰小花。马的一前蹄和一后蹄提起，作疾步前行的姿态。马蹄下方为莲蓬状花鸟图案。

11

EARLY SEVENTH-CENTURY JIN, WITH YELLOW GROUND, ALIGNED-PEARL ROUNDEL ENCLOSING CONFRONTED HORSES (DRM1PM2:S17; QK 002033, TOP, AND QK 002842, BOTTOM)

QK 002033 height 9 cm, width 9 cm; QK 002842 height 10 cm, width 9.3 cm (warp direction ↔).

Warp-faced compound 2/1 S twill with three series of warps.

Warp: silk, slightly S-twisted, yellow, white, dark blue and green (the latter two arranged in stripes); c. 162 ends per cm (c. 54 ends per warp series and cm).

Weft: silk, no noticeable twist, undyed(?), very fine; c. 25 picks per cm, passed alternately through a twill shed and a pattern shed.

One selvage preserved on each fragment; loom width not preserved.

The pattern of this textile is shown in blue and green figuring on a yellow ground and with light yellow-coloured outlining. Eight-petalled small flowers are placed as knobs between roundels, and indicate the continuation of the aligned-pearl roundels. Outside the aligned-pearl roundel, four-directional flowers form supplementary patterns.

The primary motif inside the roundel is confronted horses, with wings and ribbons floating backwards from their necks. There are small flower patterns above their heads. One front hoof and one rear hoof of each horse are lifted in a galloping posture. Lotus-seedpod-style flower and bird patterns are depicted under the horses' hooves.

橙地连珠对马纹锦 （DRM1PM2:S38；QK002794） 7 世纪初

长 12.7 厘米、宽 12.1 厘米，经向 ↔。

2/1Z 斜纹经重组织。经线：弱 S 捻丝，橘黄、白、绿与褐红色交替显色。经密约 135 根／厘米（1:2，每组约 45 根／厘米）。纬线：本色无捻丝，纬密约 30 根／厘米，明纬、夹纬交替。幅边已失。

织锦以橙色作地，浅黄色勾勒，用绿色和紫红色交替显示主要花纹。连珠圈之间的十样小花与图版 No.11 的基本相同，但圈里面的对马却有较大的区别。图版 No.11 的马颈线被马头遮挡，而此块织锦中的马颈则全部显露。前者马头上为小花，飘带水平向后；后者则饰以日月形的头饰，飘带斜上向后。前者马蹄下装饰有莲蓬状物，而后者则是忍冬形饰物。从整个马的造型来看，前者线条平直有力，后者多弯曲；前者舒展，后者拥挤，显示出一种不稳定感。

12

1 组织细节 Detail

EARLY SEVENTH CENTURY JIN, WITH ORANGE GROUND, ALIGNED-PEARL ROUNDEL, CONFRONTED-HORSES PATTERN (DRM1PM2:S38; QK 002794)

Height 12.7 cm, width 12.1 cm (warp direction ↔).

12

Warp-faced compound 2/1 Z twill with three series of warps.

Warp: silk, slightly S-twisted, orange, white, green and brownish red (the latter two arranged in stripes); c. 135 ends per cm (c. 45 ends per warp series and cm).

Weft: silk, no noticeable twist, undyed(?); c. 30 picks per cm, passed alternately through a twill shed and a pattern shed.

No selvage preserved.

The weave of this textile is warp-faced compound twill with three series of warps. It uses a tangerine-orange colour as ground, with light yellow outlining, and alternating green and dark red to display the pattern. Between aligned-pearl roundels, the four-directional flowers are basically the same as the previous piece cat. no. 11, but inside the roundels the confronted horses are quite different.

The line of the horse neck on cat. no. 11 is obscured by the horse's head, whereas in cat. no. 12 it is completely exhibited and seen to be somewhat curved. Small flowers appear above the horse's head on the former, and ribbons float straight back from the horse's neck. In this textile, sun and moon appear as head decorations, while the floating ribbon falls back obliquely. Beneath the horse hooves of the former are lotus-seedpod-like motifs, whereas the latter has a honeysuckle decoration. In terms of overall style, the horse of cat. no. 11 uses vigorous straight lines, whereas the lines of this textile curve. The feeling of energy of the former motif extends outward, whereas the depiction of these horses is constricted, giving an uneasy feeling.

黄地连珠对马纹锦 （DRM1PM2:S109 - 4；QK001863）　7 世纪初

此锦长 56 厘米（部分）、宽 7 厘米，是与 DRM1PM2:S109 太阳神锦缝合在一起的，整体尺寸参见图版 No.7，经向 ↔。

2/1S 斜纹经重组织。经线：弱 S 捻丝，米、白、深蓝与浅蓝交替显色。经密约 153 根／厘米（1：2，每组约 51 根／厘米）。纬线：双股本色无捻丝，纬密约 25 根／厘米，明纬、夹纬交替。幅边已失。

织锦的色彩总体类似于图版 No.11 的黄地连珠对马纹锦。以黄、白为基色，而以蓝、绿交替显示主花纹。在花纹的造型设计上，却与图版 No.12 的橙地连珠对马纹锦类似。

EARLY SEVENTH-CENTURY JIN, WITH YELLOW GROUND, ALIGNED-PEARL CONFRONTED-HORSES PATTERN (DRM1PM2:S109-4; QK 001863)

Height 56 cm (fragmentary), width 7 cm (warp direction ↔). For overall dimensions see cat. no.7.

Warp-faced compound 2/1 S twill with three series of warps.

Warp: silk, slightly S-twisted, beige, white, dark blue, and light blue (the latter two arranged in stripes); c. 153 ends per cm (c. 51 ends per warp series and cm).

Weft: silk, no noticeable twist, undyed(?), paired; c. 25 picks per cm, passed alternately through a twill shed and a pattern shed.

No selvage preserved.

This textile was sewn together with cat. no. 7 above, the sun-god *jin*. Its colouring is in general similar to the confronted-horse *jin* of cat. no. 11. It uses beige and white as the basic colours, and exhibits pattern through the alternation of light blue and blue. However, in terms of the actual subject matter, it is more similar to the confronted–horses textile of cat. no. 12.

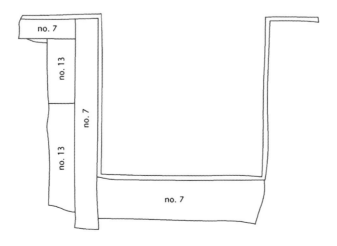

1 结构图　Numbering diagram

黄地连珠对马纹锦 （DRM1PM2:S155 – 1；QK002392、QK002797）　7 世纪初

　　总长 48 厘米、总宽 29.3 厘米，其中 QK002392 长 48 厘米、宽 17.8 厘米，QK002797 长 29.3 厘米、宽 11.5 厘米，经向 ↔。

　　2/1Z 斜纹经重组织。经线：无捻丝，黄、白、深蓝与蓝，或与绿，交替显色。经密约 162 根／厘米（1:2，每组约 54 根／厘米）。纬线：本色无捻丝，纬密约 26 根／厘米，明纬、夹纬交替，有一侧幅边存留。

　　织锦的一侧缝有另一片织锦（DRM1PM2:S155–2）。这片缝上去的织锦为 2/1Z 斜纹经重组织。经线：绿色、米色的无捻丝，经密约 120 根／厘米（1:1，每组约 60 根／厘米）。纬线：本色无捻丝，纬密约 24 根／厘米，明纬、夹纬交替，幅边已失。

　　这件缝制的幡边有一条七色平纹窄条做边饰，七色顺序为深蓝、白、红、赭、黄、绿、蓝。

　　中间的这块织锦为黄地显蓝花，与图版中的前几件大同小异。不同之处在于花纹的连珠。这片织锦中的连珠上下正中不是圆形，而是"回"字形。另外一处不同是在马头的设计上，这片锦的马头后未见绶带。

　　与其缝合在一起的另一片织锦（DRM1PM2:S155 – 2），为绿地对波连珠狮凤龙雀纹锦，和图版 No.4 的织锦非常类似。

　　这两片不同的织锦缝制在一起合成一件幡。

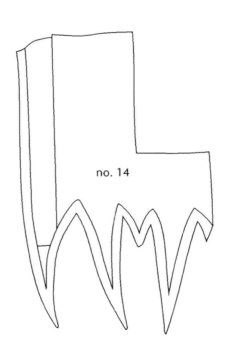

1　结构图　Numbering diagram

EARLY SEVENTH-CENTURY JIN, WITH YELLOW GROUND, ALIGNED-PEARL ROUNDELS ENCLOSING CONFRONTED-HORSES PATTERN (DRM1PM2:S155-1; QK 002392 AND QK 002797)

Overall height 48 cm, width 29.3 cm; inv. no. QK 002392: height 48 cm, width 17.8 cm; inv. no. QK 002797: height 29.3 cm, width 11.5 cm (warp direction ↔).

Warp-faced compound 2/1 Z twill with three series of warps.

Warp: silk, no noticeable twist, beige (yellow?), white, dark blue, blue, and green (the latter three arranged in stripes); c. 162 ends per cm (c. 54 ends per warp series and cm).

Weft: silk, no noticeable twist, undyed(?); c. 26 picks per cm, passed alternately through a twill shed and a pattern shed.

One selvage preserved at the upper edge.

Complemented on the left side by a fragment with find no. DRM1PM2:S155–2: Warp-faced compound 2/1 Z twill with two series of warps.

Warp: silk, no noticeable twist, green, beige; c. 120 ends per cm (c. 60 ends per warp series and cm).

[contd.]

Weft: silk, no noticeable twist, undyed(?); c. 24 picks per cm, passed alternately through a twill shed and a pattern shed.

No selvage preserved.

A band composed of seven narrow strips of plain tabby (dark blue, white, red, ochre, yellow, green, blue) is attached to the edge of the streamer.

The weave of this textile employs yellow ground and blue and green patterning; it is generally similar to the preceding examples, with minor differences. One difference is that the aligned-pearl roundels are not strictly round-shaped but are more squared off like a 回 (*hui*) character in Chinese; secondly there are no streamers floating behind the horses' heads. This piece was sewn together with DRM1PM2:S155-2, which has a green ground and opposing aligned-pearl wave-pattern framework enclosing lion, phoenix, dragon and peacock, very similar if not identical to cat. no. 4 above. The two different textiles were sewn together to form a streamer.

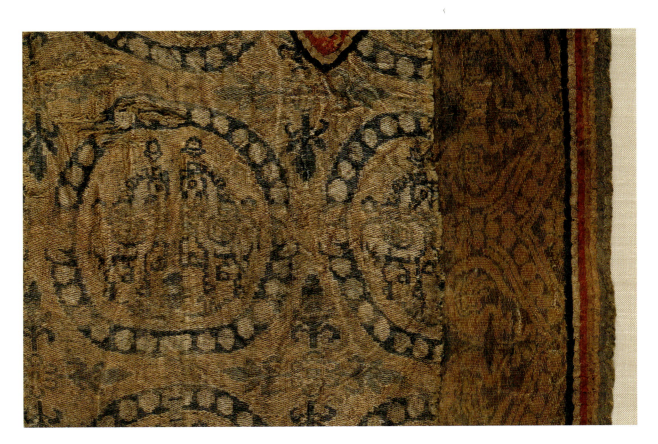

2 组织细节 Detail

黄地小窠连珠对马锦 （DRM1PM2:S150－1；QK001864B）　7世纪初

　　织锦由两片组成，其中一片为图版 No.4 中的织锦，总长 36 厘米、总宽 23 厘米。两片织锦分别长 5.8 厘米、宽 5.3 厘米，长 12.5 厘米、宽 4.5 厘米，经向 ↔。

　　2/1S 斜纹经重组织。经线：弱 S 捻丝，乳白、米、深蓝与蓝交替显色。经密约 168 根／厘米（1:2，每组约 56 根／厘米）。纬线：双股本色无捻丝，纬密约 25 根／厘米，明纬、夹纬交替。幅边已失。

　　此锦与图版 No.4 的橙地对波连珠狮凤龙雀纹锦缝合成为一件幡。与图版 No.14 的连珠对马纹锦相比，这块织锦中的连珠组成的圈较小，马头后无绶带，足踏花枝。而其他的图案设计，如前后提足、头顶日月、十样花作辅饰等都大同小异。

　　与上述对马锦相类似的锦，在吐鲁番阿斯塔那墓群中曾有多件出土。早年斯坦因在其中区 M3（625年）中已发现了一件 [12]，后来新疆维吾尔自治区博物馆在发掘 TAM302（653 年）中也发现了类似的织锦 [13]。略有区别之处只是吐鲁番所出者马足系有绶带，而都兰所出者均未见马足系绶带。故此类织锦的年代是明确的，当在初唐之际，即 7 世纪初。

15

12. New Delhi, National Museum, site no. Ast.ix.3.00.— Aurel Stein, Innermost Asia: Detailed report of explorations in Central Asia Kan-su and eastern Iran, Oxford 1928, vol.3, pl.lxxx.
13. 原藏于新疆维吾尔自治区博物馆，59TAM302.32、59TAM302.4，武敏《织绣》，图版 128、129，台北幼狮文化事业有限公司，1992 年。

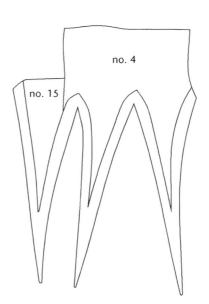

1　结构图　Numbering diagram

EARLY SEVENTH-CENTURY JIN, WITH YELLOW GROUND AND SMALL ALIGNED-PEARL ROUNDELS ENCLOSING CONFRONTED HORSES (DRM1PM2:S150-1; QK 001864 B)

Two fragments stitched together: height 5.8 cm, width 5.3 cm; height 12.5 cm, width 4.5 cm (warp direction ↔). Overall dimensions, including cat. no. 4: height 36 cm, width 23 cm.

Warp-faced compound 2/1 S twill with three series of warps.

Warp: silk, slightly S-twisted, cream, beige, dark blue and blue (the latter two arranged in stripes); c. 168 ends per cm (c. 56 ends per warp series and cm).

Weft: silk, no noticeable twist, undyed(?), paired; c. 25 picks per cm, passed alternately through a twill shed and a pattern shed.

No selvage preserved.

This textile was sewn together to form a streamer with the piece described as aligned-pearl wave-pattern framework enclosing lion, phoenix, dragon and peacock (cat. no. 4 above). Similar to cat. no. 14 described above, the aligned-pearl roundels are relatively small, there are no ribbons behind the horse heads, and the hooves prance on flowers and branches. The front and rear hooves are lifted, above the heads are sun and moon motifs, and quatrefoil flowers form a supplementary pattern. The pieces can be seen as mostly similar, with minor differences.

Many *jin* textiles similar to the above-described confronted-horses piece have been excavated at Astana in Turfan. In early years Aurel Stein found one in the central region grave M3 that was dated to 625.[13] Later, when the Xinjiang Museum was excavating TAM302, which is dated 653, they found a similar *jin*.[14] Slight differences include the fact that the pieces excavated at Turfan have ribbons on the horses' feet while those excavated at Dulan do not. Nonetheless, the dating of this *jin* weaving is clear: it should be in the neighborhood of early Tang, early seventh century.

13 New Delhi, National Museum, site no. Ast.ix.3.02. Aurel Stein, *Innermost Asia. Detailed report of explorations in Central Asia, Kan-su and eastern Iran*, Oxford 1928, vol. 3, pl. lxxx.

14 Urumqi, Xinjiang Museum, 59TAM302:22, 59TAM302:4. 武敏 Wu Min, 织绣 , *Zhixiu (Weaving and embroidery)*, Taipeh 1992, pls. 128, 129.

黄地中窠连珠对羊对雀锦 （DRM1PM2:S153；QK002032） 晋隋至初唐

长 46 厘米、宽 11 厘米，经向 ↔。

2/1Z 经重组织。经线：无捻丝，白、黄、深蓝与绿交替显色。经密约 192 根／厘米（1:2，每组 64 根／厘米）。纬线：双股本色细无捻丝，纬密 24～26 根／厘米，明纬、夹纬交替。织物一端存留幅边。

该锦保存完整，有单侧幅边。纬向长短为 46 厘米，说明该锦的幅宽应在 46 厘米以上。黄色为地，白色勾勒，蓝、绿交替分区显示主要花纹。全幅内共有四个连珠圈，沿纬向两边分开，两两对称。连珠圈上下各有一"回"字纹。在由四个方格组成的平台上，站立一对孔雀，二者下方的平台上有一簇花形。孔雀姿态矫健，展翅，大尾上翘，尾上饰有四颗圆珠。中间两窠为对孔雀，两边连珠圈中是对羊纹样。中间亦是一株花枝，枝上五叶。树用忍冬式卷草作平台，上站立一对山羊，羊颈上系有飘带，羊头清晰可见，但细长的羊角则显得不甚清晰。因为羊角用白色，与地色不易分辨。中间连珠环之间的动物是对虎，孔雀环与羊环之间的动物是对马。对羊环与幅边间的动物不清，似马又似龙。

该锦属于隋代前后风格。一是从连珠环外安置动物的情况看，吐鲁番出土的小窠连珠对孔雀锦[14]和连珠对孔雀"贵"字锦[15]的排列情况与此基本相同，亦是连珠外对兽，前者年代为 558 年，后者为 596～617 年，而且后者的连珠环形式、孔雀的造型、花的造型及花边的云彩等均与此件相同。因此，可以将这一类的织锦年代定在隋到唐初。

14 原品藏于新疆维吾尔自治区博物馆，72TAM169:34。新疆维吾尔自治区博物馆《新疆出土文物》，图版 78，文物出版社，1975 年。

15 原品藏于新疆维吾尔自治区博物馆，66TAM48:6。新疆维吾尔自治区博物馆《丝绸之路——汉唐织物》，图版 28，文物出版社，1972 年。

JIN DATED SUI TO EARLY TANG, WITH ALIGNED-PEARL ROUNDELS ON YELLOW GROUND, ENCLOSING CONFRONTED GOATS OR IBEX AND CONFRONTED PEACOCKS (DRM1PM2:S153; QK 002032)

Height 46 cm, width 11 cm (warp direction ↔).

Warp-faced compound 2/1 Z twill with three series of warps.

Warp: silk, no noticeable twist, white, yellow, dark blue and green (the latter two arranged in stripes); c. 192 ends per cm (c. 64 ends per warp series and cm).

Weft: silk, no noticeable twist, undyed(?), very fine, paired; 24–26 picks per cm, passed alternately through a twill shed and a pattern shed.

One selvage preserved at the lower edge.

This textile has been well preserved and has a selvage along one side. The weft-direction width is 46 cm, showing that this textile should have had a loom width of more than 46 cm. It employs a yellow ground, outlining in white, and alternating blue and green regions to show the main pattern.

Four aligned-pearl roundels lie across the width, the weft-direction, in two pairs. At top and bottom of each aligned-pearl roundel is a square element that resembles a 回 (*hui*) character in Chinese.

On this textile fragment, the two inner roundels have confronted peacocks, the two on the outside have confronted ibex. In the peacock roundels a pair of peacocks stands above a platform, on which is a cluster of flowers. The peacocks look grand and arrogant, with outstretched wings and great uplifted tails. Four dots decorate each tail. Inside the ibex roundel a kind of tree is depicted that uses twining honeysuckle foliage as a platform. The branches of the trees end in five leaves. The ibex face this tree, with flying ribbons on their necks. Their heads are clearly distinguished, but since their horns are woven in white they are indistinct and not clearly distinguished from the ground. In between the roundels various other animals are depicted: confronted tigers between the inner roundels, and confronted horses between the outer roundels. Animals woven next to the selvage are unclear, and may be either horses or dragons.

The style of this *jin* belongs to around the time of the Sui dynasty, indicated partly by the fact that animals are placed outside the aligned-pearl roundels. Two textiles excavated at Turfan show the same pattern: confronted peacocks in small aligned-pearl roundels[15] and in another confronted peacocks with a *gui* character (nobility).[16] Both of these also have confronted animals outside the roundels. The former is dated 558, the latter is dated 596–617. The aligned-pearl roundel style of the latter, the shape of the peacock, the flowers forms and cloud-patterns are all the same as in this Dulan piece. Because of this, we can deduce that this textile was woven in the period from Sui to early Tang.

16

15 Urumqi, Xinjiang Museum, 72TAM169:34. 新疆维吾尔自治区博物馆 Xinjiang Uighur Autonomous Region Museum (ed.), 新疆出土文物 *Xinjiang chutu wenwu (Cultural relics excavated in Xinjiang)*, Beijing 1975, pl. 78.

16 Urumqi, Xinjiang Museum, 66TAM48:6. 新疆维吾尔自治区博物馆 Xinjiang Uighur Autonomous Region Museum (ed.), 丝绸之路 —— 汉唐织物 , *Sichou zhi lu. Han Tang zhiwu (Silk Road: Han to Tang fabrics)*, Beijing 1972, pl. 28 .

1 带幅边的组织细节 Detail with selvage

2 组织细节 Weave detail

黄地连珠对羊锦 (DRM1PM2:S59；QK001855)

长 51.3 厘米、宽 10 厘米，经向 ↔。

2/1S 斜纹经重组织。经线：S 捻丝，绿、黄、米、深棕与深蓝交替显色。经密在 1:2 处约为 180 根／厘米，在 1:3 处约为 240 根／厘米，每组都约为 60 根／厘米。纬线：米色无捻丝，密度为 30 根／厘米，明纬、夹纬交替。幅边均保存完好，幅宽为 52 厘米。

这块织锦基本色彩是在连珠圈外以黄色作地，连珠圈内以紫色为地，蓝和绿变区交替使用显示主要花纹，以白色勾勒连珠。由于色彩的使用上有独到之处，该锦的风格也有些特殊。连珠圈由于用深色勾边显得十分醒目，连珠本身却由于黄白反差较小而不引人注目。用以连接各圈的是八出小花，由于花瓣方向变化及色彩有紫黄两种而显得更像蝴蝶。圈内的小羊不是中亚和西亚地区常见的带长角的羚羊，而更像是小绵羊，回首张口，咪咪而鸣。两只小羊充满了连珠圈内的绝大部分空间，加上羊足下的忍冬纹饰，更增加了图案的和谐。连珠圈之间的十样小花也有些特殊，用深色的蓝、紫、绿色显示，几何味很浓。

从技术角度看，该锦亦有特点。其经线加有较强的 S 捻，约 500 捻／米，较之一般的经锦有较大差别，可能产于受纬锦织造技术影响之后。

1 组织细节 Weave detail

JIN TEXTILE WITH YELLOW GROUND, ALIGNED-PEARL ROUNDELS ENCLOSING CONFRONTED IBEX (DRM1PM2:S59; QK 001855)

Height 51.3 cm, width 10 cm (warp direction ↔).

Warp-faced compound 2/1 S twill with four series of warps.

Warp: silk, S-twisted, green, yellow, beige, dark brown and dark blue (the latter two intermittently); c. 180 ends per cm in areas with three series of warps, c. 240 ends per cm in areas with four series of warps (c. 60 ends per warp series and cm).

Weft: silk, no noticeable twist, beige; 30 picks per cm, passed alternately through a twill shed and a pattern shed.

Both selvages preserved; loom width 52 cm.

This textile has some unique stylistic features. The colour-outlining of the aligned-pearl roundels is striking, but the pearls themselves are yellow-white and not very noticeable due to little contrast with the ground of the fabric. Patterns that look like butterflies connect the roundels: they are in fact flowers, but the change in petal direction and use of the colours purple and yellow make them appear to be butterflies. Most noticeable are the little goats depicted in the roundels. These are not the often-seen long-horned variety seen in central and western Asia, but resemble more closely little cashmere goats. They turn their heads around with open mouths, appearing to be bleating. They almost fill the space inside their roundels, although under them is a honeysuckle pattern, on which they stand.

Quatrefoil flowers that link the roundels are also quite different. Their deep shades of blue, purple, and green show a strongly geometric pattern. The overall ground of the textile is yellow outside and red inside the roundels, with blue and green used for the figuring.

In terms of technique, this *jin* has warp threads that are given a relatively strong S-twist, around 500 twists per meter. This is different from most warp-faced *jin*, and may be the result of the influence of weft-faced weaving after that technology was introduced.

蓝地连珠对饮锦　(DRM1PM2:S137；QK003594)　北朝末至隋

　　长 17.4 厘米、宽 2.6 厘米，经向 ↔。

　　平纹经重组织。经线：偶有弱 S 捻。蓝、乳白、红与绿交替显色。经密约 180 根／厘米（1:2，每组 60 根／厘米）。纬线：偶有弱 S 捻，蓝绿色，密度约 27 根／厘米，明纬、夹纬交替。残片顶端留有乳白和蓝色条的窄幅边。

　　残片整体为长条形，色彩鲜艳，蓝色作地，黄色勾边，红、绿变换显花。残存面积虽然很小，但既保留了一端的幅边，又极清晰地显示了对饮的图案。连珠圈内，一饮者头戴翘沿小帽，身穿红色窄袖长袍至膝，脚着高腰长靴。人物一手托举高足杯，面对着中间的一个巨型酒坛。坛盘口，高颈，鼓腹，通体饰横向条纹，坛高约相当于人身高的 35%。人物面目清晰，神态生动，服装为西方人装束。原锦应该是对饮图案。

18

LATE SIXTH-CENTURY JIN WITH BLUE GROUND, SHOWING PART OF A DRINKING PERSON, ONE OF A PAIR INSIDE AN ALIGNED-PEARL ROUNDEL (DRM1PM2:S137; QK 003594)

Height 17.4 cm, width 2.6 cm (warp direction ↔).

Warp-faced compound tabby with three series of warps.

Warp: silk, occasional slight S-twist, blue, cream, red and green (the latter two arranged in stripes); c. 180 ends per cm (c. 60 ends per warp series and cm).

Weft: silk, occasional slight S-twist, green-blue; c. 27 picks per cm, passed alternately through a tabby shed and a pattern shed.

Narrow selvage of one cream and one blue stripe preserved at the upper edge of the fragment.

The fragment is in the shape of a long strip. It exhibits bright colours, blue for the ground and alternating red and green for the figuring with outlining in yellow (cream). Although the fragment is small, it retains a selvage on one side and shows very clearly the original pattern of two confronted drinkers. The primary design is enclosed in an aligned-pearl roundel; the one drinker who is visible wears a small hat with uplifted brim and a narrow-sleeved long gown that reaches to his knees. He wears tall boots, and one hand lifts a tall-stemmed cup as he faces a large wine jug in the middle of the roundel. This jug has a tall neck and a drum-shaped middle and stands around one-third the height of the people. The lively expression on the face of the drinker is clear; from his attire he appears to be a westerner.

18

1 组织细节 Weave detail

两片（A、B）不同的橙地连珠对饮锦 隋至初唐

A. DRM1PM2:S93；QK002847，长 10.5 厘米、宽 7 厘米，经向 ↔。

B. DRM1PM2:S46；QK003590，长 29.5 厘米、宽 7.5 厘米，经向 ↔。

A. 2/1Z 斜纹经重组织。经线：无捻丝，淡橘、白、深蓝与浅蓝交替显色。密度约 171 根／厘米（1:2，每组约 57 根／厘米）。纬线：本色无捻丝，密度约 28 根／厘米，明纬、夹纬交替。残片顶端存留窄幅边。

B. 2/1S 斜纹经重组织。经线：Z 捻丝，白、淡橘、深蓝与浅棕交替显色。经密度约 153 根／厘米（1:2，每组约 51 根／厘米）。纬线：本色无捻丝，密度约 28 根／厘米，明纬、夹纬交替。残片顶端存留深蓝色窄幅边。

两片织锦图案相同，保存情况有所不同。DRM1PM2:S93 尚存一个连珠圈中的一半，DRM1PM2:S46 存有两个连珠圈的一半。结合起来可以看出，两个连珠圈由小团花（纬向）连接。第一连珠圈是对饮人物，头部不清，可见身穿圆领长袍，中系腰带，脚穿长靴，手持高足酒杯，一派胡人装束。中间也是盘口、高颈、鼓腹的大酒坛。第二连珠圈中也是一对人物，头戴小帽，衣着与上相仿，但不同之处为手中持有一喇叭状物。体态弯曲，似呈坐姿，臀下似有座椅之类。连珠圈之间是几何味较浓的十样花。整个织锦以橙地白勾、蓝色和棕褐色交替分区显花。

这一类的连珠对饮锦原来发现很少，已见报道的仅是出土于吐鲁番的一件，报道命名为"拂菻对饮锦"[16]。从发表的照片来看，图案为一对尖鼻卷发、身穿胡装的人正在举杯对饮，酒器为牛角杯。都兰出土的对饮锦，格局与此十分相似，但在连珠圈的构成、人物的面部形象、服饰与酒杯等方面则存在着某些差异。总体风格一致，年代亦不会相差太远，当在隋至初唐之际。

16. 藏品藏于新疆维吾尔自治区博物馆，73TAM507，Wu Min, "The Exchange of Weaving Technologies between China and Central and Western Asia from the Third to the Eighth Century Based on New Textile Finds in Xinjiang", *Central Asian Textiles and Their Contexts in the Early Middle Ages*, ed. by Regula Schorta (Riggisberger Berichte, 9), Riggisberg 2006, fig. 176.

TWO EXAMPLES (A, B) OF SUI TO EARLY-TANG JIN, WITH ORANGE GROUND AND
ALIGNED-PEARL ROUNDELS ENCLOSING OPPOSING DRINKERS

A. (DRM1PM2:S93; QK 002847). Height 10.5 cm, width 7 cm (warp direction ↔).

B. (DRM1PM2:S46; QK 003590). Height 29.5 cm, width 7.5 cm (warp direction ↔).

A. Warp-faced compound 2/1 Z twill with three series of warps.

Warp: silk, no noticeable twist, light orange, white, dark blue and light brown (the latter two arranged in stripes); c. 171 ends per cm (c. 57 ends per warp series and cm).

Weft: silk, no noticeable twist, undyed(?); c. 28 picks per cm, passed alternately through a twill shed and a pattern shed.

Narrow selvage preserved at the upper edge of the fragment.

B. Warp-faced compound 2/1 S twill with three series of warps.

Warp: silk, Z-twisted, white, orange-beige, dark blue and light brown (the latter two arranged in stripes); c. 153 ends per cm (c. 51 ends per warp series and cm).

Weft: silk, no noticeable twist, undyed(?), very fine; c. 28 picks per cm, passed alternately through a twill shed and a pattern shed.

Narrow dark blue selvage preserved at the upper edge of the fragment.

A.

These are two fragments with similar patterning but different states of preservation. S93 still has half of an aligned-pearl roundel, S46 has half of two aligned-pearl roundels. By putting these together, one can see that originally there were two aligned-pearl roundels connected in weft-direction by little flowers. The first roundel encloses opposing drinking figures. Their heads are unclear, but their bodies are clothed with long gowns tied with a sash or belt at the waist and they wear tall boots. They hold high-footed wine cups and are dressed in the manner of *hu* (barbarian) people. Between the drinkers stands a high-necked drum-bellied wine jug.

The second roundel also encloses opposing drinkers, with little hats on their heads and wearing the same robes as above, but differs from the above in that an object like a megaphone or an instrument is held in the hand. The posture of these drinkers is bent, as though they were sitting down. A chair can be seen under the buttocks. In between the roundels are quatrefoil flowers with a strongly geometric flavor. The entire textile uses an orange ground and white outlining, with blue and brown alternating in regions to form the pattern.

There have been very few discoveries of this kind of opposing-drinkers motif. Only one has been reported from excavations at Turfan; the excavation report called this a 'byzantine opposing-

1 有幅边的局部细节 (B.) Detail with selvage (B.)

B.

drinkers *jin*.[17] From photographs in the publication, it can be seen that the pattern shows a pair of pointed-nosed curly-haired drinkers lifting cups and dressed in *hu* (barbarian) attire. The wine vessels in the Turfan example are ox-horn cups. The drinkers excavated at Dulan are very similar but the structure of the aligned-pearl roundels and the faces of the people, dress, and wine cup are slightly different. Overall the style is the same, however, and the dating cannot be too different. In our opinion, therefore, the dating of this textile is in the neighborhood of Sui and early Tang.

19

17 Urumqi, Xinjiang Museum, from grave 73TAM507. Wu Min, "The Exchange of Weaving Technologies between China and Central and Western Asia from the Third to the Eighth Century Based on New Textile Finds in Xinjiang," *Central Asian Textiles and Their Contexts in the Early Middle Ages*, ed. Regula Schorta (Riggisberger Berichte 9), Riggisberg 2006, fig. 176.

2 组织细节 (B.) Detail (B.)

黄地大窠连珠狩虎锦 　(DRM1PM2:S102 ; QK002911) 　7 世纪初

20

长 98 厘米、宽 9 厘米，经向 ↕。

1/2Z 纬重组织。经线：偏红的米色 S 捻丝，夹经、明经 2∶1 交替，夹经约 18 根 / 厘米，明经约 18 根 / 厘米。纬线：无明显加捻丝，由黄、白、浅棕、深棕、绿和蓝色交替相间显色组成，并按此序循环往复，五纬一组，密度约 13 副 / 厘米。幅边已失。

织锦以黄色作地，紫褐色勾边，白色和绿色显花。在经向的长度上还能看到两个多点的连珠圈循环的部分图案。存留的连珠环内圈弦高 6 厘米、弦长 27 厘米，整个大圈的内径 38 厘米，加上 4 厘米连珠圈的宽度，全珠圈的外径约为 46 厘米。对照测算所得，其图案经向循环为 43 厘米，亦可知相差不远，也是一种大窠纬锦。团窠圈内面，一虎直身扑起。此虎形体较小，无法充塞整个画面，对照现藏于日本正仓院的绿地狩猎纹锦等图案[17]，以及吐鲁番出土的印花狩猎纹绢[18] 可以发现，这应是一件狩猎纹的团窠连珠图案，具体的狩猎对象就是老虎。在团窠连珠圈外，则是较为复杂的十样花纹，不甚清晰。

此类大窠连珠纬锦在吐鲁番所出很少。1949 年以前，日本大谷探险队发现了大窠连珠花枝对鹿锦[19]，1949 年后仅见大窠连珠一例，命名为"大窠马大球"，年代为唐武德三年（620 年）[20]。此外，在敦煌莫高窟的隋代窟第 420 窟中，见有大窠连珠纹的飞马驯虎纹织锦图案。其驯虎形象当与狩虎相差不远。由此看来，这种大窠连珠动物锦的年代当在隋至初唐时期。日本正仓院藏有一块属于大窠连珠的犀牛连珠纹织锦[21]，奈良国立博物馆则收藏了法隆寺的一块四天王狩狮织锦[22]。据日本学者考证，此类织锦的年代不会迟于武周时期。

17. 原品藏于日本奈良正仓院，Jodai gire: 7th and 8th century textiles in Japan from the Shōsō-in and Hōryū-ji, by Kaneo Matsumoto, Kyoto 1984, pl. 46.
18. 原品藏于新疆维吾尔自治区博物馆，72TAM191, 新疆维吾尔自治区博物馆《新疆出土文物》，图版 154，文物出版社，1975 年。
19. 原品藏于日本京都龙谷大学大古中亚艺术。武敏著《织绣》，图 90，台北幼狮文化事业有限公司，1992 年。
20. 武敏《吐鲁番出土蜀锦的研究》，《文物》1984 年第 6 期，图 4。
21. 原品藏于奈良正仓院。Yokohari Kazuko, "The Hōryū-ji Lion-hunting Silk and Related Silks", Central Asian Textiles and Their Contexts in the Early Middle Ages, ed. by Regula Schorta (Riggisberger Berichte, 9), Riggisberg 2006, figs. 111, 112.
22. 原品藏于奈良国立博物馆法隆寺。Yokohari 2006（同上出版物），图 105, 106。

EARLY SEVENTH-CENTURY JIN, WITH ORANGE GROUND AND LARGE ALIGNED-PEARL ROUNDEL ENCLOSING TIGER-HUNTING SCENE (DRM1PM2:S102; QK 002911)

Height 98 cm, width 9 cm (warp direction ↕).

Weft-faced compound 1/2 Z twill with five lats.

Warp: 1 pair of main warp ends to 1 binding warp end; silk, S-twisted, reddish-beige; c. 18 pairs of main warp ends and 18 binding warp ends per cm.

Weft: silk, no noticeable twist, yellow, white, dark brown, light brown, blue (latté green); straight weft sequence; c. 13 passes per cm.

No selvage preserved.

This textile has a yellow ground with purple (brown) outlining, and uses white and green to form the pattern. Only a long narrow strip of the textile remains.

Slightly more than two continuous aligned-pearl roundels can be seen on the warp-directional length. The width of the inside of the fragmentary roundel is 6 cm, the length of the arc is 27 cm. We figure that the inner diameter of the entire roundel was 38 cm; add to that 4 cm for the width of the aligned-pearl frame and the outside diameter of the entire roundel in weft direction would be around 46 cm. The pattern repeat in warp direction appears to be 43 cm, so by comparison this is not far off. This is also a large-roundel weft-faced *jin*.

A tiger can be seen inside the roundel, with stretched-out body. Since the image is small and fragmentary it is not possible to see the entire figure, but we can compare it to a textile preserved at the Shōsō-in in Japan, a *jin* with green ground and hunting pattern,[18] and also to a piece excavated from Turfan, a printed *juan* with hunting scene.[19] From these we can deduce that this too portrays a hunting scene enclosed in an aligned-pearl roundel, and that the object of the hunt is a tiger. Outside the aligned-pearl roundel is a relatively complex four-directional flower pattern, which is unclear.

This kind of large, aligned-pearl roundel, weft-faced *jin* is extremely rare in Turfan excavations. Before 1949, a *jin* textile portraying large aligned-pearl-roundels with flowers and branches and opposing deer was discovered by the Ōtani Expedition.[20] Since then only one such example has been

---

18 Nara, Shōsō-in. Kaneo Matsumoto, *Jodai-gire. 7th and 8th century textiles in Japan from the Shōsō-in and Hōryū-ji*, Kyoto 1984, pl. 45.

19 Urumqi, Xinjiang Museum, from grave 73TAM191. 新疆维吾尔自治区博物馆 Xinjiang Uighur Autonomous Region Museum (ed.), 新疆出土文物 *Xinjiang chutu wenwu (Cultural relics excavated in Xinjiang)*, Beijing 1975, pl. 154.

20 Kyoto, Ryukoku University, Ōtani Collection of Central Asian Art. 武敏 Wu Min, 织绣 , *Zhixiu (Weaving and embroidery)*, Taipeh 1992, fig. 90 on p. 157.

seen, which has been described as a 'large roundel with horse and large pearls.'[21] The dating is 620, or the third year of Wude. Other than this, in the Sui-dynasty cave 420 at the Dunhuang Grottoes the *jin* pattern of a large aligned-pearl-roundel with flying horse and docile tiger can be seen, with the shape of the tiger not too different from the one in this hunting scene. From these comparisons, we feel that this textile should be dated from Sui to early Tang. There are two silks in Japan that belong to this large tangent roundel pattern of *jin*, one of which has a rhinoceros inside an aligned-pearl pattern,[22] the other is titled 'four Heavenly Kings hunting *jin*.'[23] According to Japanese scholars, the dating of this latter piece cannot be later than the Wu Zhou period (690–705).

21 武敏 Wu Min, 吐鲁番出土蜀锦的研究 "Tulufan chutu Shu jin de yanjiu (Research on excavated Shu jin silks)," 文物 Wenwu (Cultural Relics), 6, 1984, fig. 4.

22 Nara, Shōsō-in. Yokohari Kazuko, "The Hōryū-ji Lion-hunting Silk and Related Silks," *Central Asian Textiles and Their Contexts in the Early Middle Ages*, ed. Regula Schorta (Riggisberger Berichte 9), Riggisberg 2006, figs. 111, 112.

23 Nara National Museum, from Hōryū-ji Temple. Yokohari 2006 (ibid.), figs. 105, 106.

1 组织细节 Two weave details

紫地中窠宝花立凤锦　（DRM11:S23、DRM1:S42；QK002054）　8世纪中

出土了两片同样图案的织锦，总长 28 厘米、总宽 12.7 厘米，分别长 24 厘米、4.8 厘米，经向↕。

1/2S 斜纹纬重组织。经线：很细的乳白色 S 捻丝，夹经、明经 2:1 交替，夹经约 44 根／厘米，明经约 22 根／厘米。纬线：无捻丝，由紫、黄、白、浅绿、深蓝和浅蓝交替相间显色组成，并按此序循环往复。五纬一组，纬密约 30 副／厘米。横向机头在小片织锦的底边上。

织锦显紫地，但在团窠内却是黄色作地，蓝、绿和白色显花。图案的经向循环为 16.5 厘米，纬向循环尚不能定，团窠外径 12 ～ 13 厘米。由于织作密度的关系，整个图案显得有些拉长，经向大于纬向。团窠环由 16 出花蕾构成，环内用 16 个弧作花藤连接各花，花蕾分两种，在正"十"字形的四个方向及 45 度角度处是显花瓣的花朵，而在相错 15 度角的方向上乃是带有放射线的类似柏枝叶式的花饰。团窠环中有一立凤，两足落地，相当稳健。凤冠呈火焰状，吸收了较多的西域风格。凤翅伸展，羽毛多而复杂，尾羽上翘过顶。

此锦令人想起藏于日本正仓院的紫地凤唐草圆纹锦[23]。其图案与都兰的这件还是有较大的区别的，表现在卷草葡萄环中疾走的神采飞扬的凤，但其紫地的色调、图案的主题等还是与这件锦相当接近，只是比此锦更成熟、生动。按正仓院的紫地凤唐草圆纹锦是日本天平胜宝八岁（756 年）6 月 21 日时光明皇后东大寺献纳品之一，被认为是仿自中国的产品，因此，紫地中窠宝花立凤锦的年代当是在此之前。

23　原藏藏于日本奈良正仓院。*Jodai-gire: 7th and 8th century textiles in Japan from the Shōsō-in and Hōryū-ji*, by Kaneo Matsumoto, Kyoto 1984, pl. 28, 131.

1　组织细节　Weave detail

MID-EIGHTH-CENTURY JIN, WITH PURPLE GROUND AND PRECIOUS-FLOWER ROUNDEL ENCLOSING STANDING PHOENIX (DRM1:S23 AND DRM1:S42; QK 002054)

21

Overall height 28 cm (two fragments of 24 and 4.8 cm respectively), width 12.7 cm (warp direction ↕).

Weft-faced compound 1/2 S twill with five lats.

Warp: 1 pair of main warp ends to 1 binding warp end; silk, S-twisted, cream, very fine; c. 22 pairs of main warp ends and 22 binding warp ends per cm.

Weft: silk, no noticeable twist, purple, yellow, white, light green, dark blue (latté light blue); straight weft sequence; c. 30 passes per cm.

Horizontal starting border at the lower edge of the smaller fragment.

The silk has a purple ground, but inside the roundels the ground is formed of yellow with blue, green, and white displaying the pattern. The design has a repeat of 16.5 cm in warp direction, the repeat in weft direction cannot be determined. The outer diameter of the roundels is 12–13 cm, and due to the density of the weave the pattern appears to be slightly elongated with warp-directional length greater than weft-directional. The roundel is composed of sixteen sprouting or protruding buds of two different kinds. Inside the roundels, the stems form sixteen arches connecting the flowers. Petalled flowers display at the horizontal and vertical axis and at a forty-five degree angle from them, while more feathery flowers like cypress leaves emerge from between them. The roundel encloses a phoenix with its two feet standing firmly on the ground. Its crest is portrayed in flaming style, perhaps having absorbed Western Region style. The wings of the phoenix are outstretched, with its tail feathers proudly upraised.

This textile is reminiscent of a piece in the Shōsō-in in Japan,[24] although there are fairly large differences between the two. The Shōsō-in textile depicts a phoenix on purple ground in the midst of Tang-style scrolls, but the phoenix is moving swiftly over a bed of grape tendrils. The overall subject and the purple ground, however, are similar. The Shōsō-in textile is more sophisticated, with a more lively design. It is believed that the piece in Japan was copied from a Chinese piece: it dates from 756, the eighth year Tenpyō-shōsō; on a date equivalent to June 21, the Empress Kōmyō had it formally donated among other items to the Tōdai-ji Temple. The original version must have been made in China before this time. This pattern of a standing phoenix enclosed by precious-flower roundels was highly popular during the High Tang period.

---

24 Nara, Shōsō-in. Kaneo Matsumoto, *Jodai-gire. 7th and 8th century textiles in Japan from the Shōsō-in and Hōryū-ji*, Kyoto 1984, pl. 28, 131.

黄地雁鹊穿花锦　（DRM1PM2:S47；QK003587）　8世纪中

长 8.2 厘米、宽 13.4 厘米，经向 ↕。

1/2S 斜纹纬重组织。经线：淡褐色 S 捻丝，夹经、明经 2:1 交替，夹经约 44 根／厘米，明经约 22 根／厘米。纬线：无捻丝，由米、蓝、黄、淡褐显色（褪色严重），并按此序列循环反复，四纬（？）一组，纬密约 40 副／厘米。幅边已失。在花纹边缘的顶部和底部分别有横向的 3 ～ 4 根蓝纬线和 4 根米色纬线做记号。

此锦是黄地上显花，图案为花卉卷草。花座中有三只飞禽，中间是一只小飞雁，长颈，展翅，还有两只飞禽属鹊类，故称雁鹊穿花。纬向花纹循环单位尺寸约 20 厘米。

此类锦在吐鲁番亦有出土，且有一件是与 778 年墓志同出。此锦从总体来看，是大团花四周散布飞禽和折枝花等[24]。但从局部来看，则是穿枝花的典型造型。再从敦煌壁画中的织物来看，盛唐尤多此类图案。因此可知，此类穿枝花的图案是盛唐流行的。晚唐陆龟蒙《纪锦裙》中记载了一件织锦[25]，"左有鹊二十，势若飞起……二禽大小不类而隔以花卉，均布无余地"。此类锦当与我们所叙述的穿枝花锦类似，而陆氏说此锦"纵非齐梁物，亦不下三百年"，可知其古，起码已距陆氏所在年代颇远，一样可旁证此类穿枝花锦的年代应在盛唐前后。

22

24 原品藏于新疆维吾尔自治区博物馆，68TAM381，新疆维吾尔自治区博物馆《丝绸之路汉唐织物》，图版 44，文物出版社，1972 年。
25 沈敏《吐鲁番出土蜀锦的研究》，《文物》1984 年第 6 期，79 页。

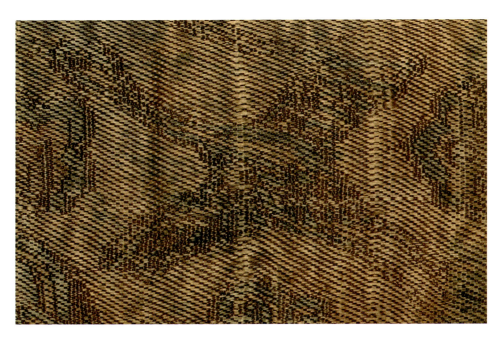

1 组织细节　Weave detail

MID-EIGHTH-CENTURY JIN, WITH YELLOW GROUND, WILD SWAN AND MAGPIE MOTIF (DRM1PM2:S47; QK 003587)

Height 8.2 cm, width 13.4 cm (warp direction ↕).

Weft-faced compound 1/2 S twill with four lats.

Warp: 1 pair of main warp ends to 1 binding warp end; silk, S-twisted, light brown; c. 22 pairs of main warp ends and 22 binding warp ends per cm.

Weft: silk, no noticeable twist, beige, blue, yellow, light brown (all heavily faded); straight weft sequence; c. 40 passes per cm.

No selvage preserved; horizontal bands of 3–4 blue and 4 beige weft passes mark the lower and upper edge of the patterned band.

Twining foliage and flowers are depicted on the once-yellow ground of this textile, together with three flying creatures among which is a small wild goose and two other goose-like birds that are perhaps magpies. The central goose has a long neck and outstretched wings. One can surmise that the weft-directional pattern repeat was around 20 cm.

This particular style has also been excavated from Turfan. One Turfan piece dated to the year 778 has bird-and-flower patterns and similarly depicts a large circle of flowers surrounded by flying creatures and interspersed with twining foliage.[25] The foliage specifically is a classic representation of what is called *chuanzhihua*, or interpenetrating branches and flowers. From the representation of textiles in Dunhuang wall paintings, it is clear that this pattern was very popular during the High Tang.

The late-Tang poem 'Notes on *jin* skirts' by Lu Guimeng cites a *jin* textile that resembles this pattern.[26] It similarly uses an interpenetrating branches and flowers motif. Lu Guimeng states that this pattern had already been known for more than three hundred years, so that we can judge its antiquity. Patterns of this type date at least to the High Tang period.

25 Urumqi, Xinjiang Museum, from grave 68TAM381. 新疆维吾尔自治区博物馆 Xinjiang Uighur Autonomous Region Museum (ed.), 丝绸之路 — 汉唐织物 , *Sichou zhi lu. Han Tang zhiwu (Silk Road: Han to Tang fabrics)*, Beijing 1972, pl. 44 (pl. 45 in the 1973 edition).

26 武敏 Wu Min, 吐鲁番出土蜀锦的研究 "Tulufanchutu Shu jin de yanjiu (Research on excavated Shu jin silks)", 文物 Wenwu(Cultural Relics), 6, 1984, p. 79. 钦定全唐文 *Qinding quan Tangwen (The official and whole collection of Tang period literature)*, Jingwei shuju, Taibei 1965, vol. 17, chapter 801, 纪锦裙 *Ji jinqun* (Notes on *jin* skirts), p. 10605b.

22

黄地团窠宝花对狮锦 (DRM1PM2:S72、DRM1PM2:S73；QK002026)　8 世纪中

　　总长 26.5 厘米、总宽 36 厘米。两件残片的长度分别为 26.5 厘米和 8 厘米，宽度分别为 18.5 厘米和 17.5 厘米。经向↕。

　　1/2Z 斜纹纬重组织。经线：红棕色 S 捻丝中间夹少量乳白色丝线，夹经、明经 2:1 交替，夹经约为 44 根／厘米，明经约 22 根／厘米。纬线：无捻丝，由蓝、白、米、黄和棕交替相间的纬线显色组成，并按此序循环往复。四纬一组，纬密约 32 副／厘米。幅边已失。

　　织锦的一侧有缝加的小块平纹衬残片，为无捻黄米色的经纬丝线织成，经密约 60 根／厘米，纬密约 34 根／厘米。

　　团窠经向循环为 17.5 厘米，纬向是 16.5 厘米，团窠外径 13.5 ～ 14 厘米。团窠共有八个藏蕾卷，四面八方均匀分布，各卷之间用藤缠接，藤枝圈之外还部分饰有花蕾。环内一对狮子相扑，均后足立地、前足悬空，神态生动。两狮之间有花卉台。团窠外的十样花是显蕾式的，中间是一朵四瓣小花。该锦狮子的造型与日本所藏四天王狩狮锦中的狮子相似[26]，而其被认为是 7 世纪下半叶的产品。吐鲁番出土一件印花绢，其上的图案也是在同一形式的宝花环中置以立鸟，风格应属同类，年代为盛唐[27]，故亦可以将此锦的年代断在盛唐前后。

26　原品藏于日本奈良国立博物馆法隆寺。Yokohan Kazuko, "The Hōryū-ji Lion-hunting Silk and Related Silks", *Central Asian Textiles and Their Contexts in the Early Middle Ages*, ed. by Regula Schorta (Riggisberger Berichte, 9), Riggisberg 2006, figs. 105, 106.
27　原品藏于新疆维吾尔自治区博物馆。72TAM191:96。武敏《织绣》第 147 页，图 116，台北幼狮文化事业有限公司，1992 年。

1　组织细节 Weave detail

23

MID-EIGHTH-CENTURY JIN, YELLOW GROUND, PRECIOUS-FLOWER ROUNDEL ENCLOSING CONFRONTED LIONS (DRM1PM2:S72 AND DRM1PM2:S73; QK 002026)

Overall height 26.5 cm, width 36 cm (two fragments of height 26.5 cm, width 18.5 cm and height 8 cm, width 17.5 cm respectively; warp direction ↕).

Weft-faced compound 1/2 Z twill with four lats.

Warp: 1 pair of main warp ends to 1 binding warp end; silk, S-twisted, reddish brown (some cream warp ends); c. 22 pairs of main warp ends and 22 binding warp ends per cm.

Weft: silk, no noticeable twist, blue, white, beige, yellow (latté brown); straight weft sequence; c. 32 passes per cm.

No selvage preserved.

Attached are fragments of a tabby lining. Warp and weft: silk, no noticeable twist, yellowish-beige; c. 60 ends and c. 34 picks per cm.

The warp-directional repeat is 17.5 cm, the weft-directional is 16.5 cm. The diameter of the outside of the roundel is between 13.5 and 14 cm.

2 组织细节 Detail

Eight hidden-bud circles are interspersed throughout the roundel, between which curl wisteria tendrils. Outside the wisteria branches are also some buds. Two lions face each other inside the roundel, crouching in vigorous fashion with rear feet on the ground and front paws in the air. Flowers and grasses serve as a platform between the lions. Outside the roundels, the quatrefoil flower is clearly bud-style, and between each is a four-petalled small flower.

The depiction of the lions in this piece is similar to the lion on a piece in Japan that shows 'four Heavenly Kings hunting lions.'[27] That textile is considered to be a product of the second half of the seventh century. Moreover, a printed *juan* excavated from Turfan is of similar style, with precious-flower roundels and standing birds inside, and is dated to around the High Tang.[28] We therefore date this piece to more or less the High Tang.

27 Nara National Museum, from Hōryū-ji Temple. Yokohari Kazuko, "The Hōryū-ji Lion-hunting Silk and Related Silks", *Central Asian Textiles and Their Contexts in the Early Middle Ages*, ed. Regula Schorta (Riggisberger Berichte 9), Riggisberg 2006, figs. 105, 106.

28 Urumqi, Xinjiang Museum, 73TAM191:96. 武敏 Wu Min, 织绣 ,*Zhixiu* (*Weaving and embroidery*), Taipeh 1992, fig.116 on p. 147.

23

黄地狮鹭衔花锦 （DRM1PM2:S60；QK002933）　8世纪末

长7厘米、宽28厘米，经向↕。

1/2S斜纹纬重组织。经线：米色Z捻丝，夹经、明经2:1交替，夹经约44根／厘米，明经约22根／厘米。纬线：无捻丝，由乳白（黄）、白、浅棕（红）、绿和深蓝交替相间显色，并按此序循环往复，四纬一组，纬密约40副／厘米。幅边已失。以浅绿和米色的横向纬线在花纹带的上下边做记号。

织锦的经向7厘米，正好是一个纹样单位，上下均有裁边。而纬向28厘米中有21厘米是一个循环单位，其中又是左右对称。黄地，白、棕、青、浅蓝色显花，其中青和浅蓝又是分区换色显花。整个图案情况是中间一个花蕾，围以卷草，类似于藏蕾式宝花花瓣。另外，还有生翼的对狮。对狮显然也是后足立地、前足腾空，但与前述的团窠宝花对狮锦（图版No.23）中的对狮有极大区别，显得敦厚可爱。对狮之外是一对栖花的鸳鸯，轻盈飞起，极有生意。从敦煌壁画中的织物图看，这种穿枝花的图案，为中唐所流行，故可将此锦的年代定在中唐时期。

LATE EIGHTH-CENTURY JIN, WITH YELLOW GROUND, LION, AND

HERON (DRM1PM2:S60; QK 002933)

Height 7 cm, width 28 cm (warp direction ↕).

Weft-faced compound 1/2 S twill with four lats.

Warp: 1 pair of main warp ends to 1 binding warp end; silk, Z-twisted, beige; c. 22 pairs of main warp ends and 22 binding warp ends per cm.

Weft: silk, no noticeable twist, cream (yellow), white, light brown (red), green (latté dark blue); straight weft sequence; c. 40 passes per cm.

No selvage preserved; horizontal bands of light green and beige weft passes mark the lower and upper edge of the patterned band.

The warp-direction height of this fragment, which is the pattern repeat, is 7 cm. Top and bottom both have cut edges. Of the 28 cm of weft-direction, 21 cm are the pattern repeat, mirrored along a vertical central axis.

On the yellow ground, white, brown, dark blue, and light blue are used for patterning, among which dark and light blue alternate in regions to display the pattern. The design is as follows: in the middle, a flower bud is wrapped or circled with curling scrolls, similar to the 'precious-flower flower petals with hidden bud' style. Then comes a pair of confronted winged lions. These clearly have their rear feet on the ground and front paws in the air, but the confronted lions described above in the precious-flower roundel cat. no.23 and this pair are totally different. These are quite robust, solid and appealing. In addition to the opposing lions is a pair of mandarin ducks perched on flowers, full of vitality and looking as though they are about to take off in flight.

This kind of interconnecting branch-and-flower pattern can be seen in Dunhuang wall paintings and is known to have been popular in the middle Tang. We place this textile in the middle Tang period.

1 组织细节 Weave detail

2 组织细节 Weave detail

绿地鸳鸯栖花锦 （DXM1:S7；QK001860） 8世纪上半叶

总长 41.5 厘米、总宽 29 厘米，其中织锦片宽 23.5 厘米，附加边条宽 5.5 厘米，经向↕。

2/1Z 斜纹经重组织。经线：弱 S 捻丝，绿、乳白，间断的褐色，绿色经线在末端是单股和双股交替。经线密度在 1:1 处约为 96 根／厘米，在 1:2 处约 144 根／厘米，每组约 48 根／厘米。纬线：本色无捻丝，密度约 28 根／厘米，明纬、夹纬交替。残片一侧保留了绿色窄幅边。织锦片上残存有一段米色平纹的装饰条。

整块织锦为绿地，黄色显花，红棕色勾边。图案循环尺寸为经向 6.3 厘米、纬向 16.5 厘米，团窠纹样为经视纹样。团窠下半部位是花盘和叶子，形成半个环。没有宾花。在花盘之上，栖卧着两只鸳鸯。织锦背面墨书汉字"薛安"。与这件锦相似的图案在正仓院所藏的螺钿上也有发现。据考证，其属于 8 世纪上半叶的产品。由此可以推断，这件织锦的年代属于盛唐时期。

1 组织细节 Weave detail

2 背面，墨书汉字"薛安"
Reverse, Chinese characters "Xue An"

FIRST HALF OF THE EIGHTH-CENTURY JIN, WITH GREEN GROUND AND MANDARIN DUCKS PERCHING ON FLOWERS (DXM1:S7; QK 001860)

Height 41.5 cm, overall width 29 cm; width of jin fabric 23.5 cm (warp direction ↕), width of attached band 5.5 cm.

Warp-faced compound 2/1 Z twill with three series of warps.

Warp: silk, slightly S-twisted, green, cream, brown (discontinuous), the green warp ends alternately single and double; c. 96 ends per cm in areas with two warp series, c. 144 ends per cm in areas with three warp series (c. 48 ends per warp series and cm).

Weft: silk, no noticeable twist, undyed(?); c. 28 picks per cm, passed alternately through a twill shed and a pattern shed.

Narrow selvage (green) preserved at the left hand side of the fragment.

Attached is a decorative fringe made from fragments of beige silk tabby.

The weave of this textile is warp-faced compound twill with three series of warps. The fragment has a preserved side selvage, green ground, yellow patterning, and red or brown outlining.

The pattern repeat is 6.3 cm in warp direction, and 16.5 cm in weft direction; the roundel pattern is depicted in line with the warp direction. Flowerpots and leaves form half a circle in the lower half of the roundel. The motifs are aligned in staggered rows, there are no accessory flowers. Two Mandarin ducks perch or are couched on the flower basin. Two Han-Chinese characters have been drawn in ink on the back of the textile: 薛安 (Xue An).

The pattern of Mandarin ducks perching on flowers is also found on a bronze mirror with mother-of-pearl and tortoiseshell inlaid back preserved in the Shōsō-in in Japan dated to the first half of the eighth century.[29] From this it can be deduced that the textile also dates from middle Tang period.

---

29 第四十回正倉院展 *47th Exhibition of Shōsō-in Treasures*, 奈良国立博物館 Nara National Museum, 1995, no. 52.

红袜 （DRM1PM2:S37；QK001854） 8 世纪中

由三种不同的面料组成袜筒、袜面和袜底三部分。总高 23.5 厘米、总宽 27.3 厘米。

袜筒（DRM1PM2:S37-1）：高 11.5 厘米、周长 32 厘米，经向 ↔。1/2Z 斜纹纬重组织[28]。经线：夹经、明经 1:1 交替，米色丝线无明显加捻。夹经、明经密度都在 24 ~ 27 根／厘米。纬线：无明显加捻，由绿蓝、乳白双色两纬一组循环显花。纬密 21 ~ 27 副／厘米。无幅边存留。织锦为蓝地，黄色显小宝花。图案经纬向循环尺寸分别是 2.8 厘米 ×2.3 厘米。纹样清秀，主花是小宝花，四簇花蕾和转向 45 度的四出小花尖；宾花为十样花，极其简单而具有几何味。

袜面（DRM1PM2:S37-2）：袜面周长 50 厘米，脚踝和脚跟处袜高 4.5 厘米。面料为绮，平纹地以 1/3Z 斜纹显花。经线：红色无明显加捻丝，经密 48 ~ 52 根／厘米。纬线：红色无明显加捻丝，纬密约 36 根／厘米。无幅边存留。袜面是红绮地上用劈针法绣制的宝花图案，以绿色圆点为中心，绣以黄色六瓣花，其外是由黄、蓝、绿、黄四层丝线绣出六个大花瓣，在大花瓣之外，再绣以六簇花瓣，所以可称宝花图案。由于是刺绣图案，因此排列显得较为自由，是全宝花而无宾花的团窠排列。

袜底（DRM1PM2:S37-3）：袜底长 31 厘米、宽 8 厘米。面料为绮，平纹地上以 1/3Z 斜纹组织显花。经线为乳白色无明显加捻丝，密度 34 ~ 36 根／厘米。纬线同为乳白色无明显加捻丝，纬密约 33 根／厘米。无幅边存留。袜底夹层面料为（2-2）并丝织出的 1/3Z 斜纹组织，且用 Z 双捻丝在袜底面料上缝出矩形格子纹。

---

28 也有研究认为这袜筒面料是斜纹经重组织。参见 *China, Dawn of a Golden Age 200-750*, ed. by James C. Y. Watt, Exhibition catalogue New York, Metropolitan Museum (New York 2004), no. 243, p. 344.

MID-EIGHTH-CENTURY RED SOCK (DRM1PM2:S37; QK 001854)

This sock consists of three parts made of different textiles: the circular shaft around the ankle, the instep, and the sole. Overall dimensions: height 23.5 cm, width 27.3 cm.

Shaft (DRM1PM2:S37-1): Height 11.5 cm, circumference 32 cm (warp direction ↔).
Weft-faced compound 1/2 Z twill with two lats.[30]

Warp: 1 main warp end to 1 binding warp end; silk, no noticeable twist, beige; c. 24–27 main warp ends and 24–27 binding warp ends per cm.

26

30 This textile has also been described as warp-faced compound twill. See *China. Dawn of a Golden Age 200-750 AD*, ed. by James C. Y. Watt, Exhibition catalogue New York, Metropolitan Museum (New York 2004), no. 243 p. 344.

袜子内衬有平纹绢。绢的经线为米色无明显加捻丝，密度 42 ~ 48 根／厘米；纬线也是米色无明显加捻丝，纬密 30 ~ 34 根／厘米。存留有一侧幅边。

袜筒和袜面交界处有一细窄的牙线条，面料为 1/2S 斜纹纬重组织。经线为米色无明显加捻丝，夹经、明经 1:1 交替，夹经、明经密度约 27 根／厘米。纬线同为无明显加捻丝，以蓝、白双色二纬一组循环显色，纬密约 30 副／厘米。无幅边存留。

在袜前面和袜后脚跟中心线上各有一条编织绦带缝缀其上。这条平纹斜编绦是用五条不同颜色的三根并股 Z 双捻丝编织成的，三根并股丝的颜色有蓝、绿、白、米和红棕色。袜面和袜底缝合处有一条很明显的刺绣边饰。

袜筒上所用的蓝地小宝花锦与吐鲁番所出的海蓝地宝相花纹锦图案非常接近[29]。其年代为 715 年。而袜面上红绮地宝花图案和敦煌第 328 窟彩塑服饰上的图案几乎完全相同[30]，是典型的盛唐风格。此物无疑应是盛唐前后的产物。

29 新疆乌鲁木齐博物馆收藏品。72TAM188:29。武敏《吐鲁番出土蜀锦的研究》，《文物》1984 年第 6 期，76 页，图 8。
30 Dunhuang. Caves of the Singing Sands. Buddhist Art from the Silk Road, text by Roderick Whitfield, Photographs by Seigo Otsuka, London 1995, vol. 1, pl. 112, 113.

Weft: silk, no noticeable twist, greenish blue, cream; straight weft sequence; c. 21–27 passes per cm.

No selvage preserved.

Blue ground, yellow pattern. The pattern repeat is 2.8 x 2.3 cm. The patterning is elegant, the main flower is of the type of a 'little precious flower,' with four clumps of flower buds and four-pointed little flower tips turned at forty-five degrees to them. The accessory motifs are quatrefoil flowers, extremely simple and geometric in flavor.

Instep (DRM1PM2:S37-2): circumference 50 cm, height at ankle and heel 4.5 cm.

Self-patterned tabby with pattern in 1/3 Z twill.

Warp: silk, no noticeable twist, red; 48–52 ends per cm.

Weft: silk, no noticeable twist, red; c. 36 picks per cm.

No selvage preserved.

1 袜筒的组织细节 Weave detail of shaft

2 袜筒和袜面交界处 Detail of piping between shaft and instep

3 袜面上的宝花刺绣图案 Instep, embroidery detail

4 袜底细节 Detail of sole

Embroidered with split stitch in silk, no noticeable twist, shades of blue, green, yellow, and red.

The fabric is a red *qi*-type weave with a precious-flowers pattern embroidered directly onto the red-coloured concentric-lozenge-patterned textile. The center of each embroidered flower is composed of green-coloured dots, surrounded by yellow six-petalled flowers, then further surrounded by petals embroidered in yellow, blue, and green silk yarn. This six-clumped-flower-petal motif can be termed the precious-flower pattern. Since this pattern was embroidered in relatively free form across the fabric, it has no accompanying flowers.

Sole (DRM1PM2:S37-3): Width 8 cm, length 31 cm.

Self-patterned tabby with pattern in 1/3 Z twill.

Warp: silk, no noticeable twist, cream; 34–36 ends per cm.

Weft: silk, no noticeable twist, cream; c. 33 picks per cm.

No selvage preserved.

Quilted with backstitch in silk, Z-ply from 2 S(?)-twisted ends, white.

The textile is a *qi*-type weave based on the 2-warp/2-weft pattern step system. It is quilted with a geometric pattern forming concentric rectangles and parallel lines.

The sock is lined with silk tabby (Warp: silk, no noticeable twist, beige; 42–48 ends per cm. Weft: silk, no noticeable twist, beige; 30–34 picks per cm. One selvage preserved).

Narrow piping is inserted between shaft and instep (weft-faced compound 1/2 S twill with two lats. Warp: 1 main warp end to 1 binding warp end; silk, no noticeable twist, beige; c. 27 main warp ends and 27 binding warp ends per cm. Weft: silk, no noticeable twist, white, blue; straight weft sequence; c. 30 passes per cm. No selvage preserved).

Braided bands are stitched along the middle line of the instep and along the heel seam, both worked in tabby oblique interlacing with 5 elements each (silk, Z-ply from 2 S(?)-twisted ends, blue, green, white, beige, reddish, tripled).

The seam between instep and sole is accentuated with a band of decorative stitching.

A textile that was excavated in Turfan has a pattern similar to the one of the shaft and was dated to the year 715. It is known as an 'ocean-blue ground with precious-flower-patterned *jin*.'[31] Comparable to the instep embroidery is a textile with almost the same pattern depicted on one of the painted dresses at Dunhuang cave 328, although that used a red ground with precious-flower embroidered pattern.[32] Without doubt, this specific style is a creation of around the time of the High Tang period.

---

31 Urumqi, Xinjiang Museum, 72TAM188:29. 武敏 Wu Min, 吐鲁番出土蜀锦的研究 "Tulufan chutu Shu jin de yanjiu (Research on excavated Shu jin silks)", 文物 Wenwu (Cultural Relics), 6, 1984, p. 76, pl. 8.

32 *Dunhuang. Caves of the Singing Sands. Buddhist Art from the Silk Road*, text by Roderick Whitfield, photographs by Seigo Otsuka, London 1995, vol. 1, pl. 112, 113.

红地鸂鶒穿花锦　(DRM1PM2:S69；QK002803)　8世纪中

长 12.4 厘米、宽 14.8 厘米、底边圆口周长 21.5 厘米，经向 ↔。

27

1/2Z 斜纹纬重组织，经线：S 捻丝，夹经、明经 2:1 交替。夹经为乳白色，约 42 根 / 厘米；明经呈米色，约 21 根 / 厘米。纬线：无明显加捻，有红（已褪色呈乳白）、白、棕、绿四色。四纬一组，纬密 26 ~ 28 副 / 厘米。幅边已失。宽侧锦边镶有四根平纹彩条饰边带（棕、绿和间夹其中的米色），而窄侧锦边则镶有七根彩条饰边带（蓝、绿、黄、米色和间夹米色的棕色）。

这件袖口形织物红色为地，白、棕、绿勾勒分区显花。该锦经向长，纬向短，经向已见两个图案循环，单个循环是 12.8 厘米，而纬向循环仅存 9.3 厘米。花卉占的比例颇大，其中能看到类似葡萄串的纹样，但整个花却不像葡萄，其中一鸟应为鸂鶒，作奔跑欲飞状，故名鸂鶒穿花锦。其年代为中唐，约当 8 世纪中叶。

MID-EIGHTH-CENTURY JIN, WITH RED GROUND, XICHI (MANDARIN DUCKS), AND INTERCONNECTING FLOWERS (DRM1PM2:S69; QK 002803)

Height 12.4 cm, width 14.8 cm, circumference at lower edge 21.5 cm (warp direction ↔).

Weft-faced compound 1/2 Z twill with four lats.

Warp: 1 pair of main warp ends to 1 binding warp end; main warp: silk, S-twisted, cream; binding warp: silk, S-twisted, beige; c. 21 pairs of main warp ends and 21 binding warp ends per cm.

Weft: silk, no noticeable twist, red (faded to cream), white, brown, green; 26–28 passes per cm. No selvage preserved.

A band composed of four narrow strips of plain tabby (twice beige, brown, green) edges the wider opening of the piece; another band of seven such strips (blue, green, yellow, beige, twice brown, beige) edges the narrower opening.

The textile is in the form of a sleeve cuff; it uses red for ground, and white, brown, and green outlining divided into areas to form the pattern. The piece of fabric used is longer in warp-direction than in weft-direction. Two pattern repeats can be seen in warp direction, each 12.8 cm high, whereas the weft-direction repeat is only 9.3 cm wide.

Flowers and scrolls predominate in this pattern, with the grapevine being one of the more recognizable elements, but the overall pattern is not exclusively grapes and among the foliage one can discern a bird, which should be called a *xichi* (Mandarin duck). It appears to be about to take off in flight. The dating of the piece can be placed in mid-Tang, or around the middle of the eighth century.

黄色对波花纹绫染缬晕绸[31] 绮 （DRM1PM2:S66、QK002023；DRM1:113-1、

QK002027；DRM1PM2:S7-1、QK002882） 7 世纪中

　　包括三块丝片，其中 QK002023 长 10.5 厘米、宽 11 厘米，经向 ↕；QK002027 长 33 厘米、宽 26.2 厘米，经向 ↕，与另外一片（参见图版 No.29）总长为 44 厘米、总宽 36 厘米；QK002882 长 28.5 厘米、宽 11 厘米，经向 ↕，与另外一片（参见图版 No.29）总长为 29.5 厘米、总宽 26 厘米。

　　面料组织同为以 1/3Z 斜纹在平纹地上显花，绫经纬线同为本色丝，无明显加捻，经密约 44 根／厘米，纬密约 40 根／厘米。有一侧存有 0.8 厘米平纹无图案幅边。织物经过染缬形成 2 ～ 3 厘米宽、与纬向平行的蓝和橘褐双色交替的彩条，蓝色染色偏重。用途不明。

　　面料图案系用藤枝形成对波环，在两个环中填以果实花纹，并如此反复连续循环，形成连绵不绝的花纹[32]。图案其纬向循环 5 厘米，经向循环 3.5 厘米。整体织物的蓝色扎染条纹明显。

31 晕绸，参见图版 No.36 中的注解。
32 此种纹饰也被认为是葡萄纹样，参见赵丰《织绣珍品》，图版 02、03，香港，1999 年。

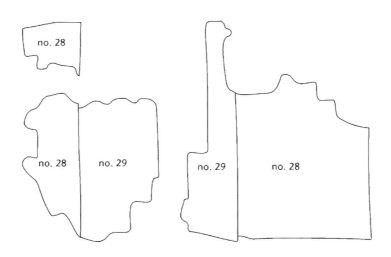

no. 28

no. 28　　no. 29

no. 29　　no. 28

1　结构图　Numbering diagram

SEVENTH- TO EIGHTH-CENTURY QI, WITH OPPOSING-WAVE PATTERN AND RESIST-DYED YUNJIAN STRIPES [33] (DRM1PM2:S66 AND QK 002023 ; DRM1:113-1 AND QK 002027 ; DRM1PM2:S7-1 AND QK 002882)

QK 002023: height 10.5 cm, width 11cm (warp direction ↕).

QK 002027: height 33 cm, width 26.2 cm (warp direction ↕). Overall dimensions including cat .no. 29: height 44 cm, width 36 cm.

QK 002882: height 28.5 cm, width 11 cm (warp direction ↕). Overall dimensions including cat .no. 29: height 29.5 cm, width 26 cm.

Self-patterned tabby with pattern in 1/3 Z twill.
Warp: silk, no noticeable twist, undyed; 44 ends per cm.
Weft: silk, no noticeable twist, undyed; 40 picks per cm.
One selvage preserved at the left hand side of the fragment, 0.8 cm wide, woven in unpatterned tabby.
Resist-dyed 2–3 cm wide alternative blue and orange-brown stripes run parallel to the warp.

Two fragments of this textile were sewn together with two fragments of cat. no. 29. It is not known what kind of object they originally formed. The pattern displays opposing undulating tendrils forming ogival compartments. Palmette-shaped flowers reminding of grapes emerge from the tangent points and protrude into the spaces formed. The pattern is continued in repeats whose size in weft-direction is 5 cm and 3.5 cm in warp direction. Altogether, however, the blue tie-resist dyed stripes dominate the woven pattern.

---

33 For the term *yunjian*, cf. cat. no. 36 below.

藤蔓纹与柿蒂纹合缀染缬晕绸绮

(DRM1:113-1、QK002027；DRM1PM2:S7-1、QK002882) 7世纪

29

QK002027长44厘米、宽9.8厘米，经向↕，与图版No.28连缀一起的总长为44厘米、总宽36厘米；QK002882长27.5厘米、宽15厘米，经向↕，与图版No.28连缀一起的总长29.5厘米、总宽26厘米。

面料组织为以1/3并S和Z替换的斜纹在平纹地上显花。经、纬线同为无染色本色，无明显加捻，经密48～50根／厘米、纬密40～44根／厘米。有一侧宽0.6厘米的无图平纹幅边存留在两块丝片的缝边之中。

面料经过染缬呈橘和棕双色晕绸效果[33]，彩条平行于经向。其平纹地上以斜纹组织显四瓣柿蒂纹，交错排列。图案以1.5厘米在纬向循环、0.8厘米经向循环。

33 晕绸，参见图版No.36注解。

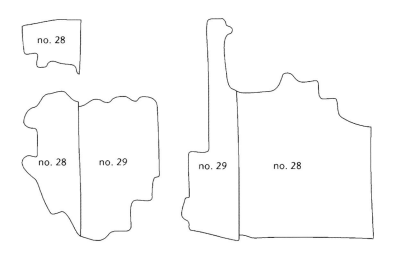

1 结构图 Numbering diagram

SEVENTH-CENTURY QI TEXTILE WITH RESIST-DYED YUNJIAN STRIPES (DRM1:S113-1

AND QK 002027; DRM1PM2:S7-1 AND QK 002882)

QK 002027: height 44 cm, width 9.8 cm (warp direction ↕). Overall dimensions including cat. no. 28: height 44 cm, width 36 cm.

QK 002882: height 27.5 cm, width 15 cm (warp direction ↕). Overall dimensions including cat. no. 28: height 29.5 cm, width 26 cm.

Self-patterned tabby with pattern in 1/3 twill in alternately S and Z direction.

Warp: silk, no noticeable twist, undyed; c. 48–50 ends per cm.

Weft: silk, no noticeable twist, undyed; c. 40–44 picks per cm.

One selvage preserved, tucked in the seam joining the two fragments, 0.6 cm wide, woven in unpatterned tabby.

Resist-dyed orange-brown stripes run parallel to the warp.

The textile displays a pattern of small four-petalled flowers, also called persimmon-calyx shapes, arranged in staggered rows. The pattern repeat is 1.5 cm in weft direction and 0.8 cm only in warp direction. In addition, it shows resist-dyed patterning of the type called *yunjian*.[34]

34 For the term *yun jian* of cat. no 36 below.

2 组织细节 Weave detail

黄色龟甲绮　(DRM1PM2:S62；QK002835)　7世纪

长 13 厘米、宽 19 厘米，经向 ↔。

面料组织为平纹地绮，以不规则斜纹组织在平纹地上显花。经线为本色 S 向轻捻丝，密度约 34 根／厘米。纬线为本色无明显加捻丝，密度为 28 根／厘米。无幅边存留。

这片绮以（经 2、纬 4）并丝出不规则斜纹在平纹地上显花，图案近似于正六边形，故称为龟甲纹，这种组织是以前出土物中未被提及的。整个图案由略显长的正六边形构成。在六边形中，沿纬向填以不同的纹样。纹样有三种。第一种是人物，变形较大，能看清首、手、身，脚下有五条线。第二种是龟形，首和四足及尾均全，龟背上还有甲花可见。第三种是几何味颇浓的花形图案。

在敦煌莫高窟第 130 窟发现的盛唐织物中，亦有龟甲绫（绮）[34]。在《新唐书·舆服志》中，也有唐太宗用龟甲绫的记载。故此龟甲绮的年代可定在初唐前后。

34 常锦涛、马世长《莫高窟发现的唐代丝织物及其它》，《文物》1972 年第 12 期，55～67 页。

1　组织细节　Weave detail

SEVENTH-CENTURY QI, WITH YELLOW GROUND AND TORTOISESHELL PATTERN (DRM1PM2:S62; QK 002835)

Height 13 cm, width 19 cm (warp direction ↔).

Self-patterned tabby with pattern in irregular twill in alternately S and Z direction (3/1-span weft floats on one side, 5/1\1/1-span warp floats on the other side).

Warp: silk, slightly S-twisted, undyed; c. 34 ends per cm.

Weft: silk, no noticeable twist, undyed; c. 28 picks per cm.

No selvage preserved.

The weave of this textile is tabby with irregular twill patterning woven according to the 2-warp/4-weft step pattern system. This kind of weave has not been mentioned before among excavated articles: it is unique.

The entire pattern is composed of slightly elongated six-sided forms, each side being composed of straight lines. Inside the hexagons, three kinds of varying patterns are added along the weft direction. The first of these is human figures that are fairly distorted: one can see the head, hands, and body clearly, but the feet are simply composed of five threads. The second is a tortoiseshell shape, with head, tail, and four legs all complete, and one can also see the pattern on the back of the tortoise. The third is geometrical-style flower patterns.

A similar pattern was discovered in cave 130 at the Dunhuang Grottoes, among the height-of-Tang textiles discovered there.[35] The *New Tang History—Chronicle of a Charioteer (Xin Tangshu—Chefuzhi)*, includes the record of tortoise-backed ling being used among the garments of emperor Tang Taizong.[36] The dating of this self-patterned tabby can therefore be set approximately in the early Tang period.

---

35 樊锦诗、马世长 Fan Jinshi, Ma Shichang, 莫高窟发现的唐代丝织物及其它 "Mogaoku faxian de Tangdai sizhiwu ji qita" (Tang-dynasty silk textiles and other things found in Mogao caves), 文物 Wenwu 12, 1972, pp. 55–67, no. K130:39 on p. 57.

36 新唐书 *Xin Tangshu (The new Book of the Tang dynasty)*, Zhonghua shuju chuban, Beijing 1975, vol. 2, book 24, chapter 志 zhi 14— 舆服 chefu, p. 527.

蓝地龟甲花织金锦带 （DRM1PM2:S125；QK001895） 7世纪

丝带长 67.5 厘米、总宽 3.8 厘米，织金带宽 3 厘米，经向↕。

经重平纹地上以隔经大循环平纹金箔纬显花。经线：绿色 Z 向强加捻丝，经密约 50 根／厘米。纬线：绿色 Z 向加捻丝和 1 毫米（不规则）宽的金箔丝交替显花，纬密约 10 根／厘米。金箔丝从一侧幅边贯通另一侧幅边，正面为平纹组织，背面则把金箔丝剪去。有双幅边，幅宽 3 厘米。织金丝带一侧有多彩（棕、双黄、双蓝）平纹饰条。

这样的织金丝带在中国尚属首次发现，图案呈龟甲状的六边形，内部是六瓣小花，排列非常整齐。其组织结构织法明显依靠了手工编织技术。在我国史料中，丝织物使用金箔的记载早在三国时已经出现。曹丕《与群臣论蜀锦书》云："自吾所织如意、虎头、连璧锦，亦有金薄，蜀薄来自洛邑，皆下恶。"但含织金的最早实物，在目前来看国内应为此件，时代亦在初唐前后。

SEVENTH-CENTURY GOLD-WOVEN RIBBON, WITH DARK GROUND AND TORTOISE-BACK PATTERN WOVEN WITH GOLD (DRM1PM2:S125; QK 001895)

Length 67.5 cm, overall width 3.8 cm, width of the gold woven band 3 cm (warp direction ↕).

Warp-faced tabby with lancé gold weft.

Warp: silk, strongly Z-twisted, dark olive green; c. 50 ends per cm.

Weft: 1 pick of every lat; ground weft: silk, Z-twisted, olive green; lancé weft: gold foil, c. 1 mm wide (irregular), c. 10 passes per cm.

The lancé weft runs from selvage to selvage. On the front it is bound in tabby by every third warp end, on the reverse it has been left floating and was cut off.

Both selvages preserved; loom width c. 3 cm.

A band composed of five narrow strips of plain tabby (brown, twice yellow, twice blue) is attached along one side of the fragment.

[contd.]

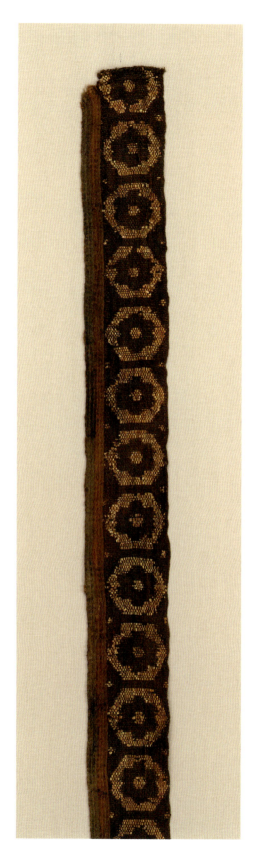

This ribbon or belt woven with gold is the first discovered in China. The silk yarn of the warp and weft are strongly twisted, the pattern is a six-sided tortoise-back pattern, inside which are six-petalled small flowers, all lined up in very orderly fashion.

The weave is tabby ground on which the pattern is shown by strips of metal foil; on the reverse, the metal foil is cut off, a method that clearly refers to hand-weaving techniques. In China's history, there is mention of using metal foil in weavings as early as the Three Kingdoms. To date, however, only a few actual items of such weaving with metal foil have been discovered in China. The dating of this piece is early Tang, more or less.

1 正面，组织细节 Weave detail, front side
（photo：Yao Qingfang 姚青芳，Ma Yanru
马燕如，2004）

2 背面，组织细节 Weave detail, back side
（photo：Yao Qingfang 姚青芳，Ma Yanru
马燕如，2004）

黄地中窠连朵宝花锦 （DRM9:S1；QK003579）　8世纪中

长 7.5 厘米、宽 23.4 厘米，经向 ↔。

1/3Z 半明斜纹纬重组织。经线：夹经、明经 1:1 交替，极细乳白色丝，无明显加捻。夹经和明经密度均约 24 根／厘米。纬线：无明显加捻，由黄、白、绿（与蓝交替显色）等色构成，并按此色序三纬一组循环显花。纬密 20 副／厘米。幅边已失。

这块纬重织锦以黄色为地，以绿色和白色显花。由于大部分白色纬线已遗失殆尽，造成织锦表面呈现局部经线浮织现象。

织锦宝花外圈由八朵侧花纽连成，花朵之间有一全侧花。宾花由变体宝花或称显蕾的十样花构成。

日本正仓院将同类图案的织锦 [35] 定在 8 世纪中叶，故可将此锦年代定在盛唐。

35. 松本包夫 Kaneo Matsumoto，正仓院裂と珐珠明寺の织物 Jodai-gire, 7th and 8th century textiles in Japan from the Shōsō-in and Hōryū-ji, Kyoto 1984, pl.11.

32

MID-EIGHTH-CENTURY JIN, WITH YELLOW GROUND AND PATTERN OF PRECIOUS FLOWERS (DRM9:S1; QK 003579)

Height 7.5 cm, width 23.4 cm (warp direction ↔).

Weft-faced compound 1/3 Z twill with three lats, weft-faced on both sides.

Warp: 1 main warp end to 1 binding warp end; silk, no noticeable twist, cream, very fine; c. 24 main and 24 binding warp ends per cm.

Weft: silk, no noticeable twist, yellow, white (nearly completely lost), green (latté blue); c. 20 passes per cm.

No selvage preserved.

The weave of this textile is weft-faced compound twill with three lats. An effect similar to warp floats results from the nearly complete loss of the white weft. The textile employs a yellow ground with green and white patterns. The outside precious-flower roundel is made up of aligned eight-flowered flower-knobs; between the flowers is a complete flower in profile. The accessory flowers are composed of irregularly shaped precious flowers or quatrefoil flowers exhibiting buds.

Patterns similar to this at the Shōsō-in in Japan[37] date to the middle of the eighth century, so this *jin* can be dated to the High Tang.

37 See, for example, Kaneo Matsumoto, *Jodai-gire. 7th and 8th century textiles in Japan from the Shōsō-in and Hōryū-ji*, Kyoto 1984, pl. 11.

组织细节 Weave detail

蓝地十样小花缂丝 　(DRM1PM2:S70；QK002020)　8世纪

长 27 厘米、宽 8 厘米，其中缂丝条宽 5.5 厘米，经向↕。

经线：两股 Z 捻丝以 S 捻合成一根（又称 S 双捻），本色，经密约 18 根／厘米。纬线：Z 向捻丝，由深蓝、黄、红褐、白等色组成，纬密 44～68 根／厘米，有双幅边，幅宽 5.5 厘米。缂丝一侧缀有四窄一宽的五色平纹绢条，颜色为浅蓝、绿、黄、赭石、褐。缂丝的另一侧则缀有三色平纹绢条，颜色为褐、黄、浅蓝三色。

缂丝又称克丝、刻丝，其名出现于宋代，但从织造技艺看，在唐代已经具备。缂丝是一种通经断纬的织物，以平纹为基本组织，依靠绕纬换彩而显花。都兰出土的这件蓝地十样小花缂丝是目前所知极少的唐代缂丝中有特别价值的一件。其纬向宽度为 5.5 厘米，尚非通幅，说明有别于唐代其他的缂丝带，但其风格又与宋代缂丝有较大区别，并不严格按照换彩需要进行缂断，有时在同一色区内亦呈镂空之状，表明了这件缂丝在缂织技术发展史上的重要地位。

1 组织细节　Weave detail

EIGHTH-CENTURY BLUE GROUND QUATREFOIL LITTLE-FLOWER KESI (DRM1PM2:S70;

QK 002020)

Height 27 cm, overall width 8 cm, width of tapestry band 5.5 cm (warp direction ↕).

33

Slit tapestry band.

Warp: silk, S-ply from 2 Z-twisted ends, undyed; c. 18 ends per cm.

Weft: silk, Z-twisted, dark blue, yellow, reddish brown, white; 44–68 picks per cm.

Both selvages preserved; loom width 5.5 cm.

A band composed of four narrow and one wider strips of plain tabby (light blue, green, yellow, ochre, brown) is attached to one long side of the fragment; a band composed of three such narrow strips (brown, yellow, light blue) is attached to the other long side.

The term *kesi* began to appear in Song-dynasty records but, from a weaving technology perspective, it was already in existence in the Tang dynasty. *Kesi* (silk tapestry) is a kind of textile that has continuous warp and discontinuous weft; it usually uses tabby as the basic weave, and relies on interlacing each weft thread only with that part of the warp where its particular colour is required by the design. At the junctions of two colour areas the two weft threads turn back about adjacent warp ends, leaving a longitudinal slit.

This piece, excavated from Dulan, is one of extremely few known to date. It is a very specially valued piece of Tang-dynasty *kesi*. The width of its weft-direction is 5.5 cm, corresponding to the loom width and showing clearly that it is quite different from the other Tang-dynasty *kesi* bands, which were always much more narrow. At the same time it is different from Song-dynasty *kesi* and is not believed to be of that later date. This piece shows less than perfect application of the technique, which allows the appearance of slits even within a single colour area. This indicates the early place of this piece in the history of *kesi* technology.

黄地染缬十字小花印花绢 (DRM1PM2:S13；QK002882) 8世纪中

长 13.5 厘米、宽 19.5 厘米，经向 ↔。

平纹组织，经、纬线同为无染本色，无明显加捻。经密约 60 根／厘米，纬密约 34 根／厘米。有可能以扎染染缬呈黄地白花。

主花是由 21 个圆点、四个方向各有 4 个十字形、每个十字形由 5 个点组成，中间还有一个圆点。宾花是一个转向 45 度的十字花，由 5 个圆点组成。此类小花图案以前未见先例，属于新发现的品种。织品年代当为盛唐。

34

MID-EIGHTH-CENTURY JUAN, WITH YELLOW GROUND AND RESIST-DYED
PATTERN OF CROSS-SHAPED LITTLE FLOWERS (DRM1PM2:S13; QK 002882)

Height 13.5 cm, width 19.5 cm (warp direction ↔).

Tabby.
Warp and weft: silk, no noticeable twist, undyed; c. 60 ends and c. 34 picks per cm.
Resist-dyed (probably tie-resist dyed) yellow.

The weave of this textile is tabby. It employs a yellow ground with white pattern. The pattern unit is composed of twenty-one round dots: four cross-shaped elements of five dots each arranged around a central dot. The accessory pattern is a similar five-dot element turned at a forty-five degree angle to the main pattern.

No precedent for this pattern has yet come to light. It is a new discovery that dates to the High Tang period.

34

黄地墨宝花印花绢　(DRM1PM2:S22；QK003596)　7～8 世纪

长 12 厘米、宽 11 厘米，经向 ↕。

经、纬丝同为乳白色，无明显加捻，但有些丝线呈弱 Z 向加捻。经密约 40 根／厘米，纬密约 30 根／厘米。无幅边存留。

面料为平纹组织。黄色绢上印有墨色宝花图案，属线描式图案。宝花是八簇花蕾，其中四簇相同，互有简繁，中心部位是八瓣团花。宾花是略为简单一些的四出十样花。

35

SEVENTH-EIGHTH CENTURY PRINTED JUAN, WITH YELLOW GROUND AND PRECIOUS-FLOWER PATTERN　(DRM1PM2:S22; QK 003596)

Height 12 cm, width 11 cm (warp direction ↕).

Tabby.

Warp and weft: no noticeable twist (some threads slightly Z-twisted), cream; c. 40 ends and c. 30 picks per cm.

No selvage preserved.

Printed with black colour.

The weave of this textile is tabby. A black precious-flower pattern is printed on the yellow *juan*. The technique belongs to the 'line-drawing style'; the precious flowers are shown as clusters of eight buds, among which four are the same, some shown in simple form, some more complex. In the center of the cluster is an eight-petalled flower. The arrangement of the precious flowers on the surface is somewhat irregular, and the interstitial flowers seem to be slightly more simple: a four-directional flower.

晕绷小花锦 (DXM1:S6－1：QK002052) 唐代

长 16 厘米、宽 46 厘米，其中三角形织锦宽 24.5 厘米，经向↕。

2/1Z 斜纹经重组织。经线：弱 S 捻丝，由黄、褐、米黄、蓝、淡蓝绿、紫等色排成两条独立系列又互相交错的晕绷彩条。经密约 114 根／厘米（1:1，每组约 57 根／厘米）。纬线：本色细无捻丝，纬密约 36 根／厘米。明纬、夹纬交替，幅边已失。

彩纹织锦内有平纹衬，经、纬线都是绿色无捻丝，密度分别为 36 根／厘米、30 根／厘米。另有一块轻薄的平纹绢和彩纹织锦对角接拼在一起。这块平纹绢的经纬线为米色无捻丝，经线密度约 48 根／厘米，纬线密度约 46 根／厘米。整块织锦外延有一条四色平纹窄带，条带颜色次序为绿、绿、米、深蓝。织锦与绢的对角接缝处覆盖有两条绿色和淡褐色的平纹织带。

彩纹织锦是斜纹经重组织，有黄、褐、米黄、蓝、淡蓝绿、紫色丝线拼成晕绷彩条。这些彩条的基本纹样有三种。第一种为四瓣正视的小花，第二种为六瓣侧视、方向向下的小花，第三种为五瓣侧视、方向向上的小花。这三种小花在纬向以 1–2–1–3–1–2–1–3 的规律错排，而在经向重复循环，具有明显条状感。

绷原是一种染缬效果。《续日本纪》云："染作晕绷色，而其色各种相间，皆横终幅。假令白次之以红，次之以赤，次之以红，次之以白，次之以缥，次之以青，次之以缥，次之以白之类，渐此浓淡，如日月晕气杂色相间之状，故谓之晕绷，以后名锦。"这段话将晕绷的来历说得十分清楚。

都兰出土物中有黄褐相间及青黄相间的染缬晕绷产品，是丝织晕绷的原型。唐代织纤十作中有绷作，当是专门织绷的作坊。都兰出土的绷采用斜纹经二重和山形斜纹两类组织。晕绷小花锦（DXM1:S6－1）属于前者，经丝的地部色彩排列为橙—黄—绿—蓝—绿—黄—橙等反复，其上再显小花，表现出锦上添花的效果，这或就是唐代史料中所提到的晕绷锦。

SEVENTH- TO EIGHTH-CENTURY YUNJIAN LITTLE FLOWER JIN (DXM1:S6-1; QK 002052)

Height 16 cm, overall width 46 cm, width of jin triangle 24.5 cm (warp direction ↕).

Warp-faced compound 2/1 Z twill with two series of warps.

Warp: silk, slightly S-twisted, yellow, orange-brown, rice-yellow, blue, light blue-green, purple; arranged in two independent but interrelated stripe patterns, one for each series of warps; c. 114 ends per cm (c. 57 ends per warp series and cm).

Weft: silk, no noticeable twist, very fine, undyed(?); c. 36 picks per cm, passed alternately through a twill shed and a pattern shed.

No selvage preserved.

The patterned silk was lined with tabby. Warp and weft: silk, no noticeable twist, green; c. 36 ends and c. 30 picks per cm.

A lightweight tabby is attached to the patterned silk along a diagonal line. Warp and weft: silk, no noticeable twist, beige; c. 48 ends and 46 picks per cm.

A band composed of four narrow strips of plain tabby (twice green, beige, dark blue) edges the whole object; the seam between patterned silk and tabby is covered by a band composed of two such strips (green, light brown).

36

1 组织细节 Weave detail

2 晕绸锦和平纹绢交界处 Detail of piping

The weave of this textile is warp-faced compound twill with two series of warps. It employs yellow, orange-brown, rice-yellow, blue, green, and blue-coloured silk yarn lined up in a *yunjian* stripes pattern. Into these stripes are woven three basic patterns: four-petalled little flowers seen frontally, six-petalled flowers seen in profile, pointing downwards, and five-petalled flowers seen in profile, pointing upwards. These three patterns are in weft-direction, lined up as 1-2-1-3-1-2-1-3, and they repeat the cycle in the warp direction with a clear and orderly regularity.

Jian was originally the result of a kind of dyeing technique. A quotation from the continuations of the *Chronicles of Japan* (*Shoku Nihongi*, Book 6, for the year 713) gives a clear explanation of its origins and techniques.[38]

Among the items excavated from Dulan are yellow-and-brown as well as blue-and-yellow striped tie-dyed *yunjian* silks, which was the model for *yunjian*-patterned woven silk textiles.

Among the ten specialized Tang-dynasty textile workshops under the management of the Imperial court there was one specifically set up for weaving *jian* fabrics. The *jian* fabrics excavated at Dulan are woven in either warp-faced compound twill or chevron twill. This *yunjian* little-flower *jin* belongs to the former. The colours of the warp threads forming the ground are lined up as orange, yellow, green, blue, green, yellow, orange and so on, repeated, on top of which are displayed little flowers, like flowers dotted over a field. This may very well be what is referred to as the *yunjian jin* in Tang-dynasty historical records.

38 "Shoku Nihongi. Chronicles of Japan, continued, from A.D. 697 to 791" [Books IV–VI], translated and annotated by J. B. Snellen, *The Transactions of the Asiatic Society of Japan*, second series, vol. 14, 1937, p. 259.

晕绸珠花锦的衣服残片 （DRM1PM2:S140；QK002898） 初唐至盛唐

总长 24 厘米、总宽 16 厘米。

A. 晕绸[36]珠花锦衣服前片（DRM1PM2:S140-1），长 14 厘米、宽 3.5 厘米，经向 ↕。2/1S 斜纹经重组织，经线：弱 S 捻丝，色彩由褐、橙、黄、米、蓝、浅蓝、绿色的各种组合构成。经密约 120 根／厘米（1:1，每组约 60 根／厘米）。纬线：本色无捻丝，纬密约 35 根／厘米。明纬、夹纬交替，幅边已失。

基本纹样亦有三种，一是四瓣柿蒂花，二是六瓣正视的梅花，三是圆珠。纬向排列是 1-3-2-3-1-3-2-3，经向则重复循环。由于圆珠纹样的密度大于其余纹样，因此，更像由直条的连珠带将第一、二种花相隔排列，条状感更加强烈。年代约在初唐和盛唐之间。

B. 蓝地小花锦领边（DRM1PM2:S140 - 2），长 25 厘米、宽 1.1 厘米，经向为对角向。2/1S 斜纹经重组织。经线：无捻丝，乳白、蓝、绿色。经密约 198 根／厘米（1:2，每组约 66 根／厘米）。纬线：本色无捻丝，纬密约 32 根／厘米。明纬、夹纬交替，幅边已失。

花锦为蓝地，显绿、黄、紫色花。由八瓣和四瓣小花组成。

C. 褐色绢衣服背面（DRM1PM2:S140 - 3），长 15 厘米、宽 8 厘米，经向 ↔。平纹组织，经纬线为米色无捻丝，经密约 60 根／厘米，纬密约 40 根／厘米。一侧保留了 0.5 厘米宽的幅边。

此绢和前两片彩锦缝合在一起。

D. 肩部的彩条锦（DRMPM12:S140 - 4），长 4 厘米、宽 1.5 厘米，经向 ↕。

1/2Z 斜纹纬重组织。经线：弱 S 捻丝，夹经、明经 1:1 交替。夹经为黄色，约 19 根／厘米。明经为棕色，约 19 根／厘米。纬线：无明显加捻，黄、浅棕、绿（与蓝交替显色）色构成。三纬一组，纬密 38 副／厘米。幅边已失。

36 参见图版 No. 36 文字说明。

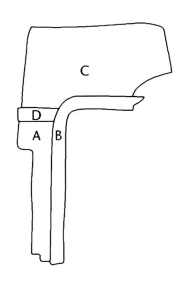

1 结构图 Numbering diagram

FRAGMENT OF A GARMENT MADE FROM DIFFERENT SILKS, AMONG THEM A YUNJIAN PEARL-FLOWER JIN, FROM EARLY TANG TO HIGH TANG PERIOD (DRM1PM2:S140; QK 002898)

Overall height 24 cm, overall width 16 cm.

A. (DRM1PM2:S140-1) Front of the garment, yunjian pearl-flower jin.[39] *Height 14 cm, width 3.5 cm (warp direction ↕).*

Warp-faced compound 2/1 S twill with two series of warps.

Warp: silk, slightly S-twisted, brown, orange, yellow, beige, blue, light blue, green in various combinations; c. 120 ends per cm (c. 60 ends per warp series and cm).

Weft: silk, no noticeable twist, undyed(?); c. 35 picks per cm, passed alternately through a twill shed and a pattern shed.

No selvage preserved.

2 组织细节 Weave detail

The weave of this textile is warp-faced compound twill with two series of warps. Colours employed include orange, yellow, blue, green and so on, in three basic patterns: four-petalled persimmon-base flowers, six-petalled plum flowers seen frontally, and round pearls.

The pattern sequence in weft direction is 1-3-2-3-1-3-2-3, while the motifs are simply repeated in warp direction. The round pearl-motifs are less spaced than the other pattern elements, strengthening the feel of verticality and contributing strongly to the striped effect of the whole pattern. The dating is roughly early Tang or between early Tang and height-of-Tang.

B. (DRM1PM2:S140-2) Neckline binding. Length of strip 25 cm, width 1.1 cm (warp direction taken diagonally).

Warp-faced compound 2/1 S twill with three series of warps.

Warp: silk, no noticeable twist, cream, blue, green; c. 198 ends per cm (c. 66 ends per warp series and cm).

Weft: silk, no noticeable twist, undyed(?); c. 32 picks per cm, passed alternately through a twill shed and a pattern shed.

No selvage preserved.

The silk used as neckline binding utilizes a blue ground with little-flower pattern. On the blue ground, the patterns of eight-petalled and four-petalled flowers are shown in green, white, and blue.

C. (DRM1PM2:S140-3) Back of the garment. Length 15 cm, width 8 cm (warp direction ↔).

Tabby.

Warp and weft: silk, no noticeable twist, beige; c. 60 ends and 40 picks per cm.

Selvage preserved on one side (0.5 cm wide).

A third piece was also sewn together with the two previous silk fragments. This is a brown juan, with a tabby weave.

D. (DRM1PM2:S140-4) Narrow shoulder strip. Length 4 cm, width 1.5 cm (warp direction ↕).

Weft-faced compound 1/2 Z twill with four lats.

Warp: 1 main warp end to 1 binding warp end; main warp: silk, slightly S-twisted, yellow; binding warp: silk, slightly S-twisted, brown; c. 19 main warp ends and 19 binding warp ends per cm.

Weft: silk, no noticeable twist, yellow, light brown, green latté blue; c. 38 passes per cm.

No selvage preserved.

39 For the term *yunjian* see above cat. no. 36.

绊 (DRM9:S6－1；QK002039) 8～9世纪

长92厘米、宽8.2厘米，经向↕。和图版No.39缝缀在一起，总长93厘米、宽36.5厘米。

平纹组织扎经染色。经线呈弱S向捻，本色扎染成蓝、棕两色，经密40根／厘米。纬线为弱S向捻丝，无染色，纬密15根／厘米。无幅边存留。

这条织物为平纹组织，将经丝分组扎经染色出蓝、棕及未染的本色，然后再进行织造，称为绊。

绊是日本学者对此类扎经染色织物的通称，但论其词源，还是来自中国。《说文》中已有"绊"字，"氏人殊缕布也"。段玉裁引《华阳国志》注："殊缕布者，盖殊其缕色而相间织之。"扎经染色织物正是分组将经丝（缕）扎染形成"殊其缕色"的效果后，再并起来相间织之（绊），故而用绊来命名扎经染色织物完全恰当。这件都兰热水出土唐代绊，在国内目前属首次发现。

EIGHTH- TO NINTH-CENTURY IKAT (WARP TIE-DYED) TEXTILE (DRM9:S6-1; QK 002039)

Height 92 cm, width 8.2 cm (warp direction ↕). Overall height (including cat. no. 39) 93 cm, width 36.5 cm.

Tabby with tie-dyed warp (ikat).

Warp: silk, slightly S-twisted, natural colour, tie-dyed blue, brown; 40 ends per cm.

Weft: silk, slightly S-twisted, undyed; 15 picks per cm.

No selvage preserved.

This textile has a tie-dyed warp and tabby weave. The technique first divides the warp threads into groups and then dyes them, before weaving them into fabric. *Kasuri* 绊 is the term Japanese

[contd.]

scholars give to this kind of warp tie-dyed textile in general, but the term originally comes from China. The character 絣, pronounced *beng* in Chinese, already appears in the second-century analytical dictionary *Shuowen jiezi*. Specifically, the Shuowen explains, in early classical Chinese, 'Di people (that is, generally non-Han Chinese) [use] *shulü* fabric.'[40] Duan Yucai, commenting on the *Shuowen jiezi,* quotes the *Huayangguo zhi* (Records of the Lands South of Mount Hua): 'Fabric called *shulü* [can be defined as] groups [of threads] are dyed according to colours and then woven.'[41]

Dying the warp threads precisely describes this process: dividing the warp yarn *(luo)* into groups and dying it into different colours, then putting them together, weaving the textile. It is totally appropriate, therefore, to use the term *beng* to describe this specific piece.

This is the first time a Tang-dynasty *beng* silk has been discovered inside China.

40 说文解字注 *Shuowen jiezi zhu (Explaining simple and analysing compound characters, with comments* [of DuanYucai]), Guji chubanshe, Shanghai 1981, chapter 13a, 系部 *xibu* / 素部 *subu*, p. 662a.

41 *Shuowen jiezi zhu* (see note 40), chapter 13a, 系部 *xibu* / 素部 *subu*, p. 662a.

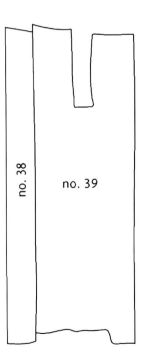

1 结构图 Numbering diagram

黄色对波葡萄花叶绫 (DRM9:S6 - 2；QK002039)　8～9世纪

长91厘米、宽28.3厘米，经向↕。与图版No.38缝缀在一起，总长93厘米、总宽36.5厘米。

这片面料组织以3/1Z斜纹为地，以1/3S斜纹显花。经线为很细的米色丝线，无明显加捻，经密约50根／厘米。纬线也是无明显加捻的米色丝线，纬密约25根／厘米。与另一片织物（参见图版No.38）缝合处存留了0.6厘米宽无图案的平纹幅边。

整片织物呈米黄色，图案骨架为对波缠枝。从现存半幅多的宽度可以看出，图案包括有三组对波环，一环中置果实，一环置叶，一环置花。在另一个半幅中，是与其对称的重复图案。这样图案纬向只有一个循环，宽约48厘米。而经向有六组对波纹，循环尺寸只有7厘米。

1　组织细节　Weave detail

EIGHTH- TO NINTH-CENTURY LING DAMASK WITH OPPOSING-WAVE PATTERN (DRM9:S6-2; QK 002039)

39

Height 91 cm, width 28.3 cm (warp direction ↕). Overall height (including cat. no. 38) 93 cm, width 36.5 cm.

Damask with ground in 3/1 Z twill and pattern in 1/3 S twill.

Warp: silk, no noticeable twist, beige, very fine; c. 50 ends per cm.

Weft: silk, no noticeable twist, beige, very fine; c. 25 picks per cm.

One selvage preserved, 0.6 cm wide, tucked in the seam joining the fragment to cat. no. 38, woven in unpatterned tabby.

The textile is a yellowish beige *ling*, with opposing wave-patterns enclosing grapes, flowers, and leaves. What remains in this fragment is more than half a loom width, and three opposing wave arcs can be seen. One encloses fruit, one leaves, and one flowers. In warp direction, the pattern repeat is short, only 7 cm, whereas in the weft-direction there is only one repeat, spreading over the whole loom width. The latter can be reconstructed to have been 48 cm.

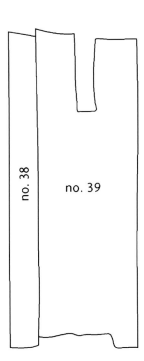

2 结构图 Numbering diagram

no. 38

no. 39

连缀绮、绢丝片 (QK002924) 7~9 世纪

总长 19 厘米、总宽 12.5 厘米。

由十八片方形或是长方形大小不同的绮连缀在一起，每块织物都是平纹绮，即在平纹地上以 3/1 斜纹出花纹组织。经线：无明显加捻丝，由米、黄、浅棕、深棕等色构成。经密 26 ~ 40 根 / 厘米。纬线：同样是无明显加捻丝，也是由米、黄、浅棕、深棕等色组成。纬密 40 ~ 50 根 / 厘米。有几块在缝边上还存有原织物的幅边。

在织物的右上角有一块浅绿色绢片（长约 7.6 厘米、宽 2.5 厘米）。其淡绿色的经、纬丝都无明显加捻，经密约 50 根 / 厘米，纬密约 30 根 / 厘米。

织物背面衬有米色绢片，经、纬丝都无明显加捻乳白色丝，经密约 60 根 / 厘米，纬密约 30 根 / 厘米。整块织物所有织片都用棕色 Z 双捻丝仔细缝合连缀在一起，组成格子状绢片。

FRAGMENTS OF QI AND JUAN SEWN TOGETHER, SEVENTH TO NINTH CENTURY (QK 002924)

Overall height 19 cm, overall width 12.5 cm.

Patchwork made from eighteen pieces of several textiles, three of them self-patterned 3/1 S twill with pattern in 1/3 Z twill, the others self-patterned tabby with pattern in 1/3 Z twill.

Warp: silk, no noticeable twist, beige, yellowish, light brown, dark brown; 26–40 ends per cm.

Weft: silk, no noticeable twist, beige, yellowish, light brown, dark brown; 40–50 picks per cm.

Several pieces preserve selvages in their seam allowances.

A piece of light green tabby (height 7.6 cm, width 2.5 cm) forms the upper right corner. Warp and weft: silk, no noticeable twist, light green; c. 50 ends and c. 30 picks per cm.

Lining of beige tabby. Warp and Weft: silk, no noticeable twist, cream; c. 60 ends and c. 30 picks per cm.

All stitching is done with neat overcast stitches (silk, Z-ply from 2 S-twisted ends, brown).

All fragments are woven in damask with 3/1 twill patterning on tabby. They have either square or oblong shape and have been carefully sewn together. The colours are subtle shades of greenish-yellow, brown, beige, and so on.

40

紫色柿蒂绮 (DRM1:S4；QK002875) 7~9世纪

整件织物包括边饰总长18厘米、总宽26厘米，其中平纹紫地绮长13.5厘米、宽20厘米，经向↔。

其组织为平纹地上以1/3Z斜纹显结构。经、纬线同为紫色，无明显加捻丝，经密约40根／厘米，纬密40根／厘米。无幅边存留。

紫绮的两侧缝缀有两条米色2/1S经重组织的锦带残片，其经向与锦带宽度同向。经线无明显加捻，有黄、浅棕和浅绿（与浅蓝相互交替）色。经密约180根／厘米（1:2，每组约60根／厘米）。纬线是米色，元明显加捻丝，明纬、夹纬交替，纬密约26根／厘米。无幅边存留。

此绮由斜纹在平纹地上起花，组成四瓣花交错排列的菱格形图案，属传统的柿蒂纹。

SEVENTH- TO NINTH-CENTURY PURPLE QI, WITH PATTERN OF SMALL FOUR-PETAL

FLOWERS (DRM1:S4; QK 002875)

Height 13.5 cm, width 20 cm (warp direction ↔); overall height (including attached band) 18 cm, width 26 cm.

Self-patterned tabby with pattern in 1/3 Z twill.

Warp: silk, no noticeable twist, purple; c. 40 ends per cm.

Weft: silk, no noticeable twist, purple; c. 40 picks per cm.

No selvage preserved.

41

Attached are two bands (c. 5.5 cm wide, warp direction running across the bands) of warp-faced compound 2/1 S twill with three series of warps.

Warp: silk, no noticeable twist, yellow, light brown, light green (striped light blue); c. 180 ends per cm (c. 60 ends per warp series and cm).

Weft: silk, no noticeable twist, beige; c. 26 picks per cm, passed alternately through a twill shed and a pattern shed.

No selvage preserved.

The basic weave of this textile is the damask-like *qi*-structure, with twill pattern on tabby ground. The displayed pattern consists of lozenge- or diamond-shaped elements formed by four-petalled flowers. This is probably what was called persimmon-base pattern in ancient times, in analogy to the fruit's calyx with four sepals.

1 组织细节 Weave detail

褐黄缃道素绫 （DRM1PM2:S56；QK002919）

由两块织物缝缀在一起，总长 15.5 厘米、总宽 26 厘米，经向↕。

3/1 浮经山形斜纹组织。山形斜纹以 16 根经线（9 根上行 7 根下行）组成一个山形单元。经线：S 向弱捻线，米黄色和褐色间隔排列，每色条约 16 根经线，显双色条，可称为间（缃）道，经密约 56 根／厘米。纬线：米色 S 向弱捻线，纬密约 42 根／厘米。无幅边存留。

都兰出土还有一块绿褐缃道素绫（DRM1PM2:S90，QKL106；无图），同为 3/1 浮经山形斜纹组织，只是以绿色与褐色双色相间排列。

缃道与晕缃的区分在于晕缃有色调过渡（参见图版 No.36），而缃道没有。

BROWN AND YELLOW STRIPED TEXTILE (DRM1PM2:S56; QK 002919)

Height 15.5 cm, width 26 cm (two fragments of the same fabric stitched together; warp direction ↕)

3/1 warp chevron twill; point entering over 16 warp ends (9 ends straight unit, 7 ends reverse unit).

Warp: silk, slightly S-twisted, beige and brown in stripes of 16 ends each; c. 56 ends per cm.

Weft: silk, slightly S-twisted, beige; c. 42 picks per cm.

No selvage preserved.

In Chinese terminology, this twill-woven silk is a brown and yellow-striped *jian*; among the textiles found in Dulan there is another fragment (DRM1PM2:S90, QKL 106; not illustrated) which is a green and brown-striped *jian*. Both line up two different colours of silk yarn to form a distinctly two-colour fabric that can be called striped. Both use a 3/1 chevron twill. The difference between this striped approach and textiles called *yunjian* (cf. cat. no. 36) is that *yunjian* has a shaded, somewhat blurry transition between colour stripes, whereas these pieces do not.

山形斜纹黄地绫　(DRLM1:S11－4；QK002887)

由同样组织的三块面料缝缀在一起，总长 32 厘米、总宽 38 厘米，经向↕。

经线为米色，无明显加捻，50～52 根／厘米。纬线同为无明显加捻米色丝，纬密约 34 根／厘米。织物一侧有 0.7 厘米宽平纹无图案幅边存留。该织物组织较为特殊，为 3/1、3/1、1/1、1/1 浮经显山形斜纹，每组山形纹单元由 52 根经线组成，27 根上行，25 根下行。

整片织物组织图案显山形花纹排列，单个花纹的高和宽均为 1 厘米左右，连绵不断，富有立体感。此片织物为露斯沟采集品。

43

YELLOW ZIGZAG-PATTERNED DAMASK (DRLM1:S11-4; QK 002887)

Height 32 cm, width 38 cm (three fragments of the same fabric stitched together; warp direction ↕).

Composite 3/1, 3/1, 1/1, 1/1 warp chevron twill; point entering over c. 52 warp ends (c. 27 ends straight unit, c. 25 ends reverse unit).

Warp: silk, no noticeable twist, beige; 50–52 ends per cm.

Weft: silk, no noticeable twist, beige; c. 34 picks per cm.

One selvage preserved, 0.7 cm wide, woven in unpatterned tabby.

This textile weave is relatively special. It is a chevron twill, and the entire design reminds of a repeated 山 ren-character pattern. Both height and width of the "character" are around 1 cm. Repeated continuously, this exhibits a very three-dimensional aspect. This textile was collected at Lusigou.

1 组织细节 Weave detail

蓝地团花夹缬绢 （DRLC:S20；QK001890） 7~9世纪

长 11.5 厘米、宽 27.7 厘米，经向↕。与黄地小花夹缬绢（图版 No.45）缝缀在一起，总长 22 厘米、总宽 28 厘米。

平纹组织，经、纬线同为无染本色，无明显加捻。经密 50 根／厘米，纬密 40 根／厘米。

与图版 No.45 为相同质地不同花色，地为蓝色平纹，夹缬染成黄色团花，直径经纬循环为 8 厘米。色彩和图案艳丽精美。

44

SEVENTH- TO NINTH-CENTURY CLAMP-RESIST-DYED JUAN TEXTILE WITH BLUE GROUND AND FLOWER-ROUNDEL PATTERN (DRLC:S20; QK 001890)

Height 11.5 cm, width 27.7 cm (warp direction ↕). Overall dimensions, including cat. no. 45 below: height 22 cm, width 28 cm.

Tabby.

Warp: silk, no noticeable twist, undyed; c. 50 ends per cm.

Weft: silk, no noticeable twist, undyed; c. 40 picks per cm.

No selvage preserved.

Clamp-resist dyed blue and reddish brown.

This textile has been sewn together with the juan cat. no. 45 below. It has the same underlying ground but different coloured patterning. Its basic weave is tabby, the ground is dyed blue, and the clamp-resist dyed forms make up red rounds of flowers on undyed background. The diameter of the flowers in warp and weft direction is 8 cm, and they are arranged in staggered rows. The colours and patterns of this piece are exquisitely beautiful.

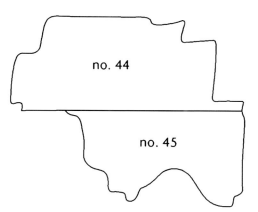

1 结构图 Numbering diagram

黄地小花夹缬绢 （DRLC：S19；QK001890） 7~9 世纪

长 11.5 厘米、宽 20.3 厘米，经向 ↕。与蓝地团花夹缬绢（图版 No.44）缝缀在一起，总长 22 厘米、总宽 28 厘米。

平纹组织，经、纬线同为无染本色，无明显加捻。经密 50 根 / 厘米，纬密 40 根 / 厘米。有一侧存留有幅边。

面料以黄色地上夹缬印成绿和红双色小花，图案为绿色的棱叶辅以三朵红花，团窠大小约为 4.2 厘米 ×2.5 厘米，略有褪色。

SEVENTH- TO NINTH-CENTURY CLAMP-RESIST-DYED JUAN TEXTILE WITH YELLOW GROUND AND LITTLE-FLOWER PATTERN (DRLC:S19; QK 001890)

Height 11.5 cm, width 20.3 cm (warp direction ↕). Overall dimensions, including cat. no. 45: height 22 cm, width 28 cm.

Tabby.
Warp: silk, no noticeable twist, undyed; c. 50 ends per cm.
Weft: silk, no noticeable twist, undyed; c. 40 picks per cm.
One selvage preserved at the left side of the fragment.
Clamp-resist dyed blue-green and brownish red.

This textile was sewn together with cat. no.44 described above. Its weave is tabby. The design is created by using the clamp-resist dyeing technique for 'printing' the green and red small-flower pattern: branches are composed of green diamonds and flowers are three-diamond clusters. The resulting flower arrangements measure around 4.2 cm x 2.5 cm. The piece exhibits some colour fading.

绯色葡萄纹绮 　(DRLC:S7；QK002812)　8~9世纪

长 32.5 厘米、宽 28.5 厘米，经向 ↔。

面料是以 3/1S 斜纹在平纹地上起花的绮[37]，经、纬线均为红色无明显加捻丝，经密约 48 根／厘米，纬密 34 ~ 36 根／厘米。残片底部存有 0.8 厘米左右的幅边。

织物颜色非常鲜艳，为绯红色。图案为葡萄、宝花缠枝及唐草。以宝花为中心，四瓣叶子向四方展开，宝花之间有向上及向下生长的两串葡萄，又由唐草缠枝连接两串弯弯的葡萄。图案对称工整，十分生动。

46

37 也有称这种组织结构为绫或其他名称，参见徐铮《单色织物》，赵丰主编《敦煌丝绸艺术全集》，中国纺织大学出版社，2007 年，160~163 页。

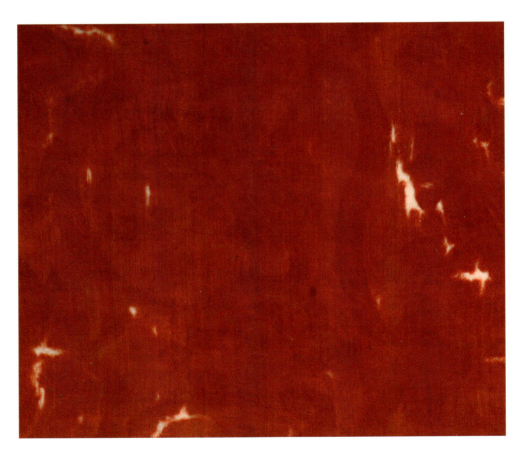

1　组织细节　Weave detail

EIGHTH- TO NINTH-CENTURY QI TEXTILE WITH GRAPE PATTERNING, WOVEN IN OVERALL RED COLOUR (DRLC:S7; QK 002812)

Height 32.5 cm, width 28.5 cm (warp direction ↔).

Self-patterned tabby with pattern in 3/1 S twill.
Warp: silk, no noticeable twist, red; c. 48 ends per cm.
Weft: silk, no noticeable twist, red; 34–36 picks per cm.
One selvage partly preserved at the bottom of the fragment, at least 0.8 cm wide.

The colour of this rather special textile is extremely bright, woven in an unusual shade of red. This structure is best described as *qi* in Chinese, although its denomination in historic sources can vary.[42] The pattern shows grapes, precious flowers, twining branches, grape tendrils, and Tang scrolls. The design is exquisite and very lively.

46

42 Xu Zheng, "Monochrome woven silk," *Textiles from Dunhuang in UK Collections*, Zhao Feng (ed.), Shanghai 2007, pp. 160–163.

由五片不同绮和绫组成的织物　（DRLC:S11-1；QK003577）　8~9世纪

整块织物总长 36.5 厘米、总宽 60.5 厘米，五块织物从左至右分别介绍如下（A~E）。

A. 绿蓝色织物，长 31.5 厘米、宽 3.5 厘米，经向 ↔。

B. 米色织物，长 38.5 厘米、宽 11 厘米，经向 ↕，是两片同组织缝在一起的绮。

C. 绿蓝色织物，长 36.5 厘米、宽 11.7 厘米，经向 ↔。

D. 长 33 厘米、宽 31.5 厘米，经向 ↕。

E. 长 29.5 厘米、宽 11 厘米，经向 ↔。

A. 面料基本组织是绮，以 3/1S 斜纹在平纹地上起花。经、纬线同为绿蓝色，无明显加捻丝，经密 60 根 / 厘米，纬密 30 根 / 厘米。有一段宽 0.8 厘米平纹的幅边带存留。

蓝绿绮上显菱形交错排列花纹。

B. 3/1Z 斜纹在平纹地上显花。经、纬线同为米色，无明显加捻丝，经密、纬密都为 54 根 / 厘米。右边织物有 0.6 厘米无图案平纹幅边存留。

米色绮图案呈菱形，交错排列。图案循环尺寸约纬向 3.8 厘米、经向 1.7 厘米。

C. 面料组织为绫，以 3/1Z 斜纹在 1/3S 斜纹地上显花。经、纬线同为绿蓝色，无明显加捻丝，经密约 60 根 / 厘米，纬密约 40 根 / 厘米。无幅边存留。

这片绿蓝色绫的图案是一排小团花，间隔一排对飞的大雁，雁作展翅飞翔状。在每组飞雁的下方，有一组多角形的小花点缀其中。

D. 面料组织为绿蓝色绮，以 3/1S 斜纹在平纹地上显花。经、纬线同为绿蓝色，无明显加捻丝，经密约 52 根 / 厘米，纬密约 40 根 / 厘米。右侧有 0.6 厘米宽的无图案平纹幅边。

织物呈绿蓝色柿蒂花，花间交错排列，四瓣柿蒂花如同一菱纹。图案循环尺寸经向为 1.3 厘米，纬向为 2.8 厘米。

E. 面料组织为蓝绿色绮，平纹地上以 3/1S 斜纹显花。经、纬线同为蓝绿色，无明显加捻丝，经密约 52 根 / 厘米，纬密约 30 根 / 厘米。无幅边存留。

可惜这片蓝绿色残绮上的图案已无法识别。

FIVE DIFFERENT EIGHTH- TO NINTH-CENTURY QI AND LING FABRICS STITCHED TOGETHER (DRLC:S11-1; QK 003577))

Overall dimensions: height 36.5 cm, width 60.5 cm. Individual fabrics numbered A through E from left to right.

A. Height 31.5 cm, width 3.5 cm, warp direction ↔). Self-patterned tabby with pattern in 3/1 S twill.

B. Height 38.5 cm, width 11 cm (two fragments of the same fabric stitched together; warp direction ↕).

C. Height 36.5 cm, width 11.7 cm (warp direction ↔). Damask with ground in 1/3 S twill and pattern in 3/1 Z twill.

D. Height 33 cm, width 31.5 cm (warp direction ↕). Self-patterned tabby with pattern in 3/1 S twill.

E. Self-patterned tabby with pattern in 3/1 S twill (height 29.5 cm, width 11 cm, warp direction ↔).

A. Warp: silk, no noticeable twist, greenish blue; c. 60 ends per cm.

Weft: silk, no noticeable twist, greenish blue; c. 30 picks per cm.

One selvage preserved, 0.8 cm wide, woven in unpatterned tabby.

The greenish-blue silk displays a small-scale pattern of lozenge-shaped elements in staggered rows.

Self-patterned tabby with pattern in 3/1 Z twill.

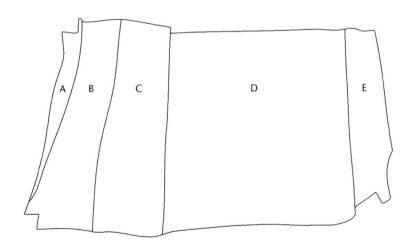

1 结构图 Numbering diagram

B. Warp: silk, no noticeable twist, beige; c. 54 ends per cm.

Weft: silk, no noticeable twist, beige; c. 54 picks per cm.

One selvage preserved at the right hand side of the fragment, 0.6 cm wide, woven in unpatterned tabby.

Beige *qi* textile with lozenge- or diamond-shaped patterning. The pattern repeat is 3.8 cm in weft direction and 1.7 cm only in warp direction.

C. Warp: silk, no noticeable twist, greenish blue; c. 60 ends per cm.

Weft: silk, no noticeable twist, greenish blue; c. 40 picks per cm.

No selvage preserved.

Because ground and pattern are both twill structures, in Chinese this textile can be classified as *ling*. It is of greenish-blue colour and shows a pattern of small flying wild geese amidst groups of flowers.

2 组织细节（B.），经向↕ Weave detail (B), warp direction↕

3 组织细节（C.），经向↔ Weave detail (C), warp direction ↔

47

4 组织细节（D.），经向↕ Weave detail (D), warp direction ↕

5 幅边（D.），其经向↕与局部放大组织细节（E.），其经向↔ Selvage (D.), warp direction ↕, and weave detail (E.), warp direction ↔

D. Warp: silk, no noticeable twist, greenish blue; c. 52 ends per cm.

Weft: silk, no noticeable twist, greenish blue; c. 40 picks per cm.

One selvage preserved at the right side of the fragment, 0.6 cm wide, woven in unpatterned tabby.

The design of this textile is formed by a four-petalled flower recalling the shape of a persimmon calyx that results in a diamond-shaped pattern. The cycle of the pattern is repeated at 1.3 cm in the warp direction and 2.8 cm in the weft direction.

E. Warp: silk, no noticeable twist, bluish green; c. 52 ends per cm.

Weft: silk, no noticeable twist, bluish green; c. 30 picks per cm.

No selvage preserved.

Extensive wear has misaligned many threads of this silk so that its pattern is no longer recognizable.

红地大窠桃形纹锦 (DRLC:S3；QK002840)　8~9 世纪

48

三片织锦分别为长 84 厘米、宽 8.5 厘米，长 100 厘米、宽 2.8 厘米，长 32 厘米、宽 2.7 厘米；经向 ↕。

1/2S 斜纹纬重组织。经线：深棕色 Z 向捻丝。夹经、明经 3:1 交替。夹经 42 ~ 45 根 / 厘米，明经 14 ~ 15 根 / 厘米。纬线：无明显加捻丝，由红、白、黄、浅蓝、深蓝、浅绿六色构成，并按此色序七纬一组循环。纬密约 28 副 / 厘米。幅边已失。背面有纬线浮织组织（抛梭现象）。

纬锦以红色作地，以蓝、绿、黄色显花。内外以多层连珠纹相夹，形成中心桃形花纹，构成团窠环。因环形巨大，其主题图案残缺不全。此锦图案设计和色彩织法和阿贝格基金会收藏的织锦（馆藏 4861、4862）有极其相似之处 [38]。

38 阿贝格基金会收藏品参见 Karel Otavsky, "Stoffe der Seidenstrasse", Entlang der Seidenstrasse. Fruhmittelalterliche Kunst zwischen Persien und China in der Abegg-Stiftung, Riggisberg 1998 (Riggisberger Berichte, 6), pp. 28-30 (Karel Otavsky), p.78 (Regula Schorta).

EIGHTH- TO NINTH-CENTURY JIN, RED GROUND, WITH LARGE ROUNDELS WITH HEART-SHAPED PETAL BORDER (DRLC:S3; QK 002840)

Three fragments: height 84 cm, width 8.5 cm; height 100 cm, width 2.8 cm; height 32 cm, width 2.7 cm (warp direction ↕).

Weft-faced compound 1/2 S twill with six(?) lats.

Warp: 1 group of three main warp ends to 1 binding warp end; silk, Z-twisted, dark brown; step: 2 groups of three main warp ends; c. 14–15 groups of three main warp ends and 16–17 binding warp ends per cm.

[contd.]

Weft: silk, no noticeable twist, red, white, yellow, light blue, dark blue, light green; straight weft sequence; c. 28 passes per cm.

No selvage preserved.

Weft floats on the reverse.

The pattern is depicted mainly in blue, green, and yellow on a red ground. The design of the silk presents large medallions of which only part of the framework is preserved. It is formed by narrow bands of aligned dots that frame a larger band decorated with heart–shaped flower buds. A very closely comparable, perhaps identical, textile in the Abegg–Stiftung Collection (inv. nos. 4861 and 4862) is woven with eight lats, adding beige and dark green to the sequence of colours.[43]

43 Karel Otavsky, "Stoffe der Seidenstrasse," *Entlang der Seidenstrasse. Frühmittelalterliche Kunst zwischen Persien und China in der Abegg-Stiftung*, ed. Karel Otavsky, Riggisberg 1998 (Riggisberger Berichte 6), pp. 28–30. Regula Schorta, "Beobachtungen zu frühmittelalterlichen Webtechniken," ibid., p. 78.

48

1 组织细节　Weave detail

多色三角形连缀绢边饰 (DRM1PM2:S187；QK002860) 7~9 世纪

长 6 厘米、宽 33 厘米。

由深蓝、深褐、红、黄、绿等不同颜色的三角形绢片连缀在一起，面料组织均为平纹。经、纬线均无明显加捻，经密为 60 根／厘米，纬密 40 根／厘米。无幅边存留。

每小块三角形绢片尺寸一致，同为高 0.5 厘米、宽 1.2 厘米。每片绢片都仔细收边后，缝在做底衬的一条深蓝平纹绢上，再连缀成一体作边饰。整条绢饰由不同颜色三角形绢片拼成，极具装饰色彩。

49

SEVENTH- TO NINTH-CENTURY JUAN TEXTILE OF TRIANGULAR PATCHES STITCHED TOGETHER AS BORDER ORNAMENTATION (DRM1PM2:S187; QK 002860)

Height 6 cm, width 33 cm.

Patchwork made from plain tabby in dark blue, dark brown, red, cream, beige, and green. Warp and weft: silk, no noticeable twist; c. 60 ends and c. 40 picks per cm. No selvage preserved.

The border is worked in horizontal stripes. First, the tiny triangles (height 0.5 cm, width 1.2 cm) have their edges neatly folded back and are stitched to a dark blue tabby band. Then, these bands are stitched together matching exactly the triangles. The colours are arranged to form a kind of meander pattern.

1 组织细节 Detail

多色三角形连缀绢边饰 （DRM1PM2:S189；QK002862） 7~9 世纪

长 5.5 厘米、宽 25 厘米。

由深蓝、绿、褐、赭石等色绢连缀在一起。经、纬线都无明显加捻，经密约 60 根／厘米，纬密约 40 根／厘米。无幅边存留。

整体面料均为平纹，每块三角同为高 0.4 厘米、宽 0.7 厘米，收边后缝在做底衬的一条深蓝平纹绢上，再连缀成一体作边饰。绢条中心撕裂致其成为两块。

50

SEVENTH- TO NINTH-CENTURY JUAN TEXTILE OF TRIANGULAR PATCHES STITCHED TOGETHER AS BORDER ORNAMENTATION (DRM1PM2:S189; QK 002862)

Height 5.5 cm, width 25 cm.

Patchwork made from plain tabby in dark blue, green, brown, and ochre.
Warp and weft: silk, no noticeable twist; c. 60 ends and c. 40 picks per cm.
No selvage preserved.

This weave is a tabby (*juan*). The triangles (height 0.4 cm, width 0.7 cm) have their edges neatly folded back and are stitched to a dark blue ground, forming a border. A deep tear along the middle divides the border in half.

多色三角直线连缀绢边饰 （DRM1PM2:S192；QK003598） 7~9世纪

长 6.5 厘米、宽 17.5 厘米。

由深蓝、米、棕色绢条连缀而成。经、纬线都无明显加捻。经密约60根／厘米，纬密35～40根／厘米。无幅边存留。

面料均为平纹绢，由绿、米、棕、蓝等色绢裁剪成三角形和长条形，缝缀成条带作边饰。在条带中心图案两侧，各有一组由米黄、红、浅黄、绿四色组成的装饰条纹。其最外两侧都有深蓝色绢边。条带上米色、黄色的变化有可能是褪色造成，原色可能区别更明显。

正面和背面　Frant side (top) and back side (bottom)

SEVENTH- TO NINTH-CENTURY JUAN TEXTILE OF TRIANGULAR PATCHES STITCHED TOGETHER WITH STRAIGHT STRIPS, AS BORDER ORNAMENTATION (DRM1PM:S192; QK 003598)

Height 6.5 cm, width 17.5 cm.

Patchwork made from plain tabby in dark blue, beige, and brown.

Warp and weft: silk, no noticeable twist; c. 60 ends and 35–40 picks per cm.

No selvage preserved.

Bands composed of four narrow strips of plain tabby (yellow, red, light yellow, green) are attached to the long sides of the fragment, followed by a wider strip of dark blue tabby.

This weave is a tabby. The textile is composed of green, yellow, brown, blue *juan*, cut into triangular shapes and strips and patched together. The different shades of beige might be the result of fading of colours that originally were more strongly differentiated.

51

1　背面组织细节　Back side detail

菱形、直线形多色连缀绢边饰 　(DRM1PM2:S195；QK002857)　7~9世纪

长7厘米、宽21.2厘米。

由深褐、米、深蓝、蓝绿、赭石、浅黄、浅绿和绿色等多种色块平纹绢连缀成条饰。经、纬线都无明显加捻。经密约60根／厘米，纬密约40根／厘米。无幅边存留。

边饰条由多种深浅色调不同的蓝、绿、褐等色三角形和长条形绢片缝缀，拼成菱形和条形。其中三角形尺寸为高0.5厘米、宽1.2厘米，各色长条宽约0.4厘米。条带中心为拼色菱形装饰。

52

SEVENTH- TO NINTH-CENTURY JUAN TEXTILE OF DIAMOND SHAPES AND STRIPS, STITCHED TOGETHER AS BORDER ORNAMENTATION (DRM1PM2:S195; QK 002857)

Height 7 cm, width 21.2 cm.

Patchwork made from plain tabby in dark brown, beige, dark blue, blue-green, ochre, light yellow, light green and green.

Warp and weft: silk, no noticeable twist; c. 60 ends and c. 40 picks per cm.

No selvage preserved.

Triangles: height 0.5 cm, width 1.2 cm; horizontal bands: width c. 0.4 cm.

This weave is a tabby. It is composed of fabrics in several shades of blue, green, and yellow sewn together, with a row of diamond-shaped decorations down the middle.

直线形边饰绢带 （DRM1PM2:S199；QK002894） 7世纪

长6厘米、宽46厘米。

经、纬线同为米色，无明显加捻，经密约70根／厘米，纬密约40根／厘米。无幅边存留。

条带由两侧各有一条六色（两绿、两褐、深蓝、米黄）和四色（两褐、两绿）的平纹绢条组成，一侧最外边加缝有一条米黄色平纹绢。

整块织物由蓝、绿和米黄色绢裁剪成条缝缀为装饰条带。条带中心绢及其两侧装饰线上有不规则黑色印纹，很可能是金属物件比如银器留下的痕迹。

53

SEVENTH- TO EIGHTH-CENTURY JUAN TEXTILE IN BELT OR RIBBON

SHAPE (DRM1PM2:S199; QK 002894)

Height 6 cm, width 46 cm.

Tabby (*juan*).
Warp and weft: silk, no noticeable twist, beige; c. 70 ends and c. 40 picks per cm.
No selvage preserved.
Bands composed of six (bottom) or four (top) narrow strips of plain tabby (bottom: twice green, twice ochre, dark blue, beige; top: twice ochre, twice green) are attached to the long sides of the fragment, followed at the bottom by a wider strip of beige tabby.

[contd.]

53

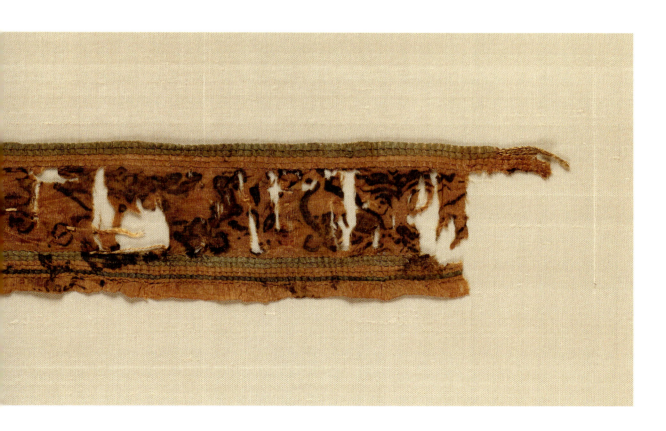

This object is composed of blue, green, and yellow *juan* tabby, cut to form strips, then patched together and stitched to a beige *juan* band to form a belt or ribbon decoration. The central band of tabby shows a black imprint of a metal object (probably silver) on all its length, extending onto the attached bands at some occasions. The patterning is probably not intentional.

1 组织细节 Detail

黄地大窠宝花锦 （DRM1PM2:S21－1；QK002361A） 8世纪

长90厘米、宽16厘米，经向‡。与另一片织物（图版No.55）缝缀在一起，总宽36.5厘米。

1/2Z纬重组织。经线为棕色S捻丝，夹经、明经2:1交替。夹经约38根／厘米，明经约19根／厘米。纬线由黄、白、深蓝、棕四色无明显捻丝构成，纬密16～17副／厘米。无幅边存留。但织物下侧一端存留一条素色织纹。

这片织锦黄地上显蓝、白、棕色花。纹样保存尚属完好，比较清晰，花窠甚大，主花图案直径达33厘米，经向循环为34.5厘米。主花中心是蓝色圆形，周围绕以白色连珠纹。然后是六出巨大的蘑菇形花蕊，在蘑菇状花蕊之间伸出六朵侧面的花。其外包有卷状花瓣，花瓣之间从后面又生出朵花，层叠反复，显得饱满浑厚。可惜宾花图案已不完整，仅露出花瓣的尖角。

no. 55　no. 54

1 结构图 Numbering diagram　　　2 组织细节 Detail

EIGHTH-CENTURY JIN TEXTILE WITH YELLOW GROUND AND LARGE PRECIOUS-FLOWER ROUNDEL (DRM1PM2:S21-1; QK 002361 A)

Height 90 cm, width 16 cm (warp direction ↕). Overall width, including cat. no. 55: 36.5 cm.

Weft-faced compound 1/2 Z twill with four lats.

Warp: 2 main warp ends to 1 binding warp end; silk, S-twisted, brown; c. 38 main warp ends per cm, c. 19 binding warp ends per cm.

Weft: silk, no noticeable twist, yellow, white, dark blue, brown; 16–17 passes per cm.

No selvage preserved. Unpatterned horizontal finishing border at the lower edge.

This textile is stitched to cat. no. 55.

This textile employs a yellow ground with blue, white, and brown patterning. The pattern is well preserved and clear, the roundels large, the main flower pattern has a diameter of 33 cm, and a warp-direction repeat of 34.5 cm. Blue circles form the center of the main flower design, surrounded by a row of white pearls. Then follow six relatively large mushroom-like flower buds, between which are six flowers seen in profile. Outside these are curled flower petals, from behind which are again more flowers, forming a layered look. Unfortunately the accessory flower pattern is now damaged and incomplete so that only the tips of flower petals can be recognized.

黄色柿蒂纹染缬晕绸 （DRM1PM2:S21－2；QK002361B） 8世纪

长90厘米、宽19.5厘米，经向↕。与图版No.54缝缀在一起，总宽36.5厘米。

面料以3/1并在S和Z向替换的斜纹组织于平纹地上显花纹。经、纬线同为乳白色，无明显加捻丝。经密46～48根／厘米，纬密40～44副／厘米。无幅边存留。经扎染呈棕色条纹。

面料图案为四瓣小花，交错行排列，又称柿蒂纹。花纹图案循环尺寸经向为0.8厘米、纬向5厘米。丝织片经绞缬染扎成棕白晕绸两色，与图版No.29的晕绸图案非常相似。

55

EIGHTH-CENTURY JIAN TEXTILE WITH YELLOW PERSIMMON-BASE PATTERN AND TIE DYING (DRM1PM2:S21-2; QK 002361 B)

Height 90 cm, width 19.5 cm (warp direction ↕). Overall width, including cat. no. 54: 36.5 cm.

Self-patterned tabby with pattern in 3/1 twill in alternately S and Z direction.
Warp: silk, no noticeable twist, cream; 46–48 ends per cm.
Weft: silk, no noticeable twist, cream; 40–44 picks per cm.
No selvage preserved.
Resist-dyed brown stripes run parallel to the warp.
This textile is stitched to cat. no. 54.

This pattern of small four-petalled flowers, arranged in staggered rows, is also called persimmon pattern. Its repeat measures 0.8 cm in the warp direction and c. 2.5 cm in the weft direction. This piece of weaving has been dyed in shaded stripes of white and brown, which was achieved by the process of tie dying. It is very comparable if not identical to cat. no. 29.

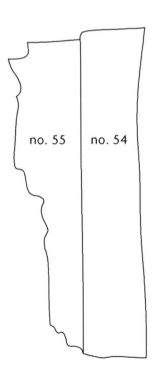

1 结构图 Numbering diagram

蓝地蜡缬绮 (QK001891) 7~8世纪

长 23.2 厘米、宽 43 厘米，经向 ↕。

面料组织为 3/1、3/1、3/1、1/1、1/1 的斜纹经线显菱形花纹。经、纬线同为无染本色，无明显加捻。经密、纬密分别为 50 根／厘米、38 ~ 40 根／厘米。一侧存留 0.4 厘米幅边。

在暗花菱形绮上施以蜡缬，印出蓝地白花纹的几何纹点、飞鸟、小花等纹样。在织物中间可以看到印花纹样的对称重复，可以推算得到其花版尺寸约为经向 10 厘米、纬向 27 厘米。由于白色花纹不清，因而推测当时采用了凸纹版印刷蜡防纹样，再在染液中染成蓝色。

56

SEVENTH- TO EIGHTH-CENTURY DIAMOND TWILL WITH BLUE GROUND AND WAX-RESIST DYED PATTERN (QK 001891)

Height 23.2cm, width 43 cm (warp direction ↕).

Composite 3/1, 3/1, 3/1, 1/1, 1/1 warp diamond twill; point entering over 28 warp ends (15 ends straight unit, 13 ends reverse unit) and point treadling over 24 picks (13 picks straight unit, 11 picks reverse unit).

Warp: silk, no noticeable twist, undyed; c. 50 ends per cm.

Weft: silk, no noticeable twist, undyed; c. 38–40 picks per cm.

One selvage preserved at the left side of the fragment, 0.4 cm wide.

Wax resist dyed indigo blue with the textile folded in half.

Wax-resist dying has been applied to the lozenge twill, making a geometric pattern of white flowers on blue ground, flying birds, small flowers, and the like. In the middle of the textile can be seen repeated mirror-imaged printed flower patterns; it can be deduced that the printing block was roughly 10 cm along the warp direction and 27 cm in the weft direction. Since the white flower pattern is unclear, it can be surmised that at the time a method of wax-resist printing with a stamp was used, and then the piece was dyed blue in a dye bath.

The weave pattern repeat measures 0.5 cm in weft and warp direction.

1 组织细节 Weave detail

蓝地蜡缬宝花绢　(QK002931)　7~8 世纪

长 12 厘米、宽 18 厘米，经向 ↕。与本色边条缝缀在一起，总长 25 厘米、总宽 18 厘米。

平纹组织，经、纬线同为本色丝，无明显加捻。经密 55 根／厘米，纬密 44 ~ 50 根／厘米。无幅边存留。蜡染蓝地显白花。

与其相连的是两条本色平纹绢，其中一条宽 9.1 厘米、存留长 13 厘米，另一条宽 9.8 厘米、长 3.7 厘米，两条对接有 1.5 厘米。其经、纬线均为漂白过的本色，无明显加捻。经、纬密度分别为 55 根／厘米、40 根／厘米。无幅边存留。几片织物均以宽平卷边缝缀在一起。

蓝地织物为平纹绢上施以蜡缬，印出蓝地白花纹。纹样为四瓣组成的小花，由六瓣花四朵与三瓣花四朵隔位交错，中心亦为四瓣花组成宝花，反复连续循环。由于白色花纹不清，推测亦采用了凸纹版印刷蜡防纹样，再在染液中染成蓝色。

SEVENTH- TO EIGHTH-CENTURY TABBY WITH BLUE GROUND AND WAX-RESIST DYED PRECIOUS-FLOWER PATTERN (QK 002931)

Height 12 cm, width 18 cm (warp direction ↕). Overall dimensions (including attached bands): height 25 cm, width 18 cm.

Tabby.

Warp and weft: silk, no noticeable twist, undyed; c. 55 ends and 44–50 picks per cm.

No selvage preserved.

Wax-resist dyed indigo blue.

Attached are two bands of unpatterned tabby; one is 9.1 cm wide, preserved on a length of 13 cm; the other is 9.8 cm wide, preserved on a length of 3.7 cm; overlapping each other by 1.5 cm.

Warp and weft: silk, no noticeable twist, undyed (bleached); c. 55 ends and c. 40 picks per cm.

No selvage preserved.

[contd.]

All pieces are neatly hemmed by rolling, and joined to each other by a flat seam.

This textile employs a wax-resist patterning on tabby, so that white patterning appears on a blue ground. The patterning results in four-petalled small flowers, interspersed with larger flowers. Since the white patterning is indistinct, it is surmised that what was used to apply the wax was a stamp-like printing block, and then the fabric was dyed blue.

57

1 组织细节 Weave detail

黄地宝花绣鞯 （QK001861） 8世纪

58

长36.8厘米、宽51.2厘米。

由两片不同的平纹丝拼在一起。第一片织物经、纬线同为棕色，无明显加捻。经密50根／厘米，纬密32～36根／厘米。第二片织物经、纬线同为无明显加捻的米色丝线，经密约60根／厘米，纬密约40根／厘米。织物存留一侧用劈针绣包住的幅边，丝线为S双捻丝线，有白、棕、蓝、绿等多种色调。

这块织物为置于马鞍下鞯的残片，以米色和棕色绢为地，其上用S双捻粗细为0.3～0.4毫米的白、棕、蓝、绿等色丝线以劈针绣法勾勒出艳丽的唐草宝花图案。花纹图案拼接仔细，呈竖向对称排列，估计是用在穿过膝靴子的大腿位置附近。

1 刺绣细节 Embroidery detail

EIGHTH-CENTURY EMBROIDERY WITH MULTICOLOUR PRECIOUS FLOWERS (QK 001861)

Height 36.8 cm, width 51.2 cm.

Split-stitch embroidery on tabby ground patched from two fragments of two different textiles.

(1) Warp: silk, no noticeable twist, brown; c. 50 ends per cm. Weft: silk, no noticeable twist, brown; c. 32–36 picks per cm. One selvage preserved.

(2) Warp: silk, no noticeable twist, beige; c. 60 ends per cm. Weft: silk, no noticeable twist, beige; c. 40 picks per cm. One selvage preserved.

Split-stitch embroidery covering the whole surface. Silk, S-plied from 2 Z-twisted ends, white, brown, blue, green in many shades.

This is a fragment of a textile that was put under a horse saddle, with brown and beige *juan* as ground, on which many shades of white, brown, blue, and green thread with a thickness of 0.3 to 0.4 mm are used in split stitch embroidery to make beautiful Tang-style floral scrolls and precious flowers. The pattern is carefully arranged into the outline shape of the piece and mirrored along a vertical axis. As an alternative, one could imagine that its intended use was for the leg part of a knee-high boot.

58

2 刺绣细节　Embroidery detail

3 刺绣细节　Embroidery detail

黄地宝花对鸟纹锦 (QK002391) 8世纪中

由三片织锦缝缀在一起，总长45.5厘米、总宽22厘米。其中最大一片长41.5厘米、宽14厘米，经向↕。

1/2S斜纹纬重组织。经线：偏红棕色，S加捻丝，夹经、明经1:1交替，夹经、明经约为19根/厘米。纬线：无明显加捻，由红、白、黄、蓝绿四色丝构成，并按此序四纬一组循环往复，30～34副/厘米。无幅边存留。另有一无花纹的平纹绢条缝在整块织锦的右侧边，经、纬线都无明显加捻，呈淡棕色，经密56～60根/厘米，纬密约40根/厘米。

唐代最为著名的图案类型是"陵阳公样"，是由唐初图案设计师窦师纶设计。张彦远《历代名画记》记载：高宗太祖时，内库瑞锦、对雉、斗羊、翔凤、游麟之状，创自师纶，至今传之。这种陵阳公样应该是以花卉作环、动物纹作主题的团窠图案，动物可以是独立的，也可以是成对的。此件宝花对鸟纹锦正是"陵阳公样"的实例之一。它以宝花作环、对鸟作主题，与记载中的翔凤、对雉等基本一致。图案经向循环约14厘米，纬向循环大于13厘米，团窠直径约为10.5厘米。

同墓所出还有紫地中窠宝花立凤锦（图版No.21）和黄地团窠宝花对狮锦（图版No.23），也属同类。

MID-EIGHTH CENTURY JIN, YELLOW GROUND, PRECIOUS-FLOWER ROUNDEL ENCLOSING CONFRONTED BIRDS (QK 002391)

Overall dimensions (three pieces of the silk are stitched together): height 45.5 cm, width 22 cm. Dimensions of the largest piece: height 41.5 cm, width 14 cm (warp direction ↕).

Weft-faced compound 1/2 S twill with four lats.

Warp: 1 main warp end to 1 binding warp end; silk, S-twisted, reddish brown; c. 19 main and 19 binding warp ends per cm.

Weft: silk, no noticeable twist, red, white, yellow, bluish green; straight weft sequence; c. 30–34 passes per cm.

No selvage preserved.

Stitched to the right edge of the fragment are remnants of unpatterned tabby.

Warp and weft: silk, no noticeable twist, light brown; 56–60 ends and c. 40 picks per cm.

No selvage preserved.

59

The most famous pattern in the Tang dynasty was the Duke Lingyang pattern. This was designed by the early-Tang pattern designer Dou Shilun. The *Lidai minghua ji* (Records of Famous Paintings Through the Ages) by Zhang Yanyuan records the following: 'at the times of the Emperors Gaozu [r. 618-626] and Taizong [r. 627-649], a *jin* textile was [kept] in the Treasure with opposing pheasants, opposing ibex, flying phoenixes, playing lin [mythical creature]. It was created by Dou Shilun and exists up to this time.' [44] This kind of Duke Lingyang pattern has confronted animal patterns as main subjects inside flower roundels; the animals can either be single or paired in opposition. The pattern with confronted birds in this piece is example of this Duke Lingyang pattern. It uses precious flowers as roundels, has a main subject of confronted birds, corresponding to the recorded description of flying phoenixes and opposing pheasants. In warp direction the pattern repeat of this silk is about 14 cm in height, in weft direction it is greater than 13 cm, and the diameter of the roundels is approximately 10.5 cm.

Other *jin* textiles excavated from the same tomb in Dulan have standing phoenixes (cat. no. 21) or confronted lions (cat. no. 23) in roundels of precious flowers, and belong to the same type.

44 张彦远 Zhang Yanyuan [of the Tang dynasty], 历代名画记 *Lidai minghua ji (Records of Famous Paintings through the Ages)*, Beijing 1963, vol. 1, p. 118.

1 组织细节 Weave detail

橙地小窠连珠镜花锦 （DRM1PM2:S127；QK002793） 7世纪

长 45 厘米、宽 7.4 厘米，经向 ↔。

2/1Z 向斜纹经重组织。经线：无明显加捻，偶尔有轻度 S 向加捻。由黄色、白色、蓝色（与棕色交替换色）分区显花。经密 162 ~ 171 根／厘米（1：2，每组为 54 ~ 57 根／厘米）。纬线：本色，无明显加捻，纬密 24 ~ 26 根／厘米，明纬、夹纬交替。双幅边完整，幅宽 44.5 厘米。

这块织锦以橙色为地，以白色勾纹、蓝色和棕色交替分区显花。连珠团窠环由 26 颗圆珠连成，中间小花是四出花蕾，然后转 45 度角呈四出叶尖，而团窠间的十样小花只是以六瓣小花为中心的四出花蕾。此锦图案的团窠花色彩较浓，浑然一体，很像是铜镜的背面，图案类似于唐镜中的宝花，因此，我们将其称作连珠镜花锦。

"镜花"一词来自《新唐书·地理志》，志载兖州土贡镜花绫，到宋代锦名中又有宝照锦等名，当指同类纹样。当然，宋代的宝照与唐代的镜花是有区别的。唐代的镜花图案也不止一种，类似这种镜花锦的服饰图案，在敦煌莫高窟隋到初唐的洞窟壁画 [39] 中常有发现，在吐鲁番阿斯塔那亦有出土 [40]，年代在 633 年前后。显然，此类锦流行于隋到初唐时期。

39 Dunhuang: Caves of the Singing Sands. Buddhist Art from the Silk Road, text by Roderick Whitfield, photographs by Seigo Otsuka, London 1995, vol. 1, cl. 366.
40 商品藏于新疆维吾尔自治区博物馆，73TAM211①。新疆维吾尔自治区博物馆《新疆出土文物》，图版 147，文物出版社，1975 年。

1 组织细节 Weave detail

60

SEVENTH-CENTURY JIN, WITH ORANGE GROUND AND SMALL ALIGNED-PEARL
ROUNDEL ENCLOSING MIRROR-PATTERN (DRM1PM2:S127; QK 002793)

Height 45 cm, width 7.4 cm (warp direction ↔).

Warp-faced compound 2/1 Z twill with three series of warps.

Warp: silk, no noticeable twist, occasionally slightly S-twisted, yellow, white, blue (striped brown); c. 162–171 ends per cm (54–57 ends per warp series and cm).

Weft: silk, no noticeable twist, undyed(?); 24–26 picks per cm, passed alternately through a twill shed and a pattern shed.

Both selvages preserved; loom width 44.5 cm.

This particular *jin* employs yellow ground, white outlining, alternating blue and brown regions to form the pattern. The roundels are formed by an outer border of 26 pearls, in which are four flower buds with protruding leaves at a 45-degree angle. The pattern is also truly like the precious flowers on a Tang mirror, because of that we call it an aligned-pearl mirror-patterned *jin*. The term 'mirror-patterned' comes from the Geography Volume of the New Tang History. In this is recorded how Yanhou contributed a mirror-pattern *ling*.[45] Until the Song dynasty one of the names describing *jin* fabrics was the 'precious reflection'*jin*, which referred to a similar patterning on a *jin* textile. Naturally, the precious-reflection of the Song and the mirror-pattern of the Tang were distinct; the Tang-dynasty mirror pattern was also not restricted to just this one kind.

Ornamental patterns similar to this kind of mirror-patterned *jin* have been discovered on Sui-dynasty to early Tang-dynasty wall paintings at Mogao Grottoes at Dunhuang.[46] They have also been excavated from Astana in Turfan, dating to around 633.[47] Clearly this kind of *jin* was popular in the Sui to early Tang period.

45 新唐书 *Xin Tangshu* (*The new book of the Tang Dynasty*), Zhonghua shuju chuban, Beijing 1975, vol. 4, book 38, chapter 志 / 28, 地理二 *dili er*, p. 995.

46 Dunhuang. *Caves of the Singing Sands. Buddhist Art from the Silk Road*, text by Roderick Whitfield, photographs by Seigo Otsuka, London 1995, vol. 1, pl. 366.

47 Urumqi, Xinjiang Museum, 73TAM211:9. 新疆维吾尔自治区博物馆 Xinjiang Uighur Autonomous Region Museum (ed.) 新疆出土文物 *Xinjiang chutu wenwu* (*Cultural relics excavated in Xinjiang*), Beijing 1975, pl. 147.

黄地瓣窠对马纹锦 (DXM1:S4；QK002021) 8世纪

长 10 厘米、宽 55.5 厘米，经向↕。

　　1/2S 斜纹纬重组织。经线：浅棕色 Z 捻丝，夹经、明经 2:1 交替，夹经 32 ~ 44 根／厘米，明经 16 ~ 22 根／厘米。纬线：无明显加捻，红（已褪为黄色）、米、蓝（与绿色交替）等三色组成，并按此序列三纬一组循环。纬密 26 副／厘米。幅边已失。

　　花纹图案经向循环不明，纬向 23.5 厘米。团窠为八瓣花环，窠内对马上半身已不全，仅见马身后部、尾与四足。马身有花饰，尾带束结，立于花盘之上。

EIGHTH-CENTURY JIN, NOW YELLOW GROUND WITH FLOWER-PETAL ROUNDEL ENCLOSING CONFRONTED HORSES (DXM1:S4; QK 002021)

Height 10 cm, width 55.5 cm (warp direction ↕).

Weft-faced compound 1/2 S twill with three lats.

Warp: 1 pair of main warp ends to 1 binding warp end; silk, Z-twisted, light brown; 16–22 pairs of main warp ends and 16–22 binding warp ends per cm.

Weft: silk, no noticeable twist, red (faded to yellow), beige, blue (latté green); straight weft sequence; 26 passes per cm.

No selvage preserved.

[contd.]

The pattern repeat in warp-direction is not preserved, in weft-direction it is 23.5 cm. The roundel is an eight-petalled flower, inside which are opposing horses whose bodies are incompletely preserved. The bottom part of the bodies, tails, and four hooves can be seen, however. There is patterning on the bodies, and the tails have a knot tied in them; the four hooves stand on a pedestal.

61

1 组织细节 Weave detail

红地中窠连珠对牛纹锦 (DXM1:S5；QK002036) 8~9 世纪

两片织锦尺寸分别长 19.5 厘米、宽 49 厘米，长 20.3 厘米、宽 15.2 厘米，经向↕。

1/2S 斜纹纬重组织。经线：棕色 Z 捻丝；夹经、明经 2:1 交替。夹经 40 ~ 42 根／厘米，明经 20 ~ 21 根／厘米。纬线：无明显加捻，由红、黄、蓝（与绿交替）显色或由红、黄显色组成，并以此色序三纬一组或是两纬一组反向循环。纬密 32 副／厘米。无幅边存留。

织锦的图案以约 46 颗连珠围成环形团窠，窠内主题为对牛图案。对牛头有角，大眼，颈上系丝带，尾巴翘起甩在身上，四足立于花盘之上。窠外十样小花。整个图案用深红地，白色显花，十样花，连珠圈。牛身均是白色，唯牛角、牛眼及蹄子装饰小块绿色。图案的纬向循环为 13 厘米，但经向循环应与纬向循环尺寸相差不大。这块织锦的年代应该与含绶鸟锦的盛唐大体相同（参见图版 No.65 ~ 67、图版 No.75 ~ 77）。

1 组织细节 Weave detail

EIGHTH- TO NINTH-CENTURY JIN, RED GROUND ALIGNED-PEARL ROUNDEL WITH CONFRONTED OXEN (DXM1:S5; QK002036)

Tow fragments, height 19.5 cm, width 49 cm, and height 20.3 cm, width 15.2 cm respectively (warp direction ↕).

62

Weft-faced compound 1/2 S twill with three lats.

Warp: 1 group of two main warp ends to 1 binding warp end; silk, Z–twisted, brown, C 20-21 groups of two main warp ends and 20-21 binding warp ends per cm.

Weft: silk, no noticeable twist, red, white, blue (striped green, interrupted); reversed weft sequence; 32 passes per cm.

No selvage preserved.

About 46 aligned pearls join to form a roundel, inside which the main subject is a pair of confronted oxen. These have horns on their heads, they have large eyes and ribbons on their necks, their tails are arched back over their bodies. Their four feet stand on a split–palmette pedestal. Outside the roundels are four-directional palmettes. The entire pattern uses a deep-red ground with white to form the pattern, the flowers, roundels and ox bodies are all white, only the horns and eyes and hooves are decorated with small bits of green. The pattern repeat is c. 13 cm in weft direction, in warp direction it is slightly larger. The dating of this piece should be basically similar to the bird-holding-ribbon pattern (see cat. nos. 65 to 67, 75 to 77), that is, the High Tang.

2 组织细节 Weave detail
(photo: Yao Qingfang 姚青芳, Ma Yanru 马燕如, 2004)

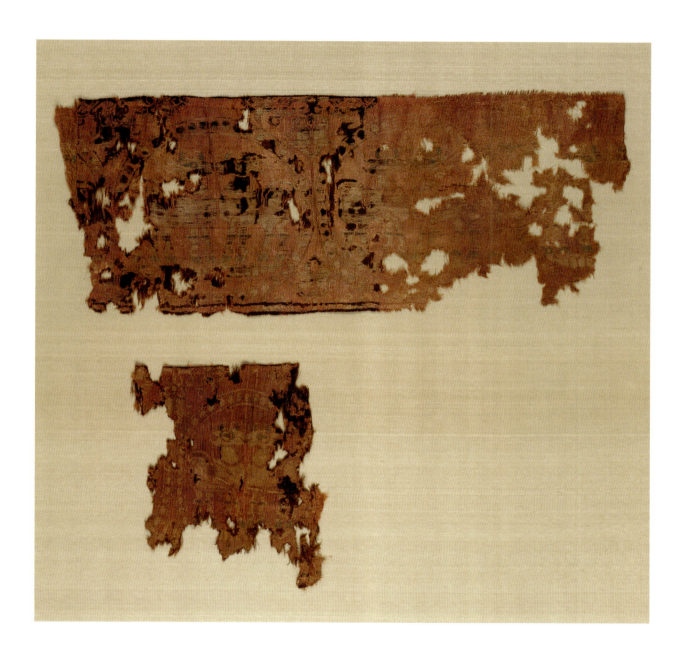

黄地中窠小花对鹰锦 (DRLC:S1；QK002029)　8~9 世纪

63

长 5 厘米、宽 36 厘米，包括缝在两端同样材质的三角片料，经向 ↕。

1/2S 斜纹纬重组织。经线：乳白色 Z 捻丝，夹经、明经 2:1 交替，夹经约 38 根 / 厘米，明经约 19 根 / 厘米。纬线：无明显加捻，红（褪色为黄色）、米、蓝三色构成，并按此序三纬一组循环。纬密约 24 副 / 厘米。幅边已失。

由黄色丝线作地，蓝色和米色纬线显花。织锦实物虽只残存一窄条，但似能见到两组对鹰，体态雄健，昂首挺胸相对而立。头部四周皆有环状物，对鹰之外以小花作团窠环，装饰味颇浓。循环纬向 7 厘米。

类似的织物在敦煌藏经洞和新疆米兰遗址也有出土[41]。

41 有关敦煌文物参见法国巴黎国家博物馆亚洲艺术收藏 EO1193/A，Krishna Riboud, Gabriel Vial, *Tissus de Touen-Houang conserves au Musée e Guimet et à la Bibliothèque Nationale*, Paris 1970 (Mission Paul Pelliot, 13), pp. 169-173，新疆米兰出土文物，参见英国伦敦维多利亚博物馆藏 M.I.vii.0017(Stein Loan 215)：Aurel Stein, *Innermost Asia. Detailed report of explorations in Central Asia, Kan-su and eastern Iran*, Oxford 1928, vol. 1 p. 481, vol. 4, pl. CXL.

1　组织细节　Weave detail

EIGHTH- TO NINTH-CENTURY JIN, YELLOW GROUND, PETAL ROUNDELS ENCLOSING CONFRONTED EAGLES (DRLC:S1; QK 002029)

Height 5 cm, width 36 cm, including two triangular fragments of the same fabric stitched to the right and left edges (warp direction ↕).

Weft-faced compound 1/2 S twill with three lats.

Warp: 1 pair of main warp ends to 1 binding warp end; silk, Z-twisted, cream; c. 19 pairs of main warp ends and 19 binding warp ends per cm.

Weft: silk, no noticeable twist, red (faded to yellow), beige, blue; straight weft sequence; c. 24 passes per cm.

No selvage preserved.

The ground of the textile is made of yellow-coloured silk threads, probably faded from red, while blue and beige (once green?) threads are used in the weft to show the pattern. Only a narrow strip remains of this silk, but one can see two groups of confronted eagles, their forms masculine and vigorous, their uplifted heads and breasts facing each other. Each has a halo behind and surrounding the head. Outside the eagles, the roundels are made of small petals, with a strongly ornamental pattern. The weft-directional pattern repeat is 7 cm.

Similar textiles have been recovered from the Library Cave at Dunhuang and excavated from the Miran site in Xinjiang. [48]

---

48 From Dunhuang: Paris, National Museum of Asian Art Guimet, inv. no. EO 1193/A. Krishna Riboud, Gabriel Vial, *Tissus de Touen-Houang conservés au Musée Guimet et à la Bibliothèque Nationale*, Paris 1970 (Mission Paul Pelliot, 13), pp. 169–73. From Miran: London, Victoria and Albert Museum, site no. M.I.viii.0017 (Stein Loan 215). Aurel Stein, *Innermost Asia. Detailed report of explorations in Central Asia, Kan-su and eastern Iran*, Oxford 1928, vol. 1 p. 481, vol. 4 pl. CXI.

黄地瓣窠灵鹫纹锦　(QK001857、QK002022)　8~9 世纪

QK001857，长 18.5 厘米、宽 46.7 厘米。QK020022，包括两块织锦残片，织锦一长 22.5 厘米、宽 18.8 厘米；织锦二长 10.5 厘米、宽 37.5 厘米；经向↕。

这组织锦都是 1/2Z 斜纹纬重组织。经线：显棕色 Z 捻丝；2:1 夹经、明经交替；夹经约 24 根／厘米，明经约 12 根／厘米。纬线：无明显加捻，以棕黄、棕、灰蓝、米、白等五色构成，并按此色序五纬一组反向循环，纬密 38 ~ 39 副／厘米。幅边已失。

其中织锦二的一侧缝有显棕色的两段平纹绢细残条。

织锦中的团窠由八瓣花环组成，环中是一正面直立的灵鹫（神鹰）。头向左，有头光。两翅平展，颈与翅有连珠条饰。中间主体为其椭圆形腹部，腹中有一人形，下方饰七根尾羽。从图案及织造方法来看，这件织物与拜占庭文化有着某种联系。

图案单元纬向循环大约是 20 厘米，而经向则大于 20 厘米。

1　组织细节　Weave detail

EIGHTH- TO NINTH-CENTURY JIN, YELLOW GROUND, WITH PETAL ROUNDEL

ENCLOSING SPIRIT-RAPTOR (QK 001857 AND QK 002022)

QK 001857: Height 18.5 cm, width 46.7 cm (warp direction ↕).

QK 002022: Two fragments: (1) height 22.5 cm, width 18.8 cm, (2) height 10.5 cm, width 37.5 cm (warp direction ↕).

Weft-faced compound 1/2 Z twill with five lats.

Warp: 1 pair of main warp ends to 1 binding warp end; silk, Z-twisted, brownish; c. 12 pairs of main warp ends and 12 binding warp ends per cm.

Weft: silk, no noticeable twist, brownish yellow, brown, grayish blue, beige, white (interrupted); reversed weft sequence; 38–39 passes per cm.

No selvage preserved.

Remnants of two narrow strips of plain tabby (brownish) are attached to one side of fragment (2).

[contd.]

The roundel is composed of an eight-petalled flower, enclosing a frontal-facing spirit raptor (a kind of sacred eagle). Its head faces left and it wears a halo. Its two wings are spread out to its sides, its neck and tail are decorated with aligned pearls. Inside the oblong chest that constitutes its body is the figure of a man, underneath which are seven tail feathers. From the pattern and construction method, this weaving has various ties to the Byzantine Empire.

The pattern unit in weft direction is around 20 cm, in warp direction it is greater than 20 cm.

2 组织细节 Weave detail

一组两片（A、B）红地中窠小花对含绶鸟锦 　(DXDM8:S2)　8~9世纪

A. QK002871，两片残锦尺寸分别为（a）长 11.6 厘米、宽 17.6 厘米，（b）长 8.8 厘米、宽 11 厘米；经向↕。

B. QK002771，长 58.5 厘米、宽 4 厘米，与附加残片的总宽为 12 厘米；经向↕。

A. 织锦是 1/2S 斜纹纬重组织，经线：红褐色 Z 捻。夹经、明经 2:1 交替。夹经约 44 根 / 厘米，明经约 22 根 / 厘米。纬线：无明显加捻，由红、蓝、黄、绿等四色构成，并按此序四纬一组循环往复。纬密 30 ~ 34 副 / 厘米。残锦背面还存有纬丝浮织块，也称为抛梭现象。无幅边存留。

B. 织锦是 1/2S 斜纹纬重组织，经线：深棕色 Z 捻。夹经、明经 3:1 交替。夹经约 57 根 / 厘米，明经约 19 根 / 厘米。纬线：无明显加捻，由红、蓝、黄、绿等四色构成，并按此序四纬一组循环往复。纬密约 37 副 / 厘米。残锦背面还存有纬丝浮织块，也称为抛梭现象。无幅边存留。

附缀残片一为绫，以 3/1Z 斜纹为地，以 1/3S 斜纹组织显花。经、纬线同为红色，无明显加捻。经密 39 ~ 41 根 / 厘米，纬密 27 ~ 28 根 / 厘米。附缀残片二为平纹组织的丝衬，经、纬线同为米色，无明显加捻。经密 44 根 / 厘米，纬密 40 ~ 48 根 / 厘米。其中红绫用来做衣袍边缘，被裁成长条。

这组织锦均以红色为地，以蓝、黄、绿等色显花。图案基本可以复原，经向循环约为 26 厘米。以花瓣组成团窠环，花瓣之间伸出 14 朵折枝小花。窠内为对含绶鸟，站立于棕榈基座上。鸟身为较细密的方格纹，颈部和腹上部饰以连珠条饰，尾羽分开，上翘下钩。宾花为对称的十样花，几何味较浓。

A.

TWO (A, B) EIGHTH- TO NINTH-CENTURY JIN SILKS, RED GROUND, ROUNDEL ENCLOSING BIRDS HOLDING RIBBONS IN THEIR BEAKS (DXDM8:S2)

A. (QK 002871) Two fragments: (a) height 11.6 cm, width 17.6 cm; (b) height 8.8 cm, width 11 cm; (warp direction ↕).

B. (QK 002771) Height 58.5 cm, width 4 cm, total width including attached fragments 12 cm (warp direction ↕).

A. Weft-faced compound 1/2 S twill with four lats.

Warp: 1 pair of main warp ends to 1 binding warp end; silk, Z-twisted, reddish brown; c. 22 pairs of main warp ends and 22 binding warp ends per cm.

Weft: silk, no noticeable twist, red, blue, yellow, green; straight weft sequence; c. 30–34 passes per cm.

No selvage preserved.

Weft floats on the reverse.

B. Weft-faced compound 1/2 S twill with four lats.

Warp: 1 group of three main warp ends to 1 binding warp end; silk, Z-twisted, dark brown; c. 19 groups of three main warp ends and 19 binding warp ends per cm.

Weft: silk, no noticeable twist, red, blue, yellow, green; straight weft sequence; c. 37 passes per cm.

No selvage preserved.

Weft floats on the reverse.

Attached fragments: Damask with ground in 3/1 Z twill and pattern in 1/3 S twill.

Warp: silk, no noticeable twist, red; c. 39–41 ends per cm.

Weft: silk, no noticeable twist, red; 27–28 picks per cm.

Attached fragments of lining: Plain tabby.

Warp and weft: silk, no noticeable twist, beige; c. 44 warp ends and 40–48 weft picks per cm.

The silk has a red ground with patterning in blue, yellow, and green; on the backside one can see weft floats produced by bringing the shuttle temporarily out of the shed. The pattern can be reconstructed, the warp-directional repeat is around 26 cm. The roundel is composed of petals, between which small flowers protrude; inside the roundel is a pair of birds holding ribbons in their beaks, standing on a platform of split palmettes. The birds' bodies are woven with a finely done checker pattern, their necks and breasts are ornamented with rows of aligned pearls, their tail feathers are spread. The interstitial motifs are four-directional flowers, with a strongly geometric flavor.

Specimen (B) served as edging to a red ling damask robe, it has been cut into a long strip.

B.
[photo: Angelika Sliwka, 2018]

红地中窠小花对含绶鸟锦　(DRXM26:S2；QK002805)　8~9世纪

　　这组八块织锦残片中最大的四片（从左至右、从上至下）尺寸分别为：（A）长12厘米、宽6.5厘米，（B）长11厘米、宽11厘米，（C）长9厘米、宽19厘米，（D）长7.5厘米、宽11厘米；经向↕。

　　织锦残片为1/2S斜纹纬重组织。经线：偏红深褐色Z捻丝，夹经、明经3∶1交替。夹经约63根／厘米，明经约21根／厘米。纬线：无明显加捻，由红、蓝、乳白、绿等四色构成，并按此色序四纬一组循环往复。纬密为28副／厘米。无幅边存留。

　　其中有织锦片的边缘缀缝有四色（包括绿、淡绿和两种深浅不同的米色等四色）的平纹彩条，外加米色平纹组成的丝片做边饰。

　　织物残损严重，无法复原，但残片纹样清晰。红色为地，青、黄、绿色显花。花瓣作团窠环，花瓣之间伸出小折枝花。窠内对含绶鸟立于棕榈座上，但鸟的尾部较大，应为一对立凤，惜头部残损。尾部上方羽毛分开，尾部饰以鳞片状纹，较细密。宾花为十样花。

EIGHTH- TO NINTH-CENTURY JIN, RED GROUND, WITH ROUNDELS ENCLOSING BIRDS HOLDING RIBBONS IN THEIR BEAKS (DRXM26:S2, QK 002805)

Eight fragments: (A) height 12 cm, width 6.5 cm; (B) height 11 cm, width 11 cm; (C) height 9 cm, width 19 cm; (D) height 7.5 cm, width 11 cm; plus four smaller fragments, not illustrated (warp direction ↕).

Weft-faced compound 1/2 S twill with four lats.

Warp: 1 group of three main warp ends to 1 binding warp end; silk, Z-twisted, dark reddish brown; c. 21 groups of three main warp ends and 21 binding warp ends per cm.

Weft: silk, no noticeable twist, red, blue, cream, green; straight weft sequence; 28 passes per cm. No selvage preserved.

Several fragments have remnants of attached bands composed of four narrow strips of plain tabby (green, pale green, two shades of beige), followed by a wider strip of beige tabby.

This textile is in fragments and it is impossible to reconstruct the pattern entirely, although the patterning on the fragments itself is quite clear. It uses red as ground and patterning of dark blue, cream, and green. The roundel is composed of flower petals, among which protrude small flower buds; inside the roundels are birds with ribbons in their beaks standing on a split-palmette platform. Since the tails of the birds are relatively large, they should perhaps be considered a pair of standing phoenixes. Their heads are lost due to damage. The tails have spread feathers and the bodies are decorated with scale-shaped patterning that is finely done. The interstitial motif is a four-directional palmette.

黄地瓣窠对含绶鸟锦 （DRXM9:S2；QK002037） 8~9 世纪

由两片拼接在一起，总长 35 厘米、总宽 17 厘米。其中两片织锦的尺寸分别为长 19.5 厘米、宽 16.5 厘米，长 16.5 厘米、宽 17 厘米，经向↕。

1/2Z 斜纹纬重组织。经线：乳白色 S 捻丝，夹经、明经 2:1 交替。夹经为 44 根 / 厘米，明经约 22 根 / 厘米。纬线：无明显加捻，由黄、白、米、绿（和蓝交替）等四色显色组成，并按此序四纬一组循环。纬密约 23 副 / 厘米。幅边已失。

整块织锦以黄色为地，绿、白色显花，背部没有纬线浮织（无抛梭）。虽褪色严重，但纹样保存却较完整。以八瓣组成团窠花形，窠内径为 25 厘米，窠内为对含绶鸟立于棕榈基座上。鸟身饰以菱格形羽纹，尾部似排刷，上饰斜向条纹。宾花为十样花。

1 组织细节 Weave detail

EIGHTH- TO NINTH-CENTURY JIN, YELLOW GROUND, FLOWER-PETAL ROUNDEL ENCLOSING CONFRONTED BIRDS WITH RIBBONS IN THEIR BEAKS (DRXM9:S2; QK 002037)

Overall height 35 cm, width 17 cm; two fragments fitting together, fragment (A): height 19.5 cm, width 16.5 cm; fragment (B): height 16.5 cm, width 17 cm (warp direction ↕).

67

Weft-faced compound 1/2 Z twill with four lats.

Warp: 1 pair of main warp ends to 1 binding warp end; silk, S-twisted, beige; c. 22 pairs main warp ends and 22 binding warp ends per cm.

Weft: silk, no noticeable twist, yellow, white, beige, green (latté blue); straight weft sequence; c. 23 passes per cm.

No selvage preserved.

This textile employs yellow as ground and green, blue, and white as patterning. The backside does not exhibit weft floats. The piece is heavily faded, but the pattern is relatively well preserved. It uses eight petals to form a roundel; the inside diameter of the roundels can be reconstructed to approximately 25 cm. The roundel encloses confronted birds with ribbons in their beaks, standing on split-palmette platforms. The birds' bodies are decorated with diamond-shaped feather patterns, their tails are neatly aligned, with diagonal lines on them, the interstitial flower is a four-directional palmette.

黄地十字瓣窠对含绶鸟锦　（QK002024）　8~9世纪

　　这组六片织锦（从左至右、从上至下）尺寸分别为：（A）长10厘米，（B）长9.8厘米，（C）长17厘米，（D）长7厘米，（E）长7厘米，（F）长17厘米；宽皆为3.5厘米；经向↕。

　　1/2S斜纹纬重组织。经线：乳白色Z捻丝；夹经、明经3:1交替；夹经51~57根/厘米，明经17~19根/厘米。纬线：无明显加捻，由红（褪色至米色）、黄、深棕（与绿交替）三种显色区组成，并按此色序三纬一组循环。纬密46~48副/厘米。幅边已失。

　　这块织锦以深棕色为地，十字花瓣组成黄地团窠，中心为一对立鸟（或鸭子）站在棕榈基座上。团窠之间是大朵八瓣花饰。

　　图案单元经向约24厘米，纬向循环大于19厘米。团窠直径约19厘米。

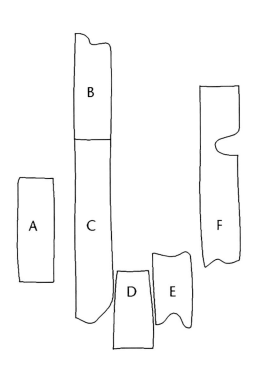

1 结构图 Numbering diagram

2 组织细节 Weave detail

EIGHTH- TO NINTH-CENTURY JIN, BROWN GROUND, PETALS WITH CROSS-SHAPES IN THEM FORMING ROUNDELS ENCLOSING CONFRONTED BIRDS

(QK 002024)

Six fragments (from left to right, top to bottom): Width 3.5 cm, height (A) 10 cm, (B) 9.8 cm, (C) 17 cm, (D) 7 cm, (E) 7 cm, (F) 17 cm (warp direction ↕).

Weft-faced compound 1/2 S twill with three lats.

Warp: 1 group of three main warp ends to 1 binding warp end; silk, Z-twisted, beige; c. 17–19 groups of three main warp ends and 17–19 binding warp ends per cm.

Weft: silk, no noticeable twist, red faded to beige, yellow, dark brown (latté green); straight weft sequence; c. 46–48 passes per cm.

No selvage preserved.

On a dark brown ground, the textile displays yellow roundels framed by petals with cross-shapes in them. Inside each roundel is a pair of confronted birds, perhaps ducks, their feet resting on a split palmette. The interstices are filled with a large eight-partite flower. The pattern unit is 24 cm in the warp direction and greater than 19 cm in the weft direction; the diameter of the roundel is approximately 19 cm.

红地中窠连珠对含绶鸟锦　(DRXM9:S20－1; QK 002762)　8~9 世纪

69

（A）与图版 No.70F 缝缀在一起，总长 8.1 厘米、总宽 19 厘米，图版中的这片锦长 8 厘米、宽 9.5 厘米；（B）长 9.7 厘米、宽 15.9 厘米。经向↕。

1/2S 斜纹纬重组织。经线：红褐色 Z 捻丝；夹经、明经 2:1 交替；夹经 48 ~ 54 根 / 厘米、明经 24 ~ 27 根 / 厘米。纬线：无明显加捻，由红、黄、蓝绿等三色构成，并按此序三纬一组循环。纬密 31 ~ 34 副 / 厘米。幅边已失。

这片织锦和图版 No.70F 缝缀在一起，以红色为地，蓝绿勾勒，黄、蓝、绿三色显花。团窠环中的连珠较小、较密，珠呈六边形。从残片看，亦为对鸟立于棕榈座上。圈外宾花为对称的十样花。但棕榈座的形式略有差异，一基座只有轮廓线，一基座中填以圆点纹。

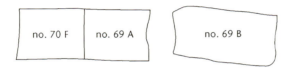

1　结构图　Numbering diagram

JIN TEXTILE WITH RED GROUND, ALIGNED-PEARL ROUNDEL ENCLOSING OPPOSING BIRDS WITH RIBBONS IN THEIR BEAKS (DRXM9:S20-1; QK 002762)

Two fragments: (A) height 8 cm, width 9.5 cm, overall dimensions, including cat. no. 70: height 8.1 cm, width 19 cm; (B) height 9.7 cm, width 15.9 cm (warp direction ↕)

Weft-faced compound 1/2 S twill with three lats.

Warp: 1 pair of main warp ends to 1 binding warp end; silk, Z-twisted, reddish brown; 24–27 pairs of main warp ends and 24–27 binding warp ends per cm.

Weft: silk, no noticeable twist, red, blue-green, yellow; 31–34 passes per cm.

No selvage preserved.

This textile is stitched to fragment (F) of cat. no. 70.

This textile uses red as ground, with blue-green outlining, and yellow and blue-green exhibiting the pattern. The linked pearls used to form the roundels are relatively small and dense, and form a hexagonal shape. From the fragment we can see that there is also a bird standing on a palmette platform; outside the roundel, flowers form an opposing cross-shaped pattern. The platforms are slightly different in that one has been designed only in outline whereas the other has a dot pattern inside.

红地中窠连珠对含绶鸟锦 (DRXM9:S20－2；QK002762) 8~9世纪

70

这组织锦由六片组成，尺寸分别为：（A）长 10.3 厘米、宽 6.6 厘米，（B）长 10.4 厘米、宽 17 厘米，（C）长 8.8 厘米、宽 14.9 厘米，（D）长 10.7 厘米、宽 9.4 厘米，（E）长 10.8 厘米、宽 4.1 厘米，经向↕；（F）在图版 No.69 的织锦上，总长 8.1 厘米、总宽 19 厘米，其中 No.70F 长 9.5 厘米、宽 8.1 厘米，经向↔。

1/2S 斜纹纬重组织。经线：红褐色 Z 捻丝；夹经、明经 2:1 交替；夹经 36 ~ 44 根 / 厘米，明经 18 ~ 22 根 / 厘米。纬线：无明显加捻，由红、黄、蓝绿等三色构成，并按此序三纬一组循环，纬密 28 ~ 34 副 / 厘米。幅边已失。

虽然此块织锦由残片组成，但其图案基本可以复原。该件连珠呈六边形，分大、小两种。连珠次序以藏青和红色相间排列。连珠圈内径为 19 厘米，外径为 21 厘米，纬向循环为 21.5 厘米。连珠圈为椭圆形，故窠内对鸟造型显得较长，鸟头已残，可见头后饰有绶带一根。鸟身羽毛用方块形装饰，尾作板刷状。织物色彩与图版 No.69 相似，亦为红色地，藏青勾勒，黄、绿两色显花。织锦背面无纬线浮织（抛梭现象）。宾花亦为椭圆形，中有藏蕾式十样花。

EIGHTH- TO NINTH-CENTURY JIN, RED GROUND, WITH ALIGNED-PEARL ROUNDELS ENCLOSING CONFRONTED BIRDS (DRXM9:S20-2; QK 002762)

Six fragments: (A) height 10.3 cm, width 6.6 cm, (B) height 10.4 cm, width 17 cm; (C) height 8.8 cm, width 14.9 cm, (D) height 10.7 cm, width 9.4 cm, (E) height 10.8 cm, width 4.1 cm (all warp direction ↕), (F) height 9.5 cm, width 8.1 cm, overall dimensions, including cat. no. 69: height 8.1 cm, width 19 cm (warp direction ↔).

Weft-faced compound 1/2 S twill with three lats.

Warp: 1 pair of main warp ends to 1 binding warp end; silk, Z-twisted, reddish brown; c. 18–22 pairs of main warp ends and 18–22 binding warp ends per cm.

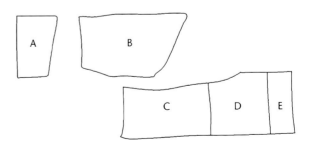

1 结构图 Numbering diagram

A.

Weft: silk, no noticeable twist, red, yellow, blue-green; straight weft sequence; c. 28–34 passes per cm.

No selvage preserved.

This textile is in fragments but the pattern can basically be reconstructed. The aligned pearls are unusual in having hexagonal shape and in being both large and small. The sequence of the pearls uses alternating blue-green and red colours. The inside diameter of the aligned-pearl roundel on this silk is 19 cm, the outer diameter is 21 cm. The pattern repeat is 21.5 cm in weft direction. The roundel itself is oblong, so that the depiction of the birds inside also seems slightly elongated. The bird's head has been damaged but one can see that behind the head there is a ribbon. The bird's feathers are ornamented in a square-shaped patterning, the tail reminds of a scrubbing brush. The colouring of the textile is similar to cat. no. 69, it shows red ground with blue-green as outline, and yellow and blue-green to exhibit the pattern. There are no weft floats on the reverse. The interstitial flower is also elongated, it has the shape of a quatrefoil with inscribed palmettes.

B.–E.
[photo: Angelika Sliwka, 2018]

红地大窠连珠对含绶鸟锦 (DRXM9:S22-1/2；QK002762)　8~9世纪

　　三片织锦（从左至右）尺寸分别为：（A）长22.5厘米、宽8.7厘米，（B）长11.5厘米、宽9厘米，（C）长29.5厘米、宽10.6厘米；经向↕。

　　1/2 S 斜纹纬重组织。经线：红褐色Z向加捻丝；夹经、明经3:1交替；夹经约75根/厘米，明经约25根/厘米。纬线：无明显加捻，由红、蓝、黄三色构成，并按此序三纬一组循环；纬密29~31副/厘米。幅边已失。其中最大一块织锦的一侧有宽约2.3厘米的无图案条带，应该是紧靠幅边的区域。最小一块织锦的背面则有局部纬丝浮织。

　　在最大织锦的短侧端缝缀有一段浅蓝色的无花纹平纹绢条，而另一较长侧端则有残留的紫色绫条。

　　这组织锦都是在深红色地上，以藏青、黄色显花。从拼对复原的图案看，这亦为连珠团窠对含绶鸟图案。观察残存宾花纹样，则是一种颇具卷草风格的大型棕榈树（生命树）纹样。据纹样高近26厘米推测，其团窠的直径起码应在30厘米以上。

EIGHTH- TO NINTH-CENTURY JIN WITH RED GROUND, LARGE ROUNDELS WITH PALMETTES AS INTERSTITIAL MOTIFS (DRXM9:S3; QK 002763)

Three fragments (from left to right): (A) height 22.5 cm, width 8.7 cm, (B) height 11.5 cm, width 9 cm, (C) height 29.5 cm, width 10.6 cm (warp direction ↕).

Weft-faced compound 1/2 S twill with three lats.

Warp: 1 group of three main warp ends to 1 binding warp end; silk, Z-twisted, reddish brown; c. 25 groups of three main warp ends and 25 binding warp ends per cm.

Weft: silk, no noticeable twist, red, blue, yellow; straight weft sequence; c. 29–31 passes per cm.

No selvage preserved, but on fragment (A) there is an unpatterned red vertical stripe, 2.3 cm wide, that immediately preceded the selvage.

Weft floats on the reverse of fragment (B).

Remnants of light blue unpatterned tabby are attached to the left side of fragment (C), and remnants of purple damask weave to its right side.

This textile is in three fragments; it employs a deep-red ground with deep blue and yellow to exhibit the pattern. From the pieced-together reconstruction of the pattern we can imagine that it probably showed roundels framed by aligned pearls enclosing, perhaps, a pair of confronted birds. From the fragmentary design of interstitial flower patterns we can see that it depicts a large palmette tree (Tree of Life) with curling leaves. By measuring the height of this pattern element, approaching 26 cm, we estimate that the diameter of the roundel was more than 30 cm.

红地大窠宝花连珠对含绶鸟锦　(DRXM9:S22-1/2; QK 002762)　8~9世纪

长 15.9 厘米、宽 9.7 厘米，经向 ↕。

织锦为 1/2S 斜纹纬重组织。经线：深红色 Z 向加捻丝。夹经、明经 3∶1 交替。夹经 57 根／厘米，明经 19 根／厘米。纬线：无明显加捻，有红、黄、蓝三色构成，并按此次序三纬一组循环；纬密29 ~ 35 副／厘米。幅边已失。织锦背面有纬丝浮织。

织锦附加的衬料边，有两种不同的平纹绢。其一，经、纬线同为米色无明显加捻丝，经密 60 根／厘米、纬密 40 ~ 44 根／厘米。其二，经、纬线同为米色无加捻丝，经密 54 根／厘米，纬密 34 根／厘米。

织锦以深红为地，以蓝和黄色显花，主要图案团窠内部已基本残缺，仅见棕榈叶座局部和鸟足，可以推测是对含绶鸟题材。该型团窠环外圈是蓝、红两色相间的连珠环，内圈是蓝地红色的八瓣宝花，故称之为复合团窠。其团窠环极大。

JIN WITH RED GROUND, LARGE ROUNDEL WITH PRECIOUS-FLOWER ALIGNED-PEARL ROUNDEL ENCLOSING OPPOSING BIRDS (DRXM9:S22-1/2; QK 002762)

Height 15.9 cm, width 9.7 cm (warp direction ↕).

Weft-faced compound 1/2 S twill with three lats.

Warp: 1 group of three main warp ends to 1 binding warp end; silk, Z-twisted, dark red; c. 19 groups of three main warp ends and 19 binding warp ends per cm.

Weft: silk, no noticeable twist, red, yellow, blue; 29–35 passes per cm.

No selvage preserved.

Weft floats on the reverse.

Attached lining: Two kinds of plain tabby. (1) Warp and weft: silk, no noticeable twist, beige; c. 60 warp ends and 40–44 weft picks per cm. (2) Warp and weft: silk, no noticeable twist, beige; c. 54 warp ends and c. 34 weft picks per cm.

This textile employs a deep red ground, with blue-green and yellow colours exhibiting the pattern. The main portion of the inside of the roundel has been lost and only the feet of the bird and a portion of a split-palmette-leaf platform can be seen, but it can be deduced that this is again a bird-with-ribbon-in-the-beak motif. The medallion frame is composed of two concentric circles, the outer one containing aligned pearls of alternating red and green colours; the inner one with red eight-petal precious flowers on green ground. This is called a composite roundel, and it can be deduced that the roundel was extremely large.

红地连珠边饰条纹锦　(DRXM9:S24；QK002770)　8~9 世纪

长 7.5 厘米、宽 18 厘米，经向↕。

1/2S 斜纹纬重组织。经线：深褐色 Z 捻丝；夹经、明经 3:1 交替；夹经约为 57 根 / 厘米，明经约 19 根 / 厘米。纬线：无明显加捻，由红、黄、绿、蓝（与棕色交替）等四色构成，并按此序两纬或四纬一组循环；纬密约 54 副 / 厘米。幅边已失。

这条横向边饰彩锦和其他几块对含绶鸟织锦同出于都兰墓葬 9 号墓（参见图版 No.70、71），极有可能同属于同类相似织物。此条织锦以红、黄两色斜纹纬重组织为地，以青、绿、黄三色显花构成织锦的彩条边饰，饰条中间为串连在一起的钺形图案，图案与纬线平行。饰条边缘为青、黄两色纬重组织，排列黄色的连珠。

EIGHTH-TO NINTH-CENTURY JIN, RED GROUND WITH DECORATIVE HORIZONTAL BORDER (DRXM9:S24; QK 002770)

Height 7.5 cm, width 18 cm (warp direction ↕).

Weft-faced compound 1/2 S twill with two to four lats.

Warp: 1 group of three main warp ends to 1 binding warp end; silk, Z-twisted, dark brown; c. 19 groups of three main warp ends and 19 binding warp ends per cm.

Weft: silk, no noticeable twist, red, yellow, green (interrupted), blue (latté brown, interrupted); c. 54 passes per cm.

No selvage preserved.

This fragment of an ornamental border was excavated from the same tomb, M9, as some fragments of the pattern with confronted birds (see, for example, cat. nos. 70 and 71). It is possible that the fragment with horizontal border was originally part of a similar textile. It employs red as ground and blue, green, and yellow for figuring. The pattern runs parallel to the weft, so in the ground areas this is a weft-faced compound weave with two lats only. Inside the central strip are floral pattern elements of tripartite leaves linked together. On both sides of the central strip run lines of green and yellow, bordering a string of yellow pearls.

黄地小花团窠对含绶鸟锦　(DRXM1:S165；QK002792)　8~9世纪

长8厘米、宽32.8厘米，经向↕。

1/2Z 斜纹纬重组织。经线：肉粉色Z捻丝，夹经、明经1:1交替，夹经14～15根／厘米，明经14～15根／厘米。纬线：无明显加捻，由黄、蓝、绿、米四色构成，并按此序四纬一组循环；纬密约25副／厘米。幅边已失。

此件织锦褪色严重，现在看到的锦以黄绿色为地，蓝色勾边及起小花。团窠环中以草绿色为地，以连续的八瓣小团花构成团窠环。纹样已经残缺，仅残存对鸟的四足，分别立于两个饰以连珠的台座上。团窠纬向循环约35厘米，与团窠环外径相差不太大。织物背面未见抛梭现象。

1 组织图 Weave detail

EIGHTH-TO NINTH-CENTURY JIN, YELLOW-GREENISH GROUND, SMALL-FLOWER
ROUNDEL ENCLOSING CONFRONTED BIRDS (DRXM1:S165; QK 002792)

Height 8 cm, width 32.8 cm (warp direction ↕).

Weft-faced compound 1/2 Z twill with four lats.

Warp: 1 main warp end to 1 binding warp end; silk, Z-twisted, salmon-pink; 14–15 main warp ends and 14–15 binding warp ends per cm.

Weft: silk, no noticeable twist, yellow-greenish, green, blue, beige; straight weft sequence; c. 25 passes per cm.

No selvage preserved.

This piece is badly faded. Today, the textile employs a yellow-greenish ground, with blue for outlines and for some of the small flowers. The medallion frame itself has a grass-green ground, laid with aligned eight-petal flowers. The central pattern has gone and all that remains are the four claws on the feet of the confronted birds. These stand atop two separate aligned-pearl platforms. The pattern repeat is about 35 cm in weft direction, not much larger than the outside diameter of the roundel. There are no weft floats on the reverse of this fragment.

三组（A、B、C）红地瓣窠含绶鸟锦 8~9世纪

A.（DRXM1PM2:S160-1；QK001859）这组织锦包括七块残片，其尺寸分别为（1）长17.3厘米、宽17厘米；（2）长15.7厘米、宽10.8厘米；（3）长13厘米、宽5厘米；（4）长5.5厘米、宽45厘米；（5）长11.3厘米、宽12.5厘米；（6）长13.5厘米、宽10.5厘米；（7）长10厘米、宽16厘米。经向↕。

B.（QK002870）这组有八块残片，其尺寸（从左至右）分别为（1）长7.3厘米、宽13.7厘米；（2）长15.2厘米、宽7厘米；（3）长9.5厘米、宽5厘米；（4）长17厘米、宽2.5厘米；（5）长12.9厘米、宽2.5厘米；（6）长18.3厘米、宽5.7厘米。六块残片的经向↕；而残片（7）和(8)则经向↔。（7）长18厘米、宽4.5厘米；（8）长18.8厘米、宽4.5厘米。

C.（DRXM1:S215；QK002867）这块织锦由三片缝在一起，有可能是一块衣料边。包括缝在一起的平纹面料其总长为11.5厘米、总宽33厘米。经向↕。每块织锦的尺寸分别为（1）长4.5厘米、宽12.5厘米；（2）长5.4厘米、宽30.5厘米；（3）长12厘米、宽4.8厘米（其经向转了90度）。

A. 1/2S斜纹经重组织。经线：红棕色Z向捻丝，夹经、明经2:1交替。夹经46~48根/厘米，明经23~24根/厘米。纬线：无明显加捻，由红、白、黄、绿、蓝等五色显花，并以此色序五纬一组循环。纬密24~26副/厘米。无幅边存留。但是在残片（1）和（5）有一段无图案竖条红带，应该是幅边的裁边。织锦的背面有纬线浮织组织（抛梭现象）。残片（1）的顶部残留有一小片米色平纹绢。残片（6）右边缘有很细致的锁边。

B. 1/2S斜纹经重组织。经线：红棕色Z向捻丝，交经、明经2:1交替。交经46~48根/厘米，明经23~24根/厘米。纬线：无明显加捻，由红、白、黄、绿、蓝等五色显花，并以此色序五纬一组循环。纬密24~26副/厘米。无幅边存留。背面有纬线浮织组织。

C.面料为1/2S斜纹经重组织，经线：深红棕色Z向捻丝，交经、明经2:1交替，交经44根/厘米，明经22根/厘米。纬线：无明显加捻，由红、白、黄、绿、蓝等五色显花，并以此色序五纬一组循环。纬密25~26副/厘米。幅边已失。背面有纬线浮织组织。

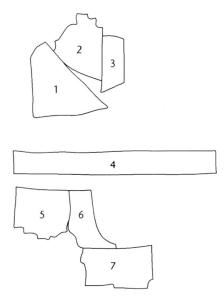

1 结构图（A.） Numbering diagram（A.）

THREE (A, B, C) EIGHTH- TO NINTH-CENTURY JIN SILKS, WITH RED GROUND, PETAL ROUNDEL ENCLOSING BIRDS WITH RIBBONS IN THEIR BEAKS

A. (DRXM1PM2:S160-1; QK 001859) Seven fragments of irregular shape: (1) height 17.3 cm, width 17 cm; (2) height 15.7 cm, width 10.8 cm; (3) height 13 cm, width 5 cm; (4) height 5.5 cm, width 45 cm; (5) height 11.3 cm, width 12.5 cm; (6) height 13.5 cm, width 10.5 cm; (7) height 10 cm, width 16 cm (warp direction ↕).

B. (QK 002870) Eight fragments of irregular shape, from left to right: (1) height 7.3 cm, width 13.7 cm; (2) height 15.2 cm, width 7 cm; (3) height 9.5 cm, width 5 cm; (4) height 17 cm, width 2.5 cm; (5) height 12.9 cm, width 2.5 cm; (6) height 18.3 cm, width 5.7 cm (all warp direction ↕); with pattern variation: (7) height 18 cm, width 4.5 cm; (8) height 18.8 cm, width 4.5 cm (both warp direction ↔).

C. (M1:S215; QK 002867) Three fragments stitched together, perhaps an edging of a garment; overall height 11.5 cm; overall width 33 cm (warp direction ↕ ; double layer, including attached tabby). Single fragments: (1) height 4.5 cm, width 12.5 cm; (2) height 5.4 cm, width 30.5 cm; (3) height 12 cm, width 4.8 cm (with warp direction turned by 90 degrees).

A. Weft-faced compound 1/2 S twill with five lats.

Warp: 1 pair of main warp ends to 1 binding warp end; silk, Z-twisted, reddish brown; c. 23–24 pairs of main warp ends and 23–24 binding warp ends per cm.

Weft: silk, no noticeable twist, red, white, yellow, green, blue; straight weft sequence; c. 24–26 passes per cm.

No selvage preserved, but on fragments (1) and (5) there is a broad, unpatterned red vertical stripe that immediately preceded the selvage.

Weft floats on the reverse.

A small piece of beige unpatterned tabby is attached to the upper edge of fragment (1), and fragment (6) is neatly hemmed along its right edge.

A.

273

75

A.

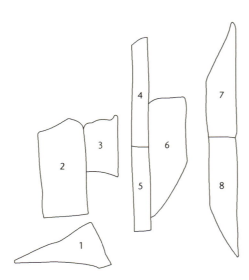

2 结构图（B.） Numbering diagram (B.)

B. Weft-faced compound 1/2 S twill with five lats.

Warp: 1 pair of main warp ends to 1 binding warp end; silk, Z-twisted, reddish brown; 23–24 pairs of main warp ends and 23–24 binding warp ends per cm.

Weft: silk, no noticeable twist, red, white, yellow, green, blue; straight weft sequence; 24–26 passes per cm.

No selvage preserved.

Weft floats on the reverse.

B.

75

C.

3 背面（C.） Back side (C.)

与其缝在一起的米色平纹面料，经、纬线都无明显加捻。经密约 60 根／厘米，纬密 34～36 根／厘米。一侧存留有幅边。

根据十余件残片可以复原得同一图案。复原之后的图案中心是一个椭圆形的团窠。团窠外环以八片花瓣纹构成，中间立一鸟。该鸟鸟身有鳞甲片状的羽纹，尾部呈板刷状，翅和尾用横条或斜条表示，翅带弯钩向上翘起，颈部饰以项圈状物，上饰连珠。翅与尾部均饰有竖向连珠的条带，两足立于平台座上。平台正面饰以横向连珠。该鸟头后生出两条平行、带结的飘带，鸟嘴衔有项链状物，其上布满连珠，下方垂有三串璎珞。宾花为对称的十样花，花中心为八瓣小团花，四周方形花，四向伸出花蕾。复原后的纹样循环约为经向 17 厘米、纬向 13 厘米（如 A）。用深红色为地，其上用藏青、灰绿、黄三色显花，配色和用色都非常讲究，晕色处按青、绿、红、黄诸色依次排列。

C. Weft-faced compound 1/2 S twill with five lats.

Warp: 1 pair of main warp ends to 1 binding warp end; silk, Z-twisted, dark reddish brown; 22 pairs of main warp ends and 22 binding warp ends per cm.

Weft: silk, no noticeable twist, red, white, yellow, green, blue; straight weft sequence; 25–26 passes per cm.

No selvage preserved.

Weft floats on the reverse.

Attached lining (?) : Tabby. Warp and weft: silk, no noticeable twist, beige; c. 60 warp ends and 34–36 weft picks per cm.

Selvage preserved on one side.

The complete pattern of these silks can be reconstructed from all these fragments. After reconstruction, the main element of the design appears to be an oval-shaped roundel. The roundel is surrounded by a frame of eight flower petals; inside the roundel stands a bird with scale-patterned feathers in some parts, and scrubbing brush-type tail. Wings and tail are decorated by using vertical bands of aligned pearls. The two feet of the bird stand on a level platform, the front of which shows a horizontal band of aligned pearls. Behind the head of the bird protrude two floating ribbons, which are knotted. In its beak, the bird holds a necklace-like object, which is packed with pearls and from which three pearl pendants hang down. Four-directional palmette flowers serve as interstitial ornament. The size of the reconstructed roundel inside the petal frame is around 17 cm in warp direction and 13 cm in weft direction (silk A). It employs a dark-red ground, on which dark blue, grey-green, beige, and yellow form the figure. The colour arrangement is exquisite, with the shading usually following the sequence blue, green, red, and yellow.

红地瓣窠含绶鸟锦 （DRXM1PM2:S167-2；QK002868） 8~9世纪

A. 长 3 厘米（其中绣片处约高 4.5 厘米）、宽 80 厘米，由四块斜裁面料花纹经向拼对缝制在一起。B. 长 4.4 厘米、宽 62 厘米，由四块面料斜裁对拼缝在一起。C. 长 4 厘米、宽 63 厘米，由三块面料斜裁对拼缝在一起。D. 长 4 厘米、宽 34.6 厘米。E. 长 3 厘米、宽 30.5 厘米。D、E. 同为经向↔。F. 长 4.3 厘米、宽 31.8 厘米，由两片缝制而成，经向↕。

这组面料为 1/2S 斜纹经重组织。经线：深红色 Z 向捻丝，夹经、明经 2:1 交替，夹经 50 ～ 60 根／厘米，明经 25 ～ 30 根／厘米。纬线：无明显加捻，由红、白、黄、绿、蓝五色构成，并以此色序五纬一组循环显花。纬密约 28 副／厘米。无幅边存留。

在 A 一处和 C 的两处靠近幅边的地方分别有大约 2 厘米宽的红色无花纹竖条。在 D 和 E 则织有横向无花纹的侧边。面料背面都有纬线浮织组织（局部抛梭现象）。

在 A 条带一侧残留带有刺绣的一小块绢。其经线为米色无明显加捻丝，密度约 60 根／厘米。纬线同为米色无明显加捻丝，密度约 30 根／厘米。覆盖其上的刺绣是由米、绿、深蓝和橘褐色的 S 双捻丝用劈针法绣制的。

这六条锦带长短不一，至少是从四块非常类似的织物上裁剪下来的。其面料有着相近的组织结构以及类似的花色设计搭配。花纹图案中的团窠都是呈椭圆或圆形，圈中仅有一只鸟。在 C 条带中团窠中的鸟嘴衔有项链状物。其上布满连珠。下方垂有三串璎珞。宾花为对称的十样花，花中心为八瓣小团花，四周方形花，四向伸出花蕾。整个团窠外亦环以八片花瓣，深红色为地。其上用藏青、灰绿、黄三色显花，配色和用色都非常讲究。

EIGHTH- TO NINTH-CENTURY JIN, RED GROUND, PETAL ROUNDEL ENCLOSING BIRDS WITH RIBBONS IN THEIR BEAKS (DRXM1PM2:S167-2; QK 002868)

From top to bottom: A. Height 3 cm, height including attached fragment of embroidery 4.5 cm, width 80 cm (stitched together from four parts, all bias-cut). B. Height 4.4 cm, width 62 cm (stitched together from three parts, all bias-cut). C. Height 4 cm, width 63 cm (stitched together from three parts, all bias-cut). D. and E. Height 4 cm, width 34.6 cm; height 3 cm, width 30.5 cm (both warp direction ↔). F. Height 4.3 cm, width 31.8 cm (stitched together from two parts; warp direction ↕).

Weft-faced compound 1/2 S twill with five lats.

Warp: 1 pair of main warp ends to 1 binding warp end; silk, Z-twisted, dark reddish brown; c. 25–30 pairs of main warp ends and 25–30 binding warp ends per cm.

Weft: silk, no noticeable twist, red, white, yellow, green blue; straight weft sequence; c. 28 passes per cm.

No selvage preserved, but on one part of band (A) and on two parts of band (C) there are unpatterned red vertical stripes, c. 2 cm wide, that immediately preceded the selvage. Unpatterned horizontal finishing border on bands (D) and (E).

Weft floats on the reverse of all bands.

A small remnant of split-stitch embroidery on tabby ground is attached to band (A). Warp: silk, no noticeable twist, cream; c. 60 ends per cm. Weft: silk, no noticeable twist, cream; c. 30 picks per cm.

Split stitch embroidery covering the whole surface. Silk, S-plied from 2 Z-twisted ends, cream, green, dark blue, orange-brown.

1 组织细节（A.、B.） Weave detail (A., B.)

279

76

Six bands of varying length, cut from at least four very similar fabrics, with close to identical weave structures, colours and patterns. The roundels are either oval-shaped or round-shaped and they enclose one bird each. The bird on band (C) holds a necklace-shaped object in its beak, on which are many linked pearls. Three jewel pendants hang down from it. The interstitial flowers are four-directional palmettes, at the center of which is an eight-petal small flower within a square shape from which four flower buds protrude. The bird roundel itself is framed by eight large flower petals. The harmonizing of colours is beautifully done with red ground and dark blue, grey-green, and yellow to form the pattern.

2 正面和背面的刺绣细节　Embroidery detail, front and back side
[photo: Yao Qingfang 姚青芳，Ma Yanru 马燕如，2004]

红地瓣窠对含绶鸟锦 （DRXM1PM2:S163；QK001859H） 8~9世纪

长4.7厘米、宽49厘米，由斜裁过的面料花纹经向拼对缝在一起。

1/2S斜纹经重组织。经线：深棕色Z向捻丝。夹经、明经2:1交替。夹经约44根／厘米，明经约22根／厘米。纬线：无明显捻丝。由红、白、黄、绿、蓝四色构成，并按此色序五纬一组循环显色。纬密约25副／厘米。无幅边存留。背面有纬线浮织组织（抛梭现象）。

这块残存的斜裁长条织锦色彩相当鲜艳。以大红为地，显藏青、黄、米白、灰绿色纹样。从残片纹样看，图案团窠颇大，团窠外亦环以花瓣。窠内一对大鸟，两两相对，共同衔着一连珠绶带。鸟的造型与前件基本相同，但也自具特点，不同之处在于鸟身羽毛以方块形来表现。鸟足以下均残，但据同类织锦图案推断，鸟亦应站立于连珠平台状座上。窠外宾花已残，推测其纹样亦同图版No.75。

1 组织细节 Weave detail

EIGHTH- TO NINTH-CENTURY JIN, RED GROUND, WITH PETAL ROUNDEL ENCLOSING CONFRONTED BIRDS WITH RIBBONS IN THEIR BEAKS

(DRXM1PM2:S163; QK 001859 H)

Height 4.7 cm, width 49 cm (bias cut; pattern depicted in line with the warp direction).

77

Weft-faced compound 1/2 S twill with five lats.

Warp: 1 pair of main warp ends to 1 binding warp end; silk, Z-twisted, dark brown; c. 22 pairs of main warp ends and 22 binding warp ends per cm.

Weft: silk, no noticeable twist, red, white, yellow, green, blue; straight weft sequence; c. 25 passes per cm.

No selvage preserved.

Weft floats on the reverse.

This remnant is a diagonally cut long strip. It uses relatively bright colours, with bright red as ground, and the pattern is shown in dark blue, yellow, whitish beige, and grey-green. Judging from the pattern of the remaining fragment, the design of the roundel was quite large. A frame of flower petals surrounded the roundel. Inside the roundel is a pair of large birds, facing each other and jointly holding an aligned-pearl ribbon in their beaks. The depiction of the birds is basically the same as above (cat. no. 75), but certain features are different. These birds have square-shaped feathers on their bodies; everything below the feet is lost, but judging from patterns of similar textiles, the birds should also be standing on an aligned-pearl platform. Interstitial flowers outside the roundel are lost, but we guess that the pattern again was the same as on cat. no. 75.

红地波斯文字锦　(DRXM1PM2:S161；QK001858)　8 世纪

长 4.1 厘米、宽 30 厘米，经向 $\updownarrow$。

1/2S 斜纹经重组织。经线：夹经、明经 2:1 交替，红色 Z 捻丝。夹经约 38 根／厘米，明经 19 根／厘米。纬线：无明显加捻，由红、黄、蓝、绿（与蓝交替）四色构成，并以此色序四纬一组在条锦花纹区循环显花。在条锦的文字区，则以红、黄双色两纬一组反向循环。纬密约为 28 副／厘米。无幅边存留。

需要特别提出的是这条文字锦与前述的几块对含绶鸟连珠花窠织锦（参见 No.75、76、77）为同一墓葬出土。经过慎重对比和研究判断，这条文字锦很可能是上述这些织锦的纬锦装饰裁边。

这条纬锦缝合为套状条带。其中条带无字一面以红色为地，以藏青、灰绿、黄三色显花，中心为一行连续桃形图案。其排列与纬线平行，图案边缘排列黄色小连珠，并以青黄双色彩条加边饰。条带的背面则是在红地上织有两行文字。经林梅村转请德国哥廷根大学东方语言学专家马坎基（David Neil MacKenzie）研究鉴定，确认这两行文字是波斯萨珊王朝所使用的婆罗钵文字。拉丁字母转写如下：

第一行：　　　MLK'nMLK'　　=ŠáhánŠáh　　　　"王中之王"
第二行：　　　LBAGOH　　　=Wuzurg xwarrah　　"伟大的，光荣的"

婆罗钵（或译排勒维）文字，其字母由阿拉美亚字母稍加变化而成，用以拼写中古波斯的婆罗钵文。文字由右而左横写，与欧洲希腊罗马系统的文字由左而右者相反。阿拉美亚字母是由腓尼基字母演化而来，是后来各国母系字母（包括景教徒所使用的叙利亚文的祖型）。安息王朝时的银币上，常见婆罗钵文字和希腊文字并列。萨珊朝时伊朗民族复兴，银币上的铭文便废除了希腊文字，专用本国文字。

1　"王中之王"铭文
　　The wording of King of Kings

正面和背面　Front side（top）and back side with inscription (bottom)

EIGHTH- TO NINTH-CENTURY JIN WITH PERSIAN LETTERING, ON RED GROUND (DRXM1PM2:S161; QK 001858)

Height. 4.1 cm, width. 30 cm (warp direction ↕).

Weft-faced compound 1/2 S twill with two to four lats.

Warp: 1 pair of main warp ends to 1 binding warp end; silk, Z-twisted, red; c. 19 pairs of main warp ends and 19 binding warp ends per cm.

Weft: silk, no noticeable twist, red, yellow, blue (interrupted), green (interrupted); weft sequence straight in pattern section, reversed in inscription section; c. 28 passes per cm.

No selvage preserved.

Special mention must be made of this piece, which was excavated from the same tomb as cat. nos. 75, 76, and 77, all three being silks with birds holding ribbons in their beaks, of the type with aligned-pearl pedestals. After careful study and comparison, we believe that this horizontal border was probably cut from one such fabric, a weft-faced compound twill, lengthwise sewn together to form a strong band. It employs a red ground with dark blue, grey-green, and yellow to form the pattern. In the center is a line of continuous tripartite leaf-shaped motifs that runs parallel to the weft threads. The unpatterned areas are woven in weft-faced compound twill with two lats only. The pattern is confined by strings of yellow-coloured pearls bordered by lines of green and yellow. A section of lettering, composed of two lines, is woven into the red ground. These two lines of woven script have been researched by Lin Meicun, Chinese Cultural Relics Research Institute, who in turn asked David Neil MacKenzie (d. 2001), Chair emeritus of Oriental Philology at the University of Göttingen (Germany), to evaluate the piece. According to Professor MacKenzie's determination, the lettering is the Pahlavi script, used by the Sasanian Dynasty of Persia. Part of the inscription can be transliterated as follows:

First line: MLK'n MLK' = Šáhánšáh (King of Kings)

Second line: LBAGOH = Wuzurg xwarrah (The Great, the Glorious)

The Persian Pahlavi script is formed from a modified Aramaic alphabet that was used to write the middle and ancient Persian Pahlavi language. The script is written horizontally from right to left, the opposite of Greek and Roman systems in Europe. The Aramaic alphabet evolved from Phoenician; it is the mother of such later scripts as Syriac, used by Nestorian devotees. Coins at the time of the Parthian Kingdom often have both Pahlavi characters as well as Greek lettering. When the Iranian people arose again at the time of the Sasanian dynasty, they did away with Greek inscriptions on their coins and used only this kind of native script.

红地方格条纹锦　(DRXM1:S162；QK002791)　8~9世纪

长6厘米、宽24厘米，经向↕。

1/2S斜纹经重组织，夹经、明经3:1交替。经线：Z向捻丝，夹经为肉粉色，明经为米色，夹经66~75根／厘米，明经22~25根／厘米。纬线：无明显加捻，以红、奶白、蓝、绿等四色构成，并以此色序四纬一组或是二纬一组循环，其中蓝绿色区分别间隔显色。纬密27~29副／厘米。无幅边存留。条纹锦一端留有一段无图案彩条，很可能是织锦幅边区。

织锦上下长边分别用两条五色平纹绢连缀作边饰，上端条绢色序从内到外为棕、红及双色调米、绿；下端绢条色序从内到外为绿、黄、米、红、棕。整块条纹锦的主要图案为菱格纹，上下两侧饰有彩条纹和连珠纹。

此块织锦的图案花纹与图版No.73、78相近，很可能是原织锦两端的装饰裁边。

EIGHTH-TO NINTH-CENTURY JIN, RED GROUND, WITH HORIZONTAL

BORDER (DRXM1:S162; QK 002791)

Height 6 cm, width 24 cm (warp direction $\updownarrow$).

Weft-faced compound 1/2 S twill with two to four lats.

Warp: 1 group of three main warp ends to 1 binding warp end; silk, Z-twisted, main warp salmon-pink, binding warp beige; 22–25 groups of three main warp ends and 22–25 binding warp ends per cm.

Weft: silk, no noticeable twist, red, cream, blue (interrupted), green (interrupted); straight weft sequence; 27–29 passes per cm.

No selvage preserved, but on the left side the pattern ends in simple colour bands, probably immediately preceding the selvage.

Bands composed of five narrow strips of plain tabby (from inside to outside, top: brown, red, beige, beige, green, bottom: green, yellow, beige, red, brown) are attached to the long sides.

The main pattern is a lozenge or diamond pattern, bordered on both sides by a coloured-stripe and aligned-pearl pattern. Similarly to cat. nos. 73 and 78 this horizontal border probably originally marked the end of a loompiece.

红地中窠连珠对含绶鸟锦 (QK002871) 8~9世纪

织锦类似袖形裁剪，长39厘米、肩部宽24厘米、袖口宽17厘米，经向↕。

1/2斜纹纬重组织，夹经、明经2:1交替。经线：偏红深棕色Z捻丝，夹经44根／厘米，明经22根／厘米。纬线：无明显加捻，红、黄、蓝三色构成，并以此序四纬一组循环。纬密24～25副／厘米。无幅边存留。

这块袖形织锦一侧宽，一侧窄，应是从同一织锦上裁剪下来的。纹样大半可辨。图案以连珠构成团窠，窠中为对鸟形象。鸟腹饰连珠，鸟尾向上翘起，鸟腿直立于棕榈座上。鸟头后无飘带。宾花位于四个连珠圈外，为对称的十样花，中心为八瓣团花，外系方形框，然后四向伸出七瓣花蕾。

织锦以深红色为地，其上用藏青、灰绿、黄等色显花，配色、用色均十分讲究。

1 背面 Back side

EIGHTH- TO NINTH-CENTURY JIN, RED GROUND WITH ALIGNED-PEARL ROUNDEL ENCLOSING CONFRONTED BIRDS (QK 002871)

Sleeve(?); length 39 cm, width at shoulder 24 cm, width at wrist 17 cm (warp direction ↕).

Weft-faced compound 1/2 S twill with three lats.

Warp: 1 pair of main warp ends to 1 binding warp end; silk, Z-twisted, dark reddish brown; c. 22 pairs of main warp ends and 22 binding warp ends per cm.

Weft: silk, no noticeable twist, red, yellow, blue; straight weft sequence; 24–25 passes per cm. No selvage preserved.

The sleeve-like shape is sewn from one rectangular piece with one large and one small inserted gore, all cut from the same fabric. Most of the pattern can be discerned from this fragment. The roundel, composed of aligned pearls, encloses a pair of birds. Their tails are uplifted, their feet stand straight on a split-palmette platform; there is no floating ribbon behind their heads. Interstitial flowers are placed outside the four aligned-pearl roundels. These are quite elaborate, with eight-petal flowers within a square-shaped box from which flower buds with seven petals are shooting out in four directions. The piece employs a deep red as ground, on which green-blue, grey-green, and yellow exhibit the pattern. The use and harmonizing of colours has been carefully considered.

2 组织细节　Weave detail

3　组织细节　Weave detail

4　组织细节　Weave detail

红地八方窠对含绶鸟锦 (QK002871) 8~9世纪

长 28 厘米、宽 39 厘米，经向 $\updownarrow$。

经线：1/2S 平纹纬重组织，交经、明经 3 : 1 交替，红褐色 Z 捻丝，交经 57 ～ 63 根／厘米，明经 19 ～ 21 根／厘米。纬线：无明显加捻，由红、黄、蓝、绿四色组成，并以此序四纬一组循环。纬密约 36 副／厘米。无幅边存留。

整块织物由一块三角形补丁将两片的织锦拼接在一起。三角形补丁是由四块不同的斜纹纬重织锦裁剪拼缝在一起的。其中一块是蓝地有连珠团窠纹饰，另一块是红地有连珠团窠和弯月小连珠环的纹饰。

其中两片大织物上的图案基本清晰可辨。图案中心是一个呈八方形的团窠，团窠环用方形连珠和连续桃形纹连接而成。转折处用四朵小花组成的宝花作组。窠中为对鸟。鸟腹部饰以连珠，鸟尾向上翘起，鸟头上方各有四瓣团花一朵，鸟腿以下残。另一块同样织锦残片（QKL147–4，无图）则显示这些鸟是站在棕榈座上的。鸟头后无飘带。宾花位于菱形窠内，为对称的十样花，由中心四向伸出花蕾。以深红色为地，其上用藏青、灰绿、黄等色勾勒和显花，配色和用色都非常讲究。

81

EIGHTH- TO NINTH-CENTURY JIN, RED GROUND, OCTAGONAL FRAME ENCLOSING CONFRONTED BIRDS (QK 002871)

Height 28 cm, width 39 cm (warp direction $\updownarrow$).

Weft-faced compound 1/2 S twill with four lats.

Warp: 1 group of three main warp ends to 1 binding warp end; silk, Z-twisted, reddish brown; c. 19–21 groups of three main warp ends and 19–21 binding warp ends per cm.

Weft: silk, no noticeable twist, red, yellow, blue, green; straight weft sequence; c. 36 passes per cm.

No selvage preserved.

The fragment is composed of two large pieces, with an inserted gore patched together from four pieces. They are cut from other weft-faced compound twills, amongst which one has blue ground and a roundel of aligned pearls, and another one has red ground, a roundel of aligned pearls, and a small roundel with crescent.

[contd.]

Although this is a patched fragment, the pattern is clear and can basically be reconstructed. The main element of the design is an octagonal frame, formed by square aligned pearls and tripartite leaves. At the corners, four-petal small flowers are used as knobs. The frame encloses a confronted pair of birds. Their breasts are decorated with aligned pearls, their tails are uplifted, and above their heads is a four-petal flower. Their legs no longer remain, but another fragment of the same textile (QKL 147-4, not illustrated) shows that they were standing on a large split-palmette platform. There are no floating ribbons behind the birds' heads. The interstices have lozenge- or diamond-shape, they enclose four-directional flowers with buds extending in all directions from the center. The ground is deep red, with green-blue, grey-green, and yellow to show the pattern. The use and harmonizing of colours has been carefully considered.

1 组织细节　Weave detail

一组四片（A、B、C、D）红地大窠连珠对含绶鸟锦

（DXDM11:S2；QK002869）　8~9 世纪

82

A.长 18 厘米、宽 9.8 厘米，经向 ↕。

B.由两块不同的锦拼接而成，分别长 15.5 厘米、宽 15.3 厘米，长 16 厘米、宽 11 厘米，经向 ↕。

C.长 7 厘米、宽 17 厘米，经向 ↕。

D.长 14 厘米、宽 9.5 厘米，经向 ↕。

A.织锦为 1/2S 斜纹纬重组织，交经、明经 2:1 交替。经线：深红棕色 Z 捻丝，交经 34 ~ 36 根／厘米，明经 17 ~ 18 根／厘米。纬线：无明显加捻，由红、绿黄、蓝三色按此序三纬一组循环，纬密约 27 ~ 29 副／厘米。无幅边存留。

B.织锦为 1/2S 斜纹纬重组织，交经、明经 2:1 交替。经线：深棕色 Z 捻丝，交经 40 ~ 42 根／厘米，明经 20 ~ 21 根／厘米。纬线：无明显加捻，由红、黄、深蓝（与绿色交替显色）四色按此序三纬一组循环，纬密 26 ~ 44 副／厘米。无幅边存留。其中一块织锦的一侧织有无图案条带，应该是紧靠幅边的区域。

C.织锦为 1/2S 斜纹纬重组织，交经、明经 2:1 交替。经线：棕色 Z 捻丝，交经 34 ~ 36 根／厘米，明经 17 ~ 18 根／厘米。纬线：无明显加捻，由红（褪至米色）、黄、蓝、绿四色按此序四纬一组循环，纬密 28 ~ 29 副／厘米。无幅边存留。但织物上侧一端存留一条素色织条。

D.织锦为 1/2S 斜纹纬重组织，交经、明经 2:1 交替。经线：深红棕色 Z 捻丝，交经 56 根／厘米，明经约 28 根／厘米。纬线：无明显加捻，由红、黄、绿、蓝四色按此序四纬一组循环，纬密约 32 副／厘米，无幅边存留。其中一块织锦的一侧织有无图案条带，应该是紧靠幅边的区域。

该锦地为红色，花为绿色和蓝色，图案为对含绶鸟。鸟首高高昂起，颈后飘着两根绶带，鸟首上部尚可见残存的棕榈座基。虽然其图案残缺，仍可看出整个团窠环尺寸较大。

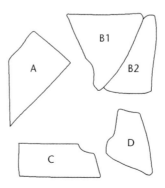

1 结构图　Numbering diagram

POSTSCRIPT

The successful publication of this bilingual research catalogue of textiles from Dulan in Qinghai Province is the culmination of a remarkable project. This collaboration between Qinghai Research Institute of Cultural Relics and Archaeology and the Abegg-Stiftung of Switzerland was a long and arduous process combining the efforts of many international scholars. Congratulations to all the participants who have contributed to the promotion of these unearthed treasures of Qinghai.

The Abegg-Stiftung is a nonprofit foundation established in the 1960s as a research institute focused on the study, conservation, and collecting of historical textiles. It maintains its own museum, publishes research books and papers on textile conservation and restoration, and offers training programs for young conservators from around the world.

The first collaboration between the Abegg-Stiftung and the Qinghai Research Institute of Cultural Relics and Archaeology began in 1999 during an international conference on Central Asian Textiles. Mr. Xu Xinguo, the director of Qinghai Research Institute at the time, presented his 1982 excavation report on Dulan Reshui Tubo tomb No.1, which is one of the largest Tubo mausoleums of the Tang dynasty located in Qinghai Province.

Since 1982, Mr. Xu Xinguo and his team, including members Su Shengxiu, Liu Xiaohe, and Zhang Changshou, have participated in many archaeological rescue excavations in the area. They excavated over 80 tombs, including the Xuewei No. 1 and surrounding tombs, and have unearthed many artifacts, including Tibetan wooden slips and objects of silk, gold, silver, lacquer, and wood.

Introduced by Mrs. Emma Bunker of Denver Art Museum and Prof. Han Rubin of the University of Science and Technology, Beijing (USTB), Mr. Dominik Keller, President of the Abegg-Stiftung, and Dr. Regula Schorta, Director of the Abegg-Stiftung, visited Qinghai Research Institute in 2003 and examined Dulan textiles for the first time. After careful examination of the unearthed textile fragments, Mr. Keller and Dr. Schorta realized that these materials contained firsthand information on how weaving technologies were exchanged among various ethnic groups along the Qinghai–Dulan trade route during the Tang dynasty. These technologies had been overlooked and not researched fully by Western scholars in the past. The importance of these unearthed textiles has been acknowledged and the Abegg-Stiftung is committed to the preservation of these findings and promoting them to Western scholars.

As a result, in 2003 the Abegg-Stiftung and Qinghai Research Institute agreed to collaborate on the restoration and conservation of these unearthed textiles. As the first step, Abegg-Stiftung invited Ms Angelika Sliwka, an experienced textile conservator, to work with Qinghai archaeologists in selecting and grouping the materials that needed immediate conservation. The Abegg-Stiftung then decided to publish the conservation results with the Qinghai Research Institute in a bilingual research catalogue for a wider international audience. During the collaboration, the Qinghai team worked closely with Ms Sliwka to learn the technical skills of conservation and establish their own state-of-the-art conservation lab for ancient textiles. Since then, the working relationship has continued to expand.

Meanwhile, Mr. Dominik Keller and Dr. Regula Schorta visited Xining several times to ensure smooth collaboration between the two institutions, especially after Director Xu retired in 2012. His successor, Ms Ren Xiaoyan (Director from 2012 to 2016), laid out a detailed plan for the archaeologists to work in their newly established lab, and ensured the original project goal of restoration. Without her support and arrangements, it would have been impossible to continue, not to mention finish, the conservation process.

The most important consideration here that I would like to address is that the restoration and conservation of any ancient textile, especially unearthed material, requires enormous dedication and patience. It is a slow process and extremely time consuming. Fortunately, the project team had many dedicated members who worked tirelessly on this delicate task. I am overwhelmed by the efforts and hours committed by the whole team.

One good example of how the collaborators worked together was during the unexpected task of last year's photo reshooting process. When the manuscript was finalized in the spring of 2017, Wenwu publishing house found that all the photos shot in 2006 for this publication were not of an adequate quality for modern digital printing. This was a total shock and devastating for all the people working on the project. After a series of discussions and meetings in Beijing, every team member agreed that it was necessary to rephotograph all the images in order to publish a high quality research book. With a very limited time window, a four-member team was quickly established, consisting of Mr. Song Chao, a professional photographer of Wenwu publishing house, Ms Wang Ge, the Chief Editor of Wenwu publishing house, Ms Angelika Sliwka, the textile conservation specialist, and Dr. Dong-Ning Wang, Adjunct Professor at Lehigh University. They immediately traveled to Xining and worked continuously for three days with the local scholars and staff at Qinghai. Their efforts paid off; the outstanding new images are available to view here in this catalogue.

Another team contribution and effort that is worthwhile to mention is the amount of translation work done for the Chinese and English manuscripts. The bulk of the translation from Chinese into English has been done by the American scholar Ms Martha Avery. The detailed weaving techniques and analysis were mainly carried out and written in English by Dr. Regula Schorta and Ms Angelika Sliwka, and then translated into Chinese by Dr. Dong-Ning Wang building on preliminary work by Ms Hu Xi. The final bilingual manuscript was proofread and edited by Drs. Schorta and Wang, and by the chief editor Ms Wang Ge at Cultural Relics Press. It was a truly international collaboration and effort by scholars from China, Switzerland, Germany, and the USA.

I am over 80 years young and fortunate enough to work with so many talented people from the beginning, and deeply touched by the enthusiasm, the devotion, and the perseverance of all the members. My special acknowledgement goes toward the team at Qinghai Research Institute of Cultural Relics and Archaeology and their three directors. Most grateful appreciation goes to the Abegg-Stiftung—without its devotion, this bilingual catalogue would not have been possible. It has been my great pleasure to work on this amazing project that contributes to communication between the East and the West. I hope this colourful and informative research catalogue brings enjoyment of the textile treasures of Dulan to all readers across different cultures and countries.

Acknowledgement is given to all the team members who have worked on this project. The name list is based on the writing strokes of their Chinese family names.

Conservation members: 卜玉凤 *Po Yufeng,* 刘杏改 *Liu Xinggai,* 刘香莲 *Liu Xianglian,* 沈跃萍 *Shen Yueping,* 严明圣 *Yan Mingsheng,* 高志伟 *Gao Zhiwei,* 崔兆年 *Cui Zhaonian.*

Storage and security members: 王倩倩 *Wang Qianqian,* 李国华 *Li Guohua,* 吴海涛 *Wu Haitao,* 李峰 *Li Feng,* 李琪美 *Li Qimei,* 李积英 *Li Jiying,* 胡学捷 *Hu Xuejie,* 张启珍 *Zhang Qizhen,* 张成志 *Zhang Chengzhi,* 段千柱 *Duan Qianzhu.*

Professor Han Rubin

Former Director of the Institute of Historical Metallurgy and Materials and Univecsity of Science and Technology Beijing

March 2018

图书在版编目（CIP）数据

都兰纺织品珍宝 ： 汉英对照 / 青海省文物考古研究
所编著 ； 许新国著 . — 北京 ： 文物出版社，2023.1

ISBN 978-7-5010-7196-8

I ． ①都… Ⅱ ． ①青… ②许… Ⅲ ． ①纺织品－出土
文物－研究－都兰县－汉、英 Ⅳ ． ① K876.94

中国版本图书馆 CIP 数据核字 (2021) 第 177263 号

都兰纺织品珍宝

编　　著	青海省文物考古研究所
著　　者	许新国　安吉莉卡·斯利弗卡
装帧设计	雅昌设计中心
出版发行	文物出版社
地　　址	北京东直门内北小街 2 号楼
邮　　编	100007
网　　址	http://www.wenwu.com
经　　销	新华书店
制版印刷	北京雅昌艺术印刷有限公司
开　　本	965 毫米 ×635 毫米　1/8
印　　张	39
版　　次	2023 年 1 月第 1 版
印　　次	2023 年 1 月第 1 次印刷
书　　号	ISBN 978-7-5010-7196-8
定　　价	680.00 元